New

Public and Community Services

STACKS

W9-CAB-947

Editorial Advisory Board

The Career Information Center includes:

- Agribusiness, Environment, and Natural Resources / 1
- Communications and the Arts / 2
- Computers, Business, and Office / 3
- Construction / 4
- Consumer, Homemaking, and Personal Services / 5
- Engineering, Science, Technology, and Social Science / 6
- Health / 7
- Hospitality and Recreation / 8
- Manufacturing / 9
- Marketing and Distribution / 10
- Public and Community Services / 11
- Transportation / 12
- Employment Trends and Master Index / 13

Public and Community Services

Career Information Center

Ninth Edition

MACMILLAN REFERENCE USA
An imprint of Thomson Gale, a part of The Thomson Corporation

THOMSON
GALE

Detroit • New York • San Francisco • New Haven, Conn. • Waterville, Maine • London

Career Information Center, Ninth Edition

Paula Kepos, Series Editor

Project Editor
Mary Rose Bonk

Editorial
Jennifer Greve

Imaging
Lezlie Light, Daniel Newell, Christine O'Bryan

Permissions
Kelly A. Quin, Tim Sisler, Andrew Specht

Manufacturing
Rhonda Dover

ISBN 0-02-866047-1 (set)
ISBN 0-02-866048-X (v.1)
ISBN 0-02-866049-8 (v.2)
ISBN 0-02-866050-1 (v.3)
ISBN 0-02-866051-X (v.4)
ISBN 0-02-866052-8 (v.5)
ISBN 0-02-866053-6 (v.6)
ISBN 0-02-866054-4 (v.7)
ISBN 0-02-866055-2 (v.8)
ISBN 0-02-866056-0 (v.9)
ISBN 0-02-866057-9 (v.10)
ISBN 0-02-866058-7 (v.11)
ISBN 0-02-866059-5 (v.12)
ISBN 0-02-866060-9 (v.13)
ISSN 1082-703X

This title is also available as an e-book.
ISBN 0-02-866099-4
Contact your Thomson Gale representative for ordering information.

Printed in the United States of America
10 9 8 7 6 5 4 3 2 1

Contents

Job Summary Chart

Job	Salary	Education/ Training	Employment Outlook	Page
Job Profiles—No Specialized Training				
Armed Services Career	Varies—see profile	Varies—see profile	Good	31
Building Custodian	Median—$23,414 per year	Training	Good	33
Day Care Worker	Average—$9.76 per hour	High school plus training	Very good	35
Electric Power Service Worker	Median—$16.60 to $25.27 per hour	None	Poor	36
Electric Power Transmission and Distribution Worker	Median—$23.61 per hour	Varies—see profile	Poor	37
Firefighter	Median—$18.43 per hour	High school plus training	Very good	39
★ Geriatric Aide	Median—$8.47 to $9.11 per hour	Training	Very good	41
★ Highway Maintenance Worker	Median—$14.21 per hour	High school plus training	Very good	43
★ Institutional Housekeeper	Median—$16,900 per year	Training	Good	44
Postal Service Worker	Varies—see profile	High school plus training	Poor	46
Power Plant Worker	Median—$52,530 per year	High school plus training	Poor	48
Refuse Worker	Median—$13.87 per hour	High school plus training	Poor	50
Security Guard	Median—$20,320 per year	High school plus training	Good	52
Job Profiles—Some Specialized Training/Experience				
Border Patrol Agent	Average—$55,000 per year	College plus training	Good	54
Correctional Officer	Median—$33,600 per year	Varies—see profile	Very good	56
Court Clerk	Median—$27,300 per year	Varies—see profile	Very good	58
Court Reporter	Median—$42,920 per year	High school plus training	Good	59
Crime Laboratory Technician	Median—$21.16 per hour	2- or 4-year college	Very good	61
Customs Worker	Median—$49,736 per year	College plus training	Good	63
Detective	Varies—see profile	High school plus training	Very good	65
Federal Government Worker	Varies—see profile	Varies—see profile	Fair	67
Institutional Child Care Worker	Median—$13.19 per hour	High school plus training	Very good	68
Legal Assistant, Corporate	Median—$39,130 per year	Varies—see profile	Very good	70
Paralegal Aide	Median—$39,130 per year	Varies—see profile	Very good	71
Police Officer	Median—$45,210 per year	High school plus training	Good	72
State Police Officer	Median—$23.55 per hour	High school plus training	Good	74
Teacher Assistant	Median—$19,410 per year	Varies—see profile	Fair	76
Teacher, Vocational Education	Median—$45,830 per year	Varies—see profile	Good	78
Youth Organization Worker	Average—$16,000 to $18,000 per year	Varies—see profile	Fair	79

★ High-growth job

Job	Salary	Education/Training	Employment Outlook	Page
Job Profiles—Advanced Training/Experience				
Adult Education Worker	Median—$14.85 per hour	College	Very good	82
City Manager	Median—$88,695 per year	College	Fair	84
College Student Personnel Worker	Median—$45,636 to $75,245 per year	College	Good	86
Criminologist	Varies—see profile	Advanced degree	Poor	87
FBI Special Agent	Varies—see profile	College plus training	Fair	89
Foreign Service Worker	Varies—see profile	Varies—see profile	Fair	91
Fund-Raiser	Median—$60,259 per year	College	Good	93
Government Inspector and Examiner	Median—$32,000 to $40,000 per year	Varies—see profile	Good	95
Internal Revenue Service Worker	Average—$36,963 to $81,417 per year	College plus training	Fair	97
Judge	Median—$93,070 per year	Advanced degree	Good	98
Lawyer	Median—$94,930 per year	Advanced degree	Good	100
Lawyer, Corporate	Average—$50,000 to $90,000 per year	Advanced degree	Good	102
Lawyer, Public Service	Varies—see profile	Advanced degree	Good	104
Librarian, Public	Median—$42,500 per year	Advanced degree	Fair	106
Librarian, School	Varies—see profile	Varies—see profile	Fair	108
Librarian, Special	Median—$60,000 per year	Varies—see profile	Fair	110
Marriage and Family Counselor	Median—$38,980 per year	College	Very good	112
Parole Officer	Median—$39,600 per year	College plus training	Good	114
Political Consultant	Varies—see profile	Advanced degree	Very good	115
Probation Officer	Median—$39,600 per year	College plus training	Good	117
☆ **Rehabilitation Counselor**	Median—$27,870 per year	College plus training	Very good	119
Religious Vocation	Varies—see profile	Advanced degree	Varies—see profile	120
School Administrator	Median—$68,340 per year	Varies—see profile	Fair	122
School Counselor	Median—$45,570 per year	College plus training	Very good	124
School Media Specialist	Median—$45,900 per year	Advanced degree	Fair	126
☆ **Social Worker**	Median—$34,820 per year	Advanced degree	Excellent	128
Teacher, College	Average—$51,800 per year	Advanced degree	Very good	129
Teacher, Preschool, Kindergarten, and Elementary	Varies—see profile	College plus training	Good	132
Teacher, Secondary School	Median—$41,400 to $45,970 per year	College plus training	Good	134
☆ **Urban and Regional Planner**	Median—$53,450 per year	Advanced degree	Very good	136
Vocational Counselor	Median—$45,570 per year	College	Very good	138

☆ **High-growth job**

Foreword

The ninth edition of the *Career Information Center* mirrors the ongoing changes in the job market caused by new technological and economic developments. These developments continue to change what Americans do in the workplace and how they do it. People have a critical need for up-to-date information to help them make career decisions.

The *Career Information Center* is an individualized resource for people of all ages and at all stages of career development. It has been recognized as an excellent reference for librarians, counselors, educators, and other providers of job information. It is ideally suited for use in libraries, career resource centers, and guidance offices, as well as in adult education centers and other facilities where people seek information about job opportunities, careers, and their own potential in the workforce.

This ninth edition updates many of the features that made the earlier editions so useful.

- A Job Summary Chart, a quick reference guide, appears in the front section of each volume to help readers get the basic facts and compare the jobs described in the volume. High-growth jobs are highlighted and identified with a star.

- Each volume of the *Career Information Center* begins with an overview of the job market in that field. These "Looking Into..." sections have been completely revised and updated. They also include new graphs, charts, and boxes providing information such as industry snapshots and the fastest-growing and top-dollar jobs in the field. The "Global View" feature tells how the new global economy is affecting jobs in the field.

- Each volume has a section called "Getting Into...," which contains useful information on entering the particular field. It offers self-evaluation tips and decision-making help, and it relates possible job choices to individual interests, abilities, and work characteristics. There is also practical information on job hunting, using the Internet and classified ads, preparing resumes, and handling interviews. "Getting Into..." also includes a section on employee rights.

- Each volume has a listing of all job profiles in the series and the volumes in which they appear, making access to profiles in other volumes easy.

- *Career Information Center* contains 694 job profiles. Each profile describes work characteristics, education and training requirements, getting the job, advancement and employment outlook, working conditions, and earnings and benefits.

- Job summaries, provided for each job profile, highlight the education or training required, salary range, and employment outlook.

- Volume 13 has been revised to reflect career concerns of the new century and employment trends through the year 2014. This volume includes updated articles on benefits, employment law, health in the workplace, job search strategies, job training, job opportunities at home, and identifying opportunities for retraining.

- More than 530 photographs provide a visual glimpse of life on the job. Photos have been selected to give the reader a sense of what it feels like to be in a specific field or job.

- Updated bibliographies in each volume include recommended readings and Web sites in specific job areas. Additional titles for the vocational counselor are included in Volume 13.

- Each volume also contains a comprehensive directory of accredited occupational education and vocational training facilities listed by occupational area and grouped by state. Directory materials are generated from the IPEDS (Integrated Postsecondary Education Data System) database of the U.S. Department of Education.

The *Career Information Center* recognizes the importance not only of job selection, but also of job holding, coping, and applying life skills. No other career information publication deals with work attitudes so comprehensively.

Using the Career Information Center

The *Career Information Center* is designed to meet the needs of many people—students, people just entering or reentering the job market, those dissatisfied with present jobs, those without jobs—anyone of any age who is not sure what to do for a living. The *Career Information Center* is for people who want help in making career choices. It combines the comprehensiveness of an encyclopedia with the format and readability of a magazine. Many professionals, including counselors, librarians, and teachers, will find it a useful guidance and reference tool.

The *Career Information Center* is organized by occupational interest area rather than in alphabetical order. Jobs that have something in common are grouped together. In that way people who do not know exactly what job they want can read about a number of related jobs. The *Career Information Center* classifies jobs that have something in common into clusters. The classification system is adapted from the cluster organization used by the U.S. Department of Labor. Each of the first twelve volumes of the *Career Information Center* explores one of twelve occupational clusters.

To use the *Career Information Center*, first select the volume that treats the occupational area that interests you most. Because there are many ways to group occupations, you may not find a particular job in the volume in which you look for it. In that case, check the central listing of all the profiles, which is located in the front of Volumes 1 through 12. This listing provides the names of all profiles and the volume number in which they appear. Volume 13 also includes a comprehensive index of all the jobs covered in the first twelve volumes.

After selecting a volume or volumes, investigate the sections that you feel would be most helpful. It isn't necessary to read these volumes from cover to cover. They are arranged so that you can go directly to the specific information you want. Here is a description of the sections included in each volume.

- **Job Summary Chart**—This chart presents in tabular form the basic data from all profiles in the volume: salary, education and training, employment outlook, and the page on which you can find the job profile. Jobs with a high growth potential are highlighted and starred.

- **Looking Into...**—This overview of the occupational cluster describes the opportunities, characteristics, and trends in that particular field.

- **Getting Into...**—This how-to guide can help you decide what jobs may be most satisfying to you and what strategies you can use to get the right job. You will learn, for example, how to write an effective resume, how to complete an application form, what to expect in an interview, how to use networking, and what to do if someone has discriminated against you.

- **Job Summary**—These summaries, located at the beginning of each profile, highlight the most important facts about the job: education and training, salary, and employment outlook.

Education and Training indicates whether the job requires no education, high school, college, advanced degree, vocational/technical school, license, or training.

Salary provides median or average salaries that may vary significantly from region to region.

Employment Outlook is based on several factors, including the Bureau of Labor Statistics' projections through the year 2014. The ratings are defined as follows: *poor* means there is a projected employment decrease of any amount; *fair* means there is a projected employment increase of 0 to 8 percent; *good* means there is a projected employment increase of 9 to 17 percent; *very good* means there is a projected employment increase of 18 to 26 percent; and *excellent* means there is a projected employment increase of 27 percent or more. The outlook is then determined by looking at the ratings and other employment factors. For example, a job with excellent projected employment growth in which many more people are entering the field than there are jobs available will have an outlook that is good rather than excellent.

For all categories, the phrase *Varies—see profile* means the reader must consult the profile for the information, which is too extensive to include in the Job Summary.

- **Job Profiles**—The job profiles are divided into three categories based on the level of training required to get the job. Each profile explores the following topics: description of the job being profiled, the education and training requirements, ways to get the job, advancement possibilities and employment outlook, the working conditions, the earnings and benefits, and places to go for more information.

Job Profiles—No Specialized Training includes jobs that require no education or previous work experience beyond high school.

Job Profiles—Some Specialized Training/Experience includes jobs that require one, two, or three years of vocational training or college, or work experience beyond high school.

Job Profiles—Advanced Training/Experience includes jobs that require a bachelor's degree or advanced degree from a college or university and/or equivalent work experience in that field.

- **Resources—General Career Information** includes a selected bibliography of the most recent books and Web sites on general career information, including how-to books on such topics as resume writing and preparing for tests. In addition, there is a special guide to readings for the career counselor in Volume 13.

- **Resources**—Each volume also contains a bibliography of books and Web sites for specific fields covered in that volume.

- **Directory of Institutions Offering Career Training**—This listing, organized first by career area, then by state, includes the schools that offer occupational training beyond high school. For jobs requiring a bachelor's degree or an advanced degree, check a library for college catalogs and appropriate directories.

- **Index**—This index, which is located at the end of each volume, lists every job mentioned in that volume. It serves not only to cross-reference all the jobs in the volume but also to show related jobs in the field. For example, under the entry OCEANOG-

RAPHER, you will find chemical oceanographer, marine biologist, and marine geophysicist.

- **Volume 13, Employment Trends and Master Index**—This volume includes several features that will help both the job seeker and the career counselor. A useful guide provides the *DOT (Dictionary of Occupational Titles)* number of most of the job profiles in the *Career Information Center*. There is also a special section on career information for Canada. The updated and revised "Employment Trends" section contains articles on health in the workplace; search strategies for finding your first job; employment trends for women, minorities, immigrants, older workers, and the physically challenged; employment demographics; benefit programs; training; employment opportunities at home; employment law; and identifying opportunities for retraining. The articles provide job seekers and career professionals with an overview of current employment issues, career opportunities, and outlooks. Finally, there is a master index to all the jobs included in all 13 volumes.

The *Career Information Center* is exactly what it says it is—a center of the most useful and pertinent information you need to explore and choose from the wide range of job and career possibilities. The *Career Information Center* provides you with a solid foundation of information for getting a satisfying job or rewarding career.

Comprehensive Job Profile List

The following list includes job profiles and corresponding volume numbers.

Accountant, Management, 3
Accountant, Public, 3
Actor, 2
Actuary, 3
Acupuncturist, 7
Administrative Assistant, 3
Admitting Interviewer, 7
Adult Education Worker, 11
Advertising Account Executive, 10
Advertising Copywriter, 2
Advertising Manager, 10
Aerospace Engineer, 6
Aerospace Engineering and Operations
    Technician, 6
Aerospace Industry, 9
Agricultural Engineer, 1
Agricultural Inspector, 1
Agricultural Technician, 1
Agronomist, 1
AIDS Counselor, 7
Air Pollution Control Technician, 1
Air Traffic Controller, 12
Air-Conditioning Engineer, 6
Air-Conditioning, Heating, and
    Refrigeration Mechanic and
    Installer, 4
Aircraft Dispatcher, 12
Aircraft Mechanic, 12
Airline Baggage and Freight Handler, 12
Airline Flight Attendant, 12
Airline Reservations Agent, 12
Airline Ticket Agent, 12
Airplane Pilot, 12
Airport Manager, 12
Airport Utility Worker, 12
Alternative Fuels Vehicle Technician, 6
Aluminum and Copper Industries, 9
Ambulance Driver, 7
Amusement and Recreation Attendant, 8
Anatomist, 6
Anesthesiologist, 7
Animal Caretaker, 8
Animal Scientist, 1
Animal Trainer, 1
Announcer, 2
Anthropologist, 6
Apparel Industry, 9
Apparel Workers, 9
Appliance Service Worker, 5
Appraiser, 5
Architect, 4
Architectural Drafter, 4
Architectural Model Maker, 4
Armed Services Career, 11
Art Director, 2
Artificial Intelligence Specialist, 6
Artist, 2
Assembler and Fabricator, 9

Astronomer, 6
Athletic Coach, 8
Athletic Trainer, 8
Auctioneer, 10
Audiologist, 7
Auditor, 3
Auto Body Repairer, 12
Auto Parts Counter Worker, 10
Auto Sales Worker, 10
Automobile Driving Instructor, 12
Automotive Exhaust Emissions
    Technician, 12
Automotive Industry, 9
Automotive Mechanic, 12
Avionics Technician, 12

Baker, 1
Bank Clerk, 3
Bank Officer and Manager, 3
Bank Teller, 3
Barber and Hairstylist, 5
Bartender, 8
Bicycle Mechanic, 12
Billing Clerk, 3
Biochemist, 6
Biological Technician, 6
Biologist, 6
Biomedical Engineer, 6
Biomedical Equipment Technician, 7
Boilermaker, 9
Bookbinder, 2
Bookkeeper, 3
Border Patrol Agent, 11
Botanist, 6
Bricklayer, 4
Bridge and Lock Tender, 12
Broadcast News Analyst, 2
Broadcast Technician, 2
Brokerage Clerk, 3
Building Custodian, 11
Building Inspector, 4
Bulldozer, Grader, or Paving Machine
    Operator, 4
Business Family and Consumer
    Scientist, 5
Business Machine Operator, 3

Cable Television and
    Telecommunications Technician, 6
Cable Television Engineer, 6
Cafeteria Attendant, 8
Camera Operator, 2
Candy Manufacturing Worker, 1
Car Rental or Leasing Agent, 12
Car Wash Worker, 12
Cardiac Monitor Technician, 7
Cardiac Perfusionist, 7
Cardiology Technologist, 7

Carpenter, 4
Cartographer, 1
Cartoonist and Animator, 2
Cashier, 10
Caterer, 8
Ceiling Tile Installer, 4
Cement Mason, 4
Ceramic Engineer, 6
Ceramics Industry, 9
Chauffeur, 5
Cheese Industry Worker, 1
Chemical Engineer, 6
Chemical Technician, 6
Chemist, 6
Child Care Worker, Private, 5
Chiropractor, 7
Choreographer, 2
City Manager, 11
Civil Engineer, 4
Civil Engineering Technician, 4
Claims Adjuster, 3
Claims Examiner, 3
Clinical Laboratory Technician, 7
Clinical Laboratory Technologist, 7
College Student Personnel Worker, 11
College/University Administrator, 3
Companion, 5
Comparison Shopper, 10
Compensation and Benefits Analyst, 3
Composer, 2
Computer and Information Systems
    Manager, 3
Computer and Office Machine
    Repairer, 3
Computer Consultant, 3
Computer Control Operator, 9
Computer Control Programmer, 9
Computer Database Administrator, 3
Computer Network Technician, 3
Computer Operator, 3
Computer Programmer, 3
Computer Security Specialist, 3
Computer Software Documentation
    Writer, 3
Computer Software Engineer, 3
Computer Support Specialist, 3
Computer Systems Analyst, 3
Conservation Scientist, 1
Construction Electrician, 4
Construction Equipment Dealer, 4
Construction Equipment Mechanic, 4
Construction Laborer, 4
Construction Millwright, 4
Construction Supervisor, 4
Consumer Advocate, 5
Consumer Credit Counselor, 5
Controller, 3
Cook and Chef, 8

Printing Machine Operator, 2
Probation Officer, 11
Producer, 2
Product Manager, 10
Professional Athlete, 8
Professional Organizer, 5
Proofreader, 2
Property, Real Estate, and Community
  Association Manager, 8
Prosthetist and Orthotist, 7
Psychiatric Aide, 7
Psychiatrist, 7
Psychologist, 7
Public Relations Manager, 2
Public Relations Specialist, 2
Purchasing Agent, 10

Quality Control Manager, 9

Radiologic Technologist, 7
Railroad Clerk, 12
Railroad Conductor, 12
Railroad Engineer, 12
Railroad Maintenance Worker, 12
Railroad Signal or Switch Operator, 12
Railroad Track Worker, 12
Real Estate Appraiser, 10
Real Estate Developer, 4
Real Estate Sales Agent and Broker, 10
Receiving, Shipping, and Traffic Clerk, 10
Receptionist, 3
Recreation Worker, 8
Recreational Therapist, 7
Recruiter, 3
Recycling and Reclamation Worker, 1
Refuse Worker, 11
Registered Nurse, 7
Rehabilitation Counselor, 11
Reinforcing Ironworker, 4
Religious Vocation, 11
Rental Clerk, 10
Respiratory Therapist, 7
Restaurant Host or Hostess, 8
Restaurant Manager, 8
Resume Writer, 3
Retail Butcher, 10
Retail Buyer, 10
Retail Store Sales Worker Supervisor, 10
Retail Store Sales Worker, 10
Rigger, 4
Robotics Engineer, 6
Robotics Technician, 6
Roofer, 4
Route Delivery Driver, 12
Rubber Industry, 9
Rug and Carpet Cleaner, 5

Safety Engineer, 6
Sailor, 12
Sales Demonstrator and Product
  Promoter, 10
Sales Engineer, 10
Sales Manager, 10

School Administrator, 11
School Bus Driver, 12
School Counselor, 11
School Media Specialist, 11
Scriptwriter, 2
Secretary, 3
Securities Broker, 3
Security Guard, 11
Semiconductor Processor, 6
Septic Tank Installer and Servicer, 4
Service Station Attendant, 12
Set and Exhibit Designer, 2
Sheet Metal Worker, 4
Shipbuilding Industry, 9
Shoe Repairer, 5
Short-Order Cook, 8
Sign Language and Oral Interpreter, 2
Singer, 2
Small Animal Breeder, 1
Small Business Owner, 10
Social Worker, 11
Sociologist, 6
Software Quality Assurance Technician
  and Analyst, 3
Software Trainer, 3
Soil Scientist, 1
Solar Energy Technician, 4
Sound Engineering Technician, 2
Special Service Bus Driver, 12
Specification Writer, 4
Speech-Language Pathologist, 7
Sports Instructor, 8
Sports Management Professional, 10
Stagehand, 2
State Police Officer, 11
Stationary Engineer and Boiler
  Operator, 9
Statistical Assistant, 3
Statistician, 3
Steel Industry, 9
Stock Clerk, 10
Stonemason, 4
Store Manager, 10
Structural Clay Products Industry, 9
Structural Steelworker, 4
Substance Abuse Counselor, 7
Supermarket Worker, 10
Surgeon, 7
Surgical Technologist, 7
Surveying Technician, 4
Surveyor, 4
Swimming Instructor and Coach, 8
Swimming Pool Servicer, 5
Systems Engineer, 6

Tax Preparer, 3
Taxi Dispatcher, 12
Taxi Driver, 12
Teacher Assistant, 11
Teacher, College, 11
Teacher, Preschool, Kindergarten, and
  Elementary, 11
Teacher, Secondary School, 11

Teacher, Vocational Education, 11
Technical Writer, 2
Telecommunications Central Office
  Technician, 6
Telecommunications Consultant, 6
Telecommunications Design Engineer, 6
Telemarketer, 10
Telephone Operator, 3
Telephone Service Representative, 3
Telephone Service Technician, 6
Textile Industry, 9
Ticket Taker, 8
Tire Changer and Repairer, 12
Title Examiner, 10
Tobacco Industry Worker, 1
Tool and Die Maker, 9
Tour Escort, 8
Tow Truck Dispatcher, 12
Tow Truck Operator, 12
Trade Show Manager, 10
Traffic Engineer, 12
Traffic Technician, 12
Training and Development Specialist, 3
Translator or Interpreter, 2
Transportation Engineer, 12
Transportation Inspector, 12
Travel Agent, Retail and Wholesale, 8
Truck and Bus Dispatcher, 12
Truck Terminal Manager, 12

Umpire and Referee, 8
Union Business Agent, 3
Urban and Regional Planner, 11
Usability Researcher, 2
Usher, 8

Vending Machine Servicer and Repairer,
  10
Veterinarian, 1
Veterinary Technician, 1
Vocational Counselor, 11

Waiter, 8
Ward Clerk, 7
Warehouse Worker, 10
Wastewater Treatment Plant Operator, 1
Watch Repairer, 5
Water Treatment Plant and System
  Operator, 1
Water Well Driller, 4
Web Designer, 2
Webmaster, 2
Wedding Consultant, 5
Welder, 4
Wholesale Sales Worker, 10
Window Cleaner, 5
Wireless Communications Technician, 6
Word Processor, 3

Youth Organization Worker, 11

Zookeeper, 8
Zoologist, 6

ublic and community services date back to the colonial era, when settlements took responsibility for the welfare of poor people and established public schools to ensure that all children could read the Bible. In some areas, they financed these efforts by collecting taxes from residents. Despite this support of public services, however, colonial citizens resisted government intervention in their lives. One of the major issues leading to the Declaration of Independence was the colonists' objection to paying taxes to Great Britain without being represented in Parliament, which decided how tax revenues would be spent. Once the citizens of the thirteen colonies had won their independence, they had no desire to give it up to another distant government.

This skepticism about governments—federal, state, and local—continues today. Americans count on public institutions and agencies to assist citizens who are vulnerable, to deliver mail, to educate their children, and to handle a wide range of crises, from quelling riots to cleaning up tornado-ravaged communities. At the same time they distrust governments and even those who do their governments's work. They watch carefully for excessive limits on their freedom and inappropriate or unnecessary taxing and spending. Increasingly, they comparison shop for alternatives to public sector services.

THE GOVERNMENT AND PUBLIC SERVICES

To protect against a too-powerful central government, the founders of the nation specifically limited its powers (and, as a result, the number of government workers). It could exercise authority over

Americans count on public institutions and agencies to provide a wide range of services from educating their children and delivering their mail to maintaining roads and protecting their property. (Royalty-Free/Photo Disc, Inc. Reproduced by permission)

Global View: Public and Community Services

Many public and community service employees—such as customs officials, foreign service workers, border police, and the military—protect U.S. interests at home and abroad. Their work is influenced by global politics and economics: they deal with health and disease, international trade, efforts to protect the environment, terrorism, and illegal drug traffic.

Some of the professions affected by the global economy are not so obvious—law and law enforcement, for example. Terrorism, a major concern in the twenty-first century, has opened up law enforcement jobs in both the United States and abroad, as has the trend in business mergers, joint ventures, and complex trade agreements. Because different countries have their own practices regarding matters such as contracts and copyrights, multinational corporations and law firms are seeking attorneys with experience in foreign legal matters.

The Internet, combined with other technological advances, has enabled law enforcement agencies worldwide to exchange information with amazing speed and to access extensive databases. Ironically, the Internet has also brought new opportunities for criminals. Policing online scams and predators has become a new specialty in the field of public service.

Teachers and librarians have been dealing with global issues for decades. An increasingly diverse population in the United States, as well as an economy that requires new skills from its workforce, has brought new challenges to these professions. The demands on educators will undoubtedly increase in the coming years, but so will the tools of their profession. For example, distance learning (courses taught via the Internet) is becoming an accepted way for students to earn their degrees.

Although communications technology has made the world smaller, those who provide public and community services are serving a larger region. This should translate into greater career opportunities.

those matters that were of interest to all states: national defense, diplomacy, coining and borrowing money, and regulating commerce between states. The states retained control over any matters not expressly delegated to the federal government, including transportation within each state, matters of marriage and divorce, and public education. Private groups, religious organizations, or individual families took care of welfare and public assistance for those in need.

The Civil War brought significant changes, including the decline of rural America. Cities grew rapidly as Americans moved away from farms and waves of immigrants poured into the country. Problems that were once handled privately were magnified in concentrated urban populations. When poverty and disease became more visible, responsibility for addressing them was gradually assumed by local governments.

As many of these problems outgrew local resources, the federal government became involved. Its ability to help, however, was limited by its ability to raise the money to pay federal employees. It was not until 1913, when the Sixteenth Amendment to the Constitution instituted a federal income tax, that the federal government was able to generate enough revenue to expand its services and its workforce.

The Establishment of the Civil Service System

In the early years of the federal government, jobs were usually apportioned according to the "spoils system," which allowed newly elected officials to give jobs to their friends and political allies—after dismissing the previous officeholders' appointees. The system satisfied those who got jobs and rewarded their friendships and political activities, but it failed to recognize the need for continuity of services and for qualified, trained government employees.

The abuses of the system became so serious that, in 1883, Congress established a civil service commission to administer competitive examinations to job applicants. Several states also passed civil service laws and began to fill jobs through similar tests. While the law has been adapted over the years, its basic premise generally holds: merit and suitability are the criteria for public employment.

An Explosion of Public Service Employment

No single event affected public sector employment more than the Great Depression of the 1930s. Because of record unemployment and devastating poverty, the federal government hired people because they needed jobs, not just because citizens

Top-Dollar Jobs in Public and Community Services

The following high-paying jobs are described in this volume. The figures represent typical salaries or earnings for experienced workers.

$100,000 or more	
	• City Manager
	• Corporate Lawyer
	• Fund-Raiser
	• Judge
	• Lawyer
	• Political Consultant
	• School Administrator

$45,000–$100,000	
	• Criminologist
	• FBI Special Agent
	• Power Plant Worker
	• Teacher, College
	• Vocational Counselor

needed services. Federal employees built roads and post offices and developed programs to conserve soil and water. Some painted murals on public buildings, while others wrote travel guides. Because federal revenues fell during the Great Depression, the government had to borrow money to pay these employees. In the past, it had gone into debt to pay for wars, but it had never used borrowed money to offset economic recession. Deficit spending in such extraordinary circumstances, it was believed, would help fuel the economy. Repaying the debt would be less burdensome when the economy improved.

However, deficit spending became an enduring feature of economic policy. It has been used regularly to bolster the economy during recessions and to engineer social change—lifting citizens out of poverty, for example. Just as regularly it has caused rancorous debate, with both politicians and taxpayers decrying governments' spendthrift ways. Debaters have called for "reinventing" and "reengineering" government to make it more cost-effective and responsive to citizens. They have argued about "downsizing," especially at the federal level, and "decentralizing," or moving the center of government away from Washington, DC. At times they have called on religious and community groups, volunteers, and families to take more responsibility for community services such as care of the poor, the elderly, and the disabled.

Some of the debate has led to successful cutbacks. But usually politicians have come up with new projects they believed their constituents might need or, at least, might remember in the voting booth. Any initiatives—either to cut back government employment or to expand it—can affect the types and numbers of public service jobs available.

CAREERS IN THE PUBLIC SECTOR

Many occupations in the public sector are also found in the private sector: engineer, health practitioner, computer technician, accountant, mechanic, and construction trade worker. Some occupations, such as legislator, revenue agent, city planner, and drill sergeant, are only found in the public sector.

Even when the jobs are similar, however, public and community service employment differs in several philosophical ways. First, private companies usually gauge success by the profits earned. Public agencies, by contrast, are more apt to measure it according to the results achieved. For example, when students buy computers, the corporations that sell those computers make money. When those same students learn to use computers in public schools, their teachers have succeeded. Second, public services are more likely than private ventures to be created in response to specific conditions or needs. Companies may develop vaccines because they are needed (and because they make money), but the public sector organizes immunization programs during flu epidemics. The government focuses on the benefits to the entire population when everyone is protected.

A third difference is accountability, workers' obligation to answer to others about job performance. Private sector workers are accountable to their managers who, in turn, answer to stockholders. In most cases, stockholders want to ensure some kind of return on their investments. In the public sector, employees answer to administrators, who report to the elected officials overseeing their agencies. Taxpayers, whose money pays the bills, may not like the way the operations are run. They are usually eager to complain about their officeholders on election day.

Federal Government

According to the U.S. Bureau of Labor Statistics, the federal government employed more than 2.5 million civilian workers in 2004. About three percent work in the legislative and judicial branches. The other ninety-seven percent work in the executive branch, which includes fourteen cabinet departments and more than ninety agencies. Two out of three federal workers have white-collar jobs, with systems analysts and computer scientists forming the largest occupational group. Although most federal departments and agencies are headquartered in Washington, DC, only fourteen percent of federal employees work in or near the nation's capital. About ninety percent of federal government employees fall under the jurisdiction of civil service laws. The remaining ten percent are mostly top-level appointees.

Individuals seeking employment with the federal government generally must take written, oral, or performance examinations related to their occupational fields. If they pass the examinations, their names are placed on waiting lists according to their scores. When vacancies occur, hiring agents may select any of the three highest-rated people on the lists. For many jobs, however, the hiring agents simply evaluate applicants on the basis of their education, training, and experience in the occupation.

The civil service system has a number of pay plans for various types of work. The General Pay Schedule, for example, covers most white-collar em-

Job openings should be plentiful for all branches of the armed services through the year 2008 since the number of people in the prime age group for recruiting has decreased. (© Terry Wild Studio. Reproduced by permission.)

ployees, while the Federal Wage System covers most blue-collar employees. Each plan consists of a series of pay grades, or levels, and a range of salary steps within each grade. Workers usually enter the system at the starting grade for their occupation. Their work is regularly evaluated, and if it is satisfactory, they advance to the next salary step.

Armed Services

In 2005 there were 2.6 million people serving in the armed services. Defending the nation in times of conflict and deterring aggression are the missions of the armed services, which include the U.S. Army (land based), the U.S. Air Force (air and space), the U.S. Navy (sea), the U.S. Marine Corps (a branch of the navy that defends against land invasions), and the U.S. Coast Guard (which enforces federal maritime laws, recovers distressed vessels and aircraft, and prevents smuggling).

Armed services personnel have a wide range of duties, including some not usually associated with the military, such as operating hospitals and programming computers. The military offers about three thousand basic and advanced occupations for enlisted personnel and about one thousand six hundred positions for officers. Although about thirty percent of these specialties are specific to the military, the remainder have civilian counterparts. Job training is perhaps the most attractive benefit for those who enter the armed services.

State and Local Government

More than 2.4 million people work in state government, and nearly 5 million others are employed in local jurisdictions (excluding education and hospitals). State governments hire more workers in managerial, administrative support, and professional occupations than do local governments. Local governments employ more workers in service occupations, such as firefighters, police officers, and sanitation workers.

Working for state and local governments is much like working for the federal government. Employees work under a merit system and advance according to set procedures and schedules, as long as they work competently. In some government positions promotions are based on seniority as well as job performance. Unlike federal employees, however, most state and local employees have the right to negotiate their wages through collective bargaining.

Education

In 2004 more than 6.1 million jobs existed for teachers from preschool to colleges and universities.

Other jobs in education include clerical and administrative workers, school librarians, social workers, health-related specialists, and counselors.

Elementary and Secondary Education Nearly 3.8 million teachers are employed at the elementary and secondary levels. More than eight of ten jobs are in the public school systems. They introduce children to learning and teach them reading, writing, geometry, even social skills. Because of their broad mission, teachers hold some of the most scrutinized jobs in the public sector. Parents, who work closely with teachers, and employers, who hire graduates of the school system, regularly complain that students are not being prepared properly. Taxpayers worry that their tax dollars are being squandered.

Many improvements have been debated or implemented over the years. Voucher programs, for instance, introduced competition into the schools. They allowed parents to apply their child's "share" of a district's funding to the school of their choice. They may select a school because of its overall academic reputation; its specialization, such as the arts; or its facilities, such as the newest computer labs. Charter schools, another option, were based on the premise that bureaucracy burdens schools and teachers and prevents them from being creative and effective. Charter schools are generally autonomous public schools that receive the same per-pupil funding as traditional schools but operate independently of school district and labor union regulations. In return for this autonomy, charter schools are expected to achieve better results.

Perhaps the most hotly debated recent effort has been the congressional mandate that ties funding for schools to students' performance on standardized achievement tests. While opponents argue that students are now being taught to take the tests, rather than prepare for their own futures, the program has had an important effect on teachers: in the past, school districts tended to hire recent graduates because they were cheaper to employ; now many administrators do what they can to retain or hire the most innovative teachers, especially those with plenty of classroom experience. New incentives, such as additional pay and tuition reimbursement, have been put in place so teachers keep their own skills current and comprehensive.

Postsecondary Education About 1.6 million teachers are employed at colleges and universities in the United States, instructing more than 14 million full-time and part-time students and conducting a significant amount of the nation's research. Nearly a third of their students are over age thirty and have returned to college to start new careers, to retrain so they can keep their jobs, or to qualify for advanced positions.

Vocational and Adult Education About five hundred thousand teachers are employed in vocational education and in community-based adult education programs. They prepare students for a variety of occupations that do not require college degrees, such as welder, machinist, mechanic, cosmetologist, and word processor. Adult education programs, which are usually run by local school districts, offer such diverse courses as reading, writing, mathematics, cooking, aerobics, investing, and dog training.

Social Work

About five hundred sixty-two thousand jobs exist in the broad field of social work, nearly forty percent of them in the public sector. Careers in social work, or human services, involve helping people cope with a wide range of problems, either through direct counseling or by referring them to specialists or placing them in assistance programs.

Sometimes social workers help the poor, disabled, and disadvantaged obtain food, shelter, and clothing; at other times they provide social rehabilitation, crisis intervention, and life-skills training. Some social workers specialize. Medical social workers, for example, help patients and their families cope with catastrophic illness. School social workers counsel troubled children and help integrate children with disabilities into the general school population. Others have found work in the corporate sector. Businesses employ them to ensure compliance with regulations that require accessible facilities or to manage employee assistance programs, such as substance-abuse counseling.

Law

Of the seven hundred thirty-four thousand lawyers in the United States today, about twenty percent hold government positions. A majority of them work at the local level. In the federal government, most jobs for lawyers are in the departments of Justice, Treasury, and Defense.

Some administrative and managerial jobs in law do not require legal training, although can be an asset. For example, to handle litigation more quickly and inexpensively, agencies are relying more on paralegal aides and legal assistants. Numbering two hundred twenty-four thousand, paralegal aides and legal assistants research law cases, prepare documents, and perform other legal work previously done by higher-priced lawyers.

Local governments are the biggest employer of police officers. (© Fat Chance Productions/Corbis.)

Industry Snapshots

GOVERNMENT

State and local governments employ more workers than any business in the United States. By 2014 government employment can be expected to grow at the state and local levels but decline at the federal level as program responsibilities shift away from the national government. The biggest job growth in state and local governments will be in community services, health services, and protective services. Population growth in the nation's cities and suburbs is also predicted to contribute to more jobs in state and local government.

MILITARY

Although the total number of personnel was reduced following the collapse of the Soviet Union, the conflicts in Afghanistan and Iraq, as well as the threats of terrorism and biological warfare in general, may mean increased numbers of active duty personnel. Many military jobs are becoming more technical and complex, so standards for new recruits may rise.

EDUCATION

Education employment is expected to rise to more than 14.2 million workers in 2010, spurred by increased enrollments of children in preschool, kindergarten, elementary school, and high schools, as well as growth in the number of older, foreign, and part-time students at the postsecondary level. Jobs for special education teachers may be plentiful because of legislation that focuses on the needs of individuals with disabilities.

SOCIAL WORK

An aging population and a growing number of individuals and families in crisis are expected to require more social services. In particular, more school social workers may be needed to respond to the adjustment problems of immigrants, children from backgrounds of poverty and abuse, and children with mental and physical disabilities. Medical social workers should find jobs plentiful because of the trend toward early discharge of patients from hospitals.

CORRECTIONS

The number of correctional officers has grown by eighty percent since 1985 and is expected to increase by as much as thirty-five percent by 2012. Thousands of job openings are generated each year. A surge in drug-related crime and a shift toward mandatory sentencing and reduced parole have increased the nation's prison population significantly and led to an overwhelming demand for correctional officers.

LAW

Demand for lawyers will grow as the population increases and as middle-income groups use more legal services. Jobs in the public sector are expected to increase because the government now provides more legal and related services to the poor and elderly. Health-care law, international law, and environmental law may be busy specialties. Despite the number of job openings, however, competition for employment will be intense because of the large number of law students graduating each year. Lawyers looking to open their own practices would probably do best in small towns or suburban areas, away from the competition of larger, established firms.

Protective Services

Workers in the field of protective services seek to safeguard people and property. These workers include about seven hundred twelve thousand police officers, detectives, and special agents; more than four hundred eighty-four thousand corrections officers; and more than three hundred fifty-three thousand firefighters. These numbers do not include volunteer firefighters, who number in the hundreds of thousands. While most police officers and firefighters are employed by local governments, the majority of correctional officers are employed at state prisons, prison camps, and reformatories. In the past the job of correctional officer consisted of enforcing the rules of the institution. More and more, however, correctional officers are assisting with inmates' rehabilitation by serving as informal counselors and by reinforcing remedial training.

TRENDS IN THE PUBLIC SECTOR

At a time when the need for public services is increasing, the resources to provide those services are decreasing. Public servants at all levels of govern-

Federal, state, and local governments contract extensively with nonprofit agencies to provide key social services for the elderly, the homeless, and youths. (© Terry Wild Studio. Reproduced by permission.)

As might be expected, unions representing public sector employees fight efforts to privatize their jobs. Even those outside the workforce fear that this trend will revive the spoils system if it is misused to reassign civil service jobs to entrepreneurs who are political allies of and campaign contributors to government officeholders.

The premise behind privatization is that business is more efficient than government. However, private companies that have a monopoly on a service or that operate without adequate government supervision can also be inefficient. Consequently, government policy is shifting from privatization to "managed competition," which requires that more than one company must be available to bid on a contract. Workers in the public sector are allowed to bid against private companies. For example, when the city of Indianapolis put the job of filling potholes up for bids, employees of the public works department figured out how they could do the job more economically than private companies and kept the task in the public sector.

Electronic Technology

The public sector lags behind the private sector in adopting Information Age technology. Even so, government at all levels now uses new electronic media for better delivery of public services.

Electronic Pathways to Government Federal, state, and local governments are using computer bulletin boards to provide quick, convenient access to information and to facilitate communication. From the comfort of their homes, citizens with computers and Internet connections can obtain the latest census statistics, read summaries of bills before the state legislature, send e-mail to the mayor, and access the card catalog at the local library. In some areas governments have installed interactive kiosks in shopping malls, grocery stores, and other central locations to provide information about city services, employment opportunities, and unemployment benefits. Some kiosks dispense marriage licenses and other government forms.

Saving Time and Money The public sector is taking advantage of new technology to cut expenses and speed up services. For example, most Departments of Motor Vehicles allow drivers to renew their licenses online. Because of the time saved, clerks can spend more time on other tasks. The Social Security Administration uses electronic technology to deposit benefits directly into retirees' bank accounts, eliminating costly paper checks. The U.S. Postal Service handles more than fifty percent of all mail at least in part through automation, resulting in enormous cost savings. Electronic mail sorting,

ment are searching for ways to perform their work more economically and efficiently. Teamwork and collaboration are becoming more common as personnel from different agencies and different levels or branches of public service find they have similar problems.

Privatization and Competition

In the United States privatization means contracting with for-profit businesses to deliver publicly funded services. A city sanitation department, for example, might replace its refuse collectors with a private company that guarantees more economical and efficient trash removal.

In some areas, private companies have always been hired to provide services or goods that governments were unable to supply. For instance, the federal government hires private contractors to make weapons and build highways. Local school boards contract cafeteria and busing services. During the 1980s and 1990s, however, governments began privatizing services traditionally managed by public sector employees, such as wastewater treatment plants, motor vehicle inspection stations, and correctional facilities. School boards in Maryland and Massachusetts have even turned poorly performing public schools over to private education companies.

Summer Jobs in Public and Community Services

GOVERNMENT

Summer jobs and internships are available at all levels of government, especially in clerical, administrative, and technical fields. The federal government employs summer staff as congressional aides and legislative assistants. State jobs are available in the capitals as well as regional offices, while summer jobs in local government include positions in county courthouses, town parks, and recreational programs and facilities such as swimming pools. Contact:

- local government offices
- governor's office and state agencies
- members of Congress and federal agencies

Sources of Information

Government Job Finder Planning/Communications
7215 Oak Ave.
River Forest, IL 60305-1935
www.planningcommunications.com

Washington Information Directory
Congressional Quarterly, Inc.
1255 Twenty-second St. NW
Washington, DC 20037
www.cq.com

SOCIAL SERVICES

Summer workers are needed in day care centers and senior centers. Institutions for children and adults with disabilities need care givers, as do hospitals and facilities for dependent children. Youth organizations need camp counselors, recreation helpers, and aides to run summer programs. Contact:

- state department of education
- child care institutions
- public and private day care centers
- social service agencies

Sources of Information

National Association for the Education of Young Children

1509 Sixteenth St. NW
Washington, DC 20036
www.naeyc.org

National Association of Social Workers/NASW Press
750 First St. NE, Ste. 700
Washington, DC 20002-4241
www.naswdc.org

PUBLIC SERVICES

Summer positions are available for aides in public and university libraries. Aides and fund-raisers are needed for public-interest groups. Municipal projects, such as highway maintenance, may require summer help, and refuse workers and firefighters may be needed to replace vacationing staff. Contact:

- local libraries
- local government agencies
- private maintenance, construction, and sanitation contractors
- public-interest groups

See individual job profiles for sources of information.

LAW

Law firms often hire summer office workers, including receptionists, typists, word processors, and researchers. Law students can work as summer associates or possibly participate in summer training programs. For details, contact:

- law firms
- legal aid associations
- company legal departments

Sources of Information

American Bar Association
321 N. Clark St.
Chicago, IL 60610
www.abanet.org

---

for example, costs only a fourth as much as sorting mail by hand. Increased automation may eliminate more than forty thousand postal jobs by 2008.

Customer Service

A growing trend in the public sector is to regard recipients of community services as customers and to approach them with courtesy, efficiency, and know-how. Many agencies provide mandatory training in customer service.

One-Stop Shopping The customer-service approach is having its most noticeable effect in the delivery of human services, where many people qualify for more than one type of aid and the system is fragmented and confusing. For instance, an elderly blind woman with medical problems may find that the resources she needs lie within four or five different agencies or departments. She must shuttle from office to office—often in different towns or even different counties—and submit to repetitive questions. After all that, she may still not receive complete assistance. Responding to clients' frustration, government officials in many areas have installed "one-stop shopping." Services such as Medicaid, employment counseling, and welfare benefits may be grouped together in an accessible location, or clients may be assigned one social worker to negotiate various branches of the system.

Plastic for Paper Some agencies issue plastic cards to welfare recipients, which they can use to pay for food or to obtain cash. Similar to bank debit cards, the cards are more secure, convenient, and efficient than paper checks and food stamp coupons.

Government Marketing

To help pay their bills many localities are now turning to "government marketing," which takes several forms. A government unit might operate a store or a mail-order catalog that sells merchandise to the public. The Los Angeles County Coroner's Office, for example, grossed about $20,000 per month in the mid-1990s through sales of key chains, coffee mugs, towels, and other merchandise. Other agencies sell advertising space on public property such as trash barrels and bicycle racks at city parks. While transit departments have long sold advertising space on buses, they now offer advertisers the entire vehicle—from headlights to taillights and from roof to road—for their "body-wrap" ads. Advertisers also donate uniforms, automobiles and vans, and other equipment—all of which bear companies' names and logos.

Some government units sell their services for profit. For example, a fire department might run ambulances—driven by firefighters—for a fee. The U.S. Department of Energy signed a contract with factories along the Mexican border to consult on pollution control.

OTHER AVENUES TO PUBLIC AND COMMUNITY SERVICES

In addition to government entities, nonprofit agencies, corporations, and volunteer organizations offer opportunities for public service.

Nonprofit Organizations

About twenty-three thousand private, nonprofit service organizations exist at the national level, and many more exist at state, county, and community levels. They operate prenatal clinics, food banks, shelters for battered women and the homeless, hospices for people with AIDS, counseling centers for troubled youth, and many other programs. Federal, state, and local governments contract extensively with nonprofit agencies to provide key services. Religious and fraternal organizations also sponsor many social service organizations.

Corporations

Many large companies have community service or public affairs divisions that direct corporate philanthropy. They donate funds or goods, such as surplus merchandise or used office equipment, to events and projects in their communities, as well as the services of executives to run civic or charitable projects. Sometimes they give their employees time off to participate in community activities or match their employees' charitable donations. Banks and other financial institutions may look for ways to invest money and other corporate resources in the community. These efforts are driven by a desire to build good public relations and the realization that a healthy community is good for business.

More and more corporations work with public and private community organizations to revive neighborhoods, improve schools, and curb violence. A good example is the Atlanta Project, launched by former president Jimmy Carter, which divided the city of Atlanta into twenty clusters and assigned a corporation to each. Residents of each cluster and corporate employees work together to try to solve problems related to housing, public safety, health, and education.

Volunteer Organizations

Nonprofit agencies, religious groups, and other community organizations offer opportunities for volunteers to perform public service. For example, volunteers are needed to construct low-income housing, clean up polluted areas, patrol neighborhoods, serve as companions to neighbors who are elderly or disabled, be mentors for disadvantaged youths, and deliver meals to the homebound. Although volunteers usually receive no pay for their work, they learn skills that may be useful in future careers.

Government programs such as Volunteers in Service to America (VISTA) and Job Corps also offer many opportunities. Some government programs provide financial assistance, health care, or other benefits. AmeriCorps, a national service program established in 1993, repays community service with grants for college tuition.

WHY PUBLIC SERVICE?

Although employment, job security, and benefits have become more variable in recent years, public service careers have not lost their main appeal: they present opportunities to individuals who want to make a difference in the quality of people's lives. Employees become a network of people who provide services their communities require.

Getting Into

Good jobs do not magically appear. Anyone who has been in the job market knows that landing the right job takes planning, preparation, perseverance, and patience. This is true whether you are looking for your first job, reentering the job market, trying to get a new job, or planning a mid-career change. This essay is designed to guide you through the process of finding a job, from helping you define your career objectives to suggesting ways to prepare yourself for interviews. Use the advice and checklists below to help identify the kind of work that fits your personality, skills, and interests. Then learn how to locate job openings that match your criteria. Finally, use these tips to help you create a resume and prepare for the interview that helps you land the job that's right for you.

PLANNING YOUR CAREER

What are your unique skills? What kind of workplace appeals to you? What do you find most rewarding in your daily life? Answering these questions can help you identify a career path that will enrich your life, financially and otherwise. Most people enjoy doing a job well. There is an inner satisfaction that comes from taking on a challenge and accomplishing something worthwhile. Whether you are just starting out in the working world or you are at the midpoint of a career, it is worth taking some time to consider whether or not you are in the right kind of work—or looking for the right kind of job. If you are unhappy or dissatisfied in your daily work and are just trying to do enough to get by, you may not be in the right job or the right field. The following ideas can help you match your skills and interests with the kind of work you will find most rewarding.

Evaluate Yourself

Before you make any career decisions, think about subjects or topics that interest you and tasks you do well. This can help you pinpoint the kind of work you would be happy doing. One way to go about this is to compile a self-inventory chart. Such a chart will be helpful as you decide which jobs you want to consider. Including details about your work history and educational background will also make the chart useful to you as you compile your resume, write cover letters, complete job application forms, and prepare for job interviews.

Begin your self-inventory chart by listing all the jobs you have ever had, including summer employment, part-time jobs, volunteer work, and any freelance or short-term assignments you have done. Include the dates of employment, the names and addresses of supervisors, and the amount of money you earned. Then compile a similar list of your hobbies and other activities, including any special experiences you have had, such as travel. Next, do the same for your educational history, listing schools attended, major courses of study, grades, special honors or awards, courses you particularly enjoyed, and extracurricular activities.

At this point, you may see a career pattern emerging: perhaps your list is already suggesting a direction for your career search. If the picture still lacks detail or focus, expand your self-inventory chart by compiling a list of standard workplace aptitudes, and rate yourself *above average*, *average*, or *below average* for each one. Some skill categories to include in your list are administrative, analytic, athletic, clerical, language, leadership, managerial, manual, mathematical, mechanical, sales, and verbal abilities. Also rate your willingness to accept responsibility and your ability to get along with people. In combination with your educational background, work history, and list of personal interests, this information should help you understand why some kinds of work appeal to you and others do not.

Evaluate Workplace Characteristics

Another tool to help you find a rewarding job is the "Work Characteristics Checklist" below. Some of these characteristics will be attractive to you. Some will not. Perhaps you will discover that having a workplace with flexible hours, for example, is more important to you than being able to work outdoors. Or maybe you will find that these are both very significant issues in your quality of life.

This checklist can be useful as a guide as you compile your own list of what is important to you in a job or workplace. Do not expect a job to meet all your requirements, however. Focusing on the job characteristics that are most important to you will

Work Characteristics Checklist

Do you want a job in which you can

- work outdoors?
- be physically active?
- work with your hands?
- be challenged mentally?
- work with machines?
- work independently?
- work on a team?
- follow clear instructions?
- earn a lot of money?
- have a chance for rapid advancement?
- have good benefits?
- travel in your work?
- work close to home?
- work regular hours?
- have a flexible schedule?
- have a variety of tasks?
- have supervisory responsibilities?
- express your own ideas?
- be a decision maker?

help you identify the type of work you would find most rewarding. It will also be helpful when it is time to decide whether or not to apply for jobs you discover during the search process.

Evaluate Career Options

Now that you've evaluated your personal skills, aptitudes, interests, and experience, and you've identified the kinds of workplace characteristics that are important to you, do you feel confident that you know what kinds of jobs you'd be good at? If not, you may wish to consult an experienced career counselor or take advantage of online resources that can help you find a good career field match.

Most high schools, vocational schools, and colleges provide vocational testing and career counseling guidance for students and alumni. Some local offices of the state employment services affiliated with the federal employment service offer free counseling. Commercial career centers also offer guidance services.

There are many tools available to test your interests and aptitudes for the purpose of career counseling. The personal profile that emerges from a skills inventory can be matched with potential career fields to show you what kinds of jobs might be good matches for your interests. These assessment tools will also show you what kind of training is necessary to qualify for jobs in these career fields. You may find programs like this online that you can try for yourself. For a more comprehensive approach, you may prefer to look into aptitude tests that are administered and interpreted by a career counselor.

Most major cities have professional career consultants and career counseling firms. You should make sure to check their reputations before paying for their services. A list of counseling services in your area is available from the American Counseling Association in Alexandria, Virginia (http://www.counseling.org).

You can also search the Internet for many services that career counselors provide. Some sites have online counselors who can help you with a variety of tasks, such as obtaining information on jobs, careers, and training. They may be able to provide information on available services, including housing assistance, day care facilities, and transportation. A list of career planning resources, including Web sites, is available at the end of this volume.

EVALUATE SPECIFIC JOBS

After you have considered what you do well and what you enjoy doing, and identified some career options that provide a good match with your interests and abilities, you're ready to focus on the specific types of jobs that may be available to you. First, make a note of all the jobs in this volume that interest you. Then examine the education and training required for these jobs. Decide whether you qualify or would be able to gain the qualifications.

If possible, talk with people who have the kinds of jobs you are considering. Firsthand information can be invaluable. Also look through the appropriate trade and professional journals listed at the end of this essay and check the section at the end of the volume called "Resources" for books and Web sites that contain more detailed information about the jobs. In addition, counselors usually are helpful. For more detailed information, you can contact the trade and professional associations listed at the end of each occupational profile.

Once you have found out all you can about a particular type of job, compare the features of the job with your work characteristics checklist. See how many characteristics of the job match your work preferences. By completing these steps for all the jobs that appeal to you, you should be able to come up with a list of jobs that match your interests and abilities.

FINDING JOB OPPORTUNITIES

Once you've decided what kind of job suits you, the next step is to look for available positions. Obviously, the more openings you can find, the better your chance of landing a job. People usually apply

Job Finder's Checklist

The following list of job-hunting tips may seem obvious, but getting all the bits and pieces in order beforehand helps when you're looking for a job.

Resume Find out whether you will need a resume. If so, bring your resume up to date or prepare a new one. Assemble a supply of neatly printed copies and have an electronic version ready to e-mail to prospective employers.

References Line up your references. Ask permission of the people whose names you would like to use. Write down their addresses, phone numbers, and job titles.

Contacts Put the word out to everyone you know that you are looking for a job.

Job market Find out where the jobs are. Make a list of possible employers in your field of interest.

Research Do a little homework ahead of time—it can make a big difference in the long run. Find out as much as you can about a job, the field, and the company before you apply. A knowledgeable job applicant makes a good impression.

Organization Keep a file on your job-hunting campaign with names and dates of employers contacted, ads answered, results, and follow-up.

Appearance Make sure that the clothes you plan to wear to an interview are neat and clean. You may need to dress more formally than you would on the job, particularly if you are visiting a personnel office or meeting with a manager. Keep in mind that people will form an opinion of you based on their first impressions.

---

for many job openings before they find the right employment match.

There are many ways to find out about or apply for job openings. Some of these job-hunting techniques are explained on the pages that follow, along with information about how to follow up on job leads.

Applying in Person

For some jobs, especially part-time or entry-level jobs, you may be able to find employment by visiting the company or companies for which you would like to work. This works best when a company is expanding or jobs are plentiful for other reasons, or when a "help wanted" sign is posted at the company. Applying in person can sharpen your interviewing techniques and give you a chance to see a variety of workplaces. This direct approach is best for hourly labor or service jobs; when applying for other types of work, it is not the method to use unless you are directed to do so. Applicants for professional or supervisory jobs should always send a letter and resume to the company.

Phone and Letter Campaigns

To conduct a phone campaign, use the business listings of your telephone directory to build a list of companies for which you might like to work. Call their personnel departments and find out whether they have any openings. This technique is not useful in all situations, and it has its drawbacks: you may not be able to make a strong impression by phone, and you will not have a written record of your contacts.

Letter writing campaigns can be very effective if the letters are well thought out and carefully prepared. Your letters should always be typed. Handwritten letters and photocopied letters convey a lack of interest or motivation.

You may be able to compile a good list of company addresses in your field of interest by reading the trade and professional publications listed at the end of this essay. Many of the periodicals publish directories or directory issues. Other sources you can use to compile lists of companies are the trade unions and professional organizations listed at the end of each job profile in this volume. The reference librarian at your local library can also help you find appropriate directories.

You can also e-mail letters to human resource departments of many companies. Be sure to follow all the same guidelines as you would for traditional letter correspondence.

Whether they are paper or electronic, your letters should be addressed to the personnel or human resources department of the organization. If possible, send the letter to a specific person. If you don't know who the correct person is, try to find the name of the personnel director through the directories in the library. You can also call on the phone and say, "I'm writing to ask about employment at your company. To whom should I address my letter?" If you can't find a name, use a standard salutation. It's a good idea to enclose a resume (described later in this essay) with the letter to give the employer a brief description of your educational and work experience.

Keep a list of all the people you write to, along with the date each letter was mailed, or keep a photocopy of each letter. Then you can follow up by writing a brief note or calling people who do not reply within about three weeks.

Job Databases Online

The World Wide Web can be an excellent resource for job hunters. The Internet currently has thousands of career-related sites where you can read about job openings or post your resume in a database for a possible match with available jobs. Some sites, such as The Monster Board (http://www.monster.com), help you build a resume and post it online as well as allow you to search through a massive database of help-wanted listings. Others employ a search engine to find jobs that match your background, then post your resume online for employers. The Web site called CareerBuilder (http://www.careerbuilder.com) uses an interactive personal search program that lets you select job criteria such as location, title, and salary; you are then notified by e-mail when a matching position is posted in the database.

Many companies post job openings in their human resource Web pages. You can usually access these lists by visiting the Web site of a company and clicking on a link called "jobs," "careers," or "employment opportunities." If you find a job that interests you during your online search, whether it's posted at a company's own Web site or on a general listing of jobs, follow the directions given for applying for the position. Some online ads will provide the contact information you need to send your resume and cover letter directly to the employer, ei-

Many career-related Web sites can be found on the Internet. This hypothetical site (for illustration purposes only) allows job-seekers to search for a position by location and job category.

ther by e-mail or by traditional mail, but other ads direct job hunters to apply directly through a link at the job description.

Job hunters can often find job listings through the Web sites of the professional associations in their career fields. State government Web sites may also provide links to job listings—or to non-government sites that list available jobs.

Help-Wanted Ads

Many people find out about job openings by reading the "help-wanted" sections of newspapers, trade journals, and professional magazines. Employers and employment agencies often, though not always, use these classified ad sections to publicize available jobs.

Classified ads use unique terms to convey basic information. You will find some common abbreviations in the chart in this essay titled "Reading the Classifieds." You can usually decode the abbreviations by using common sense, but if something puzzles you, call the newspaper and ask for a translation. Classified ads usually list the qualifications that are required for a particular job and explain how to contact the employer.

As you find openings that interest you, answer each ad using the method requested. Record the date of your contact, and if you don't hear from the employer within two or three weeks, place another call or send a polite note asking whether the job is still open. Don't forget to include your phone number and address in your initial contact.

Some help-wanted ads are "blind ads." These ads give contact information for replying but provide no name, phone number, or address that would identify the company. Employers and employment agencies may place these ads to avoid having to reply to all of the job applicants or being contacted directly by job-seekers.

Situation-Wanted Ads

Another way to get the attention of potential employers is with a situation-wanted ad. You can place one of these in the classified section of your local newspaper or of a trade journal in your field of interest. Many personnel offices and employment agencies scan these columns when they're looking for new employees. The situation-wanted ad is usually most effective for people who have advanced ed-

Reading the Classifieds

HELP WANTED

ACADEMIC AIDE—Local college needs a person to handle a variety of student services incl. academic & social counseling. Good oppty. Degree, similar exp. pfd. Call 000-0000 weekdays 10–4, Sat. 10–12.

CHILD CARE   RESIDENT DIRECTOR
Suburban child care agency needs capable person to assume direction of residential program. Must have MSW & min. 3 yrs. admin. and supervisory bkgd. Salary commensurate w/experience. Good fringe benefits. M4711 Chronicle. An Equal Oppty. Employer

CORRECTIONS OFFICER
HALFWAY HOUSE
Immediate opening for mature, reliable person to supervise and counsel residents at County Pre-Release Center in City, State. Revolving shift work will require evening and weekend hours. Apply in person.

CUSTODIAN f/p $0/hr. Mon–Fri. 2–8:30, Sun. 8–9:30. Protestant Church. Carlson Agency, Main Street

LEGAL SECY. with top qualifications to work with partner in attractive offices. Good skills essential incl. WP. Salary commensurate with ability. 000-0000.

LIBRARIAN
School year. Small private h.s. Metropolitan area. Bachelor of Library Science req. Knowledge of computerized databases helpful. Write Journal Box T 7431.

SECURITY GUARDS
Immediate openings. Full and part time. Uniform supplied. Must be U.S. resident, have no criminal convictions, have car and phone. 000-0000.

SOCIAL WORKER—Child welfare agency seeks MSW to supervise foster care program. Competitive salary, excel. benefits. Call/send resume and sal. req. to:
S. Allen
Broadfield Child Care
24 Lincoln Ave.
City, State 00000

CLASSIFIED ABBREVIATIONS

addl.	additional
admin.	administrative, administration
avail. immed.	available immediately
avg.	average
bkgd.	background
excel.	excellent
exp.	experience
fee neg.	fee negotiable (fee can be worked out with employer)
figs.	figures
f/p., f/pd.	fee paid (agency fee paid by employer)
f/t	full time
gd. bnfts.	good benefits
incl.	including
mgr.	manager
natl.	national
pfd.	preferred
p/t	part time
refs.	references
req.	required
sal.	salary
sec., secy.	secretary
temp.	temporary
trnee.	trainee
typ.	typist, typing
w/	with
WP	word processing

SITUATION WANTED

DAY CARE WORKER
seeks p/t work, 3 days/wk. Experienced, good refs. 000-0000.

PRIVATE
DETECTIVE
Available by hour, day, week, job. Confidential background, missing person, matrimonial investigations. Experienced, reasonable. 000-0000.

ELEMENTARY TEACHER
wishes to tutor child/children for summer. Any subject. Call 000-0000.

FUND RAISER
4 yrs. exp. direct mail and local campaign planning for natl. organization. Willing to travel, work odd hrs.   M3136 Times.

LEGAL SECRETARY—top skills, 3 yrs. exp. with patent attorney. Computer literate. Avail. August. Box 823, Chronicle.

LIBRARIAN
MLS & 3 yrs. technical & reference exp. seeks p/t library job metropolitan area. 000-0000.

MINISTER
DUTCH REFORMED
CHURCH
Wishes to relocate to Midwest. 8 yrs. exp., heavy youth work. Box Z47 Gazette.

SCHOOL CUSTODIAN. Avail. immed., West County area. 6 yrs. school exp. Alex Rudman, 000-0000.

YOUTH WORK
Sociology student wants f/t summer job with youth organization. Urban location preferred. Camp counselor exp. Call Chuck, 000-0000 after 6 p.m.

TEACHER—Exp. in H.S. art and computer graphics desires job in any related field. 000-0000.

ucation, training, or experience, or who are in fields where their unique skills are in great demand.

A situation-wanted ad should be brief, clear, and to the point. Its main purpose is to interest the employer enough so you are contacted for an interview. It should tell exactly what kind of job you want, why you qualify, and whether you are available for full-time or part-time work. Use the same abbreviations that employers use in classified ads.

If you are already employed and do not want it known that you are looking for a new position, you can run a blind ad. A blind ad protects your privacy by listing a box number at the publication to which all replies can be sent. They are then forwarded to you. You do not need to give your name, address, or phone number in the ad.

Networking

A very important source of information about job openings is networking. This means talking with friends and acquaintances about your area of interest. If any of them have friends or relatives in the field, ask if they would be willing to speak with you. There's nothing wrong with telling anyone who will listen that you are looking for a job—family, friends, counselors, and former employers. This will multiply your sources of information many times over.

You can use the Internet to make contacts, too. You can meet people with similar interests in news groups, which are organized by topic. Then you can correspond individually via e-mail. Many fields have professional organizations that maintain Web sites. These can help you keep current on news affecting your field, including employment opportunities.

Sometimes a contact knows about a job vacancy before it is advertised. You may have an advantage, then, when you get in touch with the employer. Don't, however, use the contact's name without permission. Don't assume that a contact will go out on a limb by recommending you, either. Once you have received the inside information, rely on your own ability to get the job.

Notes on Networking

Let people know you're looking. Tell friends, acquaintances, teachers, business associates, former employers—anyone who might know of job openings in your field.

Read newspapers and professional and trade journals. Look for news of developments in your field and for names of people and companies you might contact.

Use the World Wide Web. Make contacts through news groups, or find information on Web sites for professional organizations in your field.

Join professional or trade associations. Contacts you make at meetings could provide valuable job leads. Association newsletters generally carry useful information about people and developments in the field.

Attend classes or seminars. You will meet other people in your field at job-training classes and professional development seminars.

Participate in local support groups. You can gain information about people and places to contact through support groups such as those listed by *The Riley Guide*, available online at http://www.rileyguide.com/support.html, as well as through alumni associations.

Be on the lookout. Always be prepared to make the most of any opportunity that comes along. Talk with anyone who can provide useful information about your field.

Placement Services

Most vocational schools, high schools, and colleges have a placement or career service that maintains a list of job openings and schedules visits from companies. If you are a student or recent graduate, you should check there for job leads. Many employers look first in technical or trade schools and colleges for qualified applicants for certain jobs. Recruiters often visit colleges to look for people to fill technical and scientific positions. These recruiters usually represent large companies. Visit your placement office regularly to check the job listings, and watch for scheduled visits by company recruiters.

State Employment Services

Another source of information about job openings is the local office of the state employment service. Many employers automatically list job openings at the local office. Whether you're looking for a job in private industry or with the state, these offices, which are affiliated with the federal employment service, are worth visiting, online or in person, if there are offices locally.

State employment service offices are public agencies that do not charge for their services. They can direct you to special programs run by the government in conjunction with private industry. These programs, such as the Work Incentive Program for families on welfare, are designed to meet special needs. Some, but not all, of these offices offer vocational aptitude and interest tests and can refer interested people to vocational training centers. The state employment service can be a valuable first stop in your search for work, especially if there are special circumstances in your background. For example, if you did not finish high school, if you have had any difficulties with the law, or if you are living in a difficult home environment, your state employment service office is equipped to help you.

Private Employment Agencies

State employment services, though free, are usually very busy. If you are looking for more personal service and want a qualified employment counselor to help you find a job, you might want to approach a private employment agency.

Private employment agencies will help you get a job if they think they can place you. Most of them get paid only if they're successful in finding you a job, so you need to show them that you are a good prospect. These agencies will help you prepare a resume if you need one, and they will contact employers they think might be interested in you.

Private employment agencies are in the business of bringing together people who are looking for jobs and companies that are looking for workers. For some positions, usually mid- and higher-level jobs, the employment agency's fee is paid by the employer. In such cases, the job seeker pays no fee. In other cases, you may be required to pay the fee, which is usually a percentage of your annual salary. Paying a fee can be a worthwhile investment if it leads to a rewarding career.

Some agencies may also ask for a small registration fee whether or not you get a job through them. Some agencies may demand that you pay even if you find one of the jobs they are trying to fill through your other contacts. Be sure to read and understand the fine print of any contract you're expected to sign, and ask for a copy to take home. Since the quality of these agencies varies, check to see if an agency is a certified member of a state or national association.

Some employment agencies, called staffing services, operate in a different way. They are usually paid by employers to screen and refer good candidates for job openings. They earn money when they refer a candidate who is hired by the employer. The employee pays no fee. Staffing firms, however, only spend time on candidates they think they may be able to place.

Private employment agencies are usually helping many people at one time. They may not have the time to contact you every time they find a job opening. Therefore, you may need to phone them at reasonable intervals after you have registered.

Civil Service

In your search for work, don't forget that the civil service—federal, state, and local—may have many jobs in your field. You may contact the state employment office or apply directly to the appropriate state or federal agency. The armed services also train and employ civilians in many fields. Don't neglect these avenues for finding jobs. Civil service positions usually require you to take a civil service examination. Books are available to help you prepare for these exams, and your local civil service office can also provide information.

Unions

In certain fields, unions can be useful sources of information. If you are a member of a union in your field of interest, you may be able to find out about jobs in the union periodical or through people at the union local. If you do not belong to a union, you may contact a union in the field you are interested in for information about available employment services. You will find addresses for some unions in the job profiles in this book.

Temporary Employment

A good way to get a feel for the job market—what's available and what certain jobs are like—is to work in a temporary job. There are both private and state agencies that can help place people in short-term jobs. Some jobs are seasonal, and extra workers may be needed in the summer or at another busy time.

Temporary employment can increase your job skills, your knowledge of a particular field, and your chances of hearing of permanent positions. In today's tight labor market, many companies are using the services of temporary workers in increasing numbers. In fact, temporary agencies may sign multimillion-dollar contracts to provide businesses with a range of temporary workers. In some cases, temporary workers are in such demand that they may receive benefits, bonuses, and the same hourly wages as equivalent permanent employees. Some temporary agencies are even joining with companies to create long-term career paths for their temporary workers.

MARKETING YOURSELF

An employer's first impression of you is likely to be based on the way you present yourself on print. Whether it is in an application form or on a resume, you will want to make a good impression so that employers will be interested in giving you a personal

DO YOU KNOW YOUR RIGHTS?

JOB DISCRIMINATION—WHAT IT IS

Federal and State Law

An employer cannot discriminate against you for any reason other than your ability to do the job. By federal law, an employer cannot discriminate against you because of your race, color, religion, sex, or national origin. The law applies to decisions about hiring, promotion, working conditions, and firing. The law specifically protects workers who are over the age of forty from discrimination on the basis of age.

The law also protects workers with disabilities. Employers must make their workplaces accessible to individuals with disabilities—for example, by making them accessible to wheelchairs or by hiring readers or interpreters for blind or deaf employees.

Federal law offers additional protection to employees who work for the federal government or for employers who contract with the federal government. State law can also provide protection, for example by prohibiting discrimination on the basis of marital status, arrest record, political affiliations, or sexual orientation.

Affirmative Action

Affirmative action programs are set up by businesses that want to make a special effort to hire women and members of minority groups. Federal employers and many businesses that have contracts with the federal government are required by law to set up affirmative action programs. Employers with a history of discriminatory practices may also be required to establish affirmative action programs.

Discrimination against Job Applicants

A job application form or interviewer may ask for information that can be used to discriminate against you illegally. The law prohibits such questions. If you are asked such questions and are turned down for

the job, you may be a victim of discrimination. However, under federal law, employers must require you to prove that you are an American citizen or that you have a valid work permit.

Discrimination on the Job

Discrimination on the job is illegal. Being denied a promotion for which you are qualified or being paid less than coworkers are paid for the same job may be forms of illegal discrimination.

Sexual, racial, and religious harassment are forms of discrimination and are prohibited in the workplace. On-the-job harassment includes sexual, racial, or religious jokes or comments. Sexual harassment includes not only requests or demands for sexual favors but also verbal or physical conduct of a sexual nature.

JOB DISCRIMINATION—WHAT YOU CAN DO

Contact Federal or State Commissions

If you believe that your employer practices discrimination, you can complain to the state civil rights commission or the federal Equal Employment Opportunity Commission (EEOC). If, after investigating your complaint, the commission finds that there has been discrimination, it will take action against the employer. You may be entitled to the job or promotion you were denied or to reinstatement if you were fired. You may also receive back pay or other financial compensation.

Contact a Private Organization

There are many private organizations that can help you fight job discrimination. For example, the American Civil Liberties Union (ACLU) works to protect all people from infringement on their civil rights. The National Association for the Advancement of Colored People (NAACP), National Organization

interview. A potential employer is likely to equate a neat, well-written presentation with good work habits, and a sloppy, poorly written one with bad work habits.

Writing an Effective Resume

When you write to a company to follow up a lead or to ask about job openings, you should send information about yourself. The accepted way of doing this is to send a resume with a cover letter.

The work resume is derived from the French word résumer, meaning "to summarize." A resume does just that—it briefly outlines your education, work experience, and special abilities and skills. A resume may also be called a curriculum vitae, a personal profile, or a personal data sheet. This summary acts as your introduction by mail or e-mail, as your calling card if you apply in person, and as a convenient reference for you to use when filling out an application form or when being interviewed.

for Women (NOW), and Native American Rights Fund may negotiate with your employer, sue on your behalf, or start a class action suit—a lawsuit brought on behalf of all individuals in your situation.

WHAT TO DO IF YOU LOSE YOUR JOB

Being Fired and Being Laid Off

In most cases, an employer can fire you only if there is good cause, such as your inability to do the job, violation of safety rules, dishonesty, or chronic absenteeism.

Firing an employee because of that employee's race, color, religion, sex, national origin, or age (if the employee is over forty) is illegal. Firing an employee for joining a union or for reporting an employer's violation (called whistle-blowing) is also prohibited. If you believe you have been wrongfully discharged, you should contact the EEOC or the state civil rights commission.

At times, employers may need to let a number of employees go to reduce costs. This reduction in staff is called a layoff. Laying off an employee has nothing to do with the employee's job performance. Federal law requires employers who lay off large numbers of employees to give these employees at least two months' notice of the cutback.

Unemployment Compensation

Unemployment insurance is a state-run fund that provides payments to people who lose their jobs through no fault of their own. Not everyone is entitled to unemployment compensation. Those who quit their jobs or who worked only a few months before losing their jobs may not be eligible.

The amount of money you receive depends on how much you earned at your last job. You may receive unemployment payments for only a limited period of time and only so long as you can prove that you are actively looking for a new position.

Each claim for unemployment compensation is investigated before the state makes any payments. If the state unemployment agency decides to deny you compensation, you may ask the agency for instructions on how to appeal that decision.

OTHER PROTECTIONS FOR EMPLOYEES

Honesty and Drug Testing

Many employers ask job applicants or employees to submit to lie detector tests or drug tests. Lie detector tests are permitted in the hiring of people for high security positions, such as police officers. Some states prohibit or restrict the testing of applicants or employees for drug use. Aptitude and personality tests are generally permitted.

Other Federal Laws

The Fair Labor Standards Act prescribes certain minimum wages and rules about working hours and overtime payments. Workers' compensation laws provide payment for injuries that occur in the workplace and wages lost as a result of those injuries.

The Occupational Safety and Health Act sets minimum requirements for workplace safety. Any employee who discovers a workplace hazard should report it to the Occupational Safety and Health Administration (OSHA). The administration will investigate the claim and may require the employer to correct the problem or pay a fine.

Rights Guaranteed by Contract

Not every employee has a written contract. If you do, however, that contract may grant you additional rights, such as the right to severance pay in the event you are laid off. In addition, employees who are members of a union may have certain rights guaranteed through their union contract.

Before you sign any contract, make sure you understand every part of it. Read it thoroughly and ask the employer questions. Checking the details of a contract before signing it may prevent misunderstanding later.

A resume is a useful tool in applying for almost any job, even if you use it only to keep a record of where you have worked, for whom, and the dates of employment. A resume is required if you are being considered for professional or executive jobs. Prepare it carefully. It's well worth the effort.

The goal of a resume is to capture the interest of potential employers so they will call you for a personal interview. Since employers are busy people, the resume should be as brief and as neat as possible. You should, however, include as much relevant information about yourself as you can. This is usually presented under at least two headings: "Education" and "Experience." The latter is sometimes called "Employment History." Some people add a third section titled "Related Skills," "Professional Qualifications," or "Related Qualifications."

If you prepare a self-inventory such as the one described earlier, it will be a useful tool in preparing a resume. Go through your inventory, and select the items that show your ability to do the job or jobs in which you are interested. Plan to highlight these

RYAN RADVIK

391 Macarthy Drive
Malvern, PA 12345
(555) 123-5678
Rradvik@email.com

EXPERIENCE

Summer, 2004

Assembly Worker, Olsen Manufacturing Company, Inc., Malvern, PA.

Responsible for assembly of metal casing for lighting equipment. Served as member of inspection team on a rotating basis.

Part-time 2000 to 2003

Coach, YMCA, West Chester, PA.

Supervised training and competition matches of boys' soccer team. Planned practice sessions for beginners and experienced players. Organized competition schedule with other teams. Responsible for team safety and security of equipment.

2000

Groundskeeper, Twin Meadows Country Club, Ridgewood, NJ.

Responsible for care of golf course. Duties included fertilizing, mowing, trimming lawns, and collecting litter. Operated club vehicles and power equipment. Planted and tended ornamental flowers and shrubs.

EDUCATION

2000

Diploma, Windsor High School, Ridgewood, NJ.

General business program.

Captain, soccer and track teams.

REFERENCES

Available upon request.

- State your name, address, telephone number, and email first.
- State job objective or general career goal in a few words.
- List education and work experience in reverse chronological order, with most recent item first.

DOROTHY LEHMAN

Apartment 8
989 Cameron Boulevard
Arlington, VA 12345
(555) 123-4567
dlehman@email.com

OBJECTIVE: *Position as reference librarian in public or university library.*

EXPERIENCE:

1995 to 2003   **School Librarian**, Manchester School District, Arlington, VA.

Responsible for administration and program planning for library of midsize elementary school. Handled all acquisitions, cataloging, and maintenance of library materials. Worked with superintendent on annual library budget proposal. Organized video, film, and pamphlet collections. Supervised library study groups. Provided reference services for students and faculty.

1994 to 1995   **Cataloger**, Hamilton University Library, Richmond, VA.

Responsible for identification, cataloging, and cross-referencing of new acquisitions. Recataloged older holdings to conform to new system. Entered all data in university computer system as well as main library card file. Prepared cases and bindings for nonstandard material. Coordinated work with catalog staff in special collection libraries.

EDUCATION:

1995   **Master of Library Science**, Hamilton University, Graduate School of Library Science, Richmond, VA.

1992   **Bachelor of Arts**, University of Virginia, Charlottesville, VA. Major in Modern Languages.

RELATED SKILLS AND QUALIFICATIONS: *Reading and speaking knowledge of Spanish and German.*

Member, American Library Association.

REFERENCES: *Available upon request.*

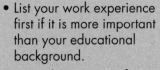

- List your work experience first if it is more important than your educational background.
- Keep descriptions of your education and work experience brief.
- List special skills and qualifications if they are relevant to the job.

items on your resume. Select only those facts that point out your relevant skills and experience.

Once you have chosen the special points to include, prepare the resume. At the top, put your name, address, and phone number. After that, decide which items will be most relevant to the employer you plan to contact.

State Your Objective Some employment counselors advise that you state a job objective or describe briefly the type of position for which you are applying. The job objective usually follows your name and address. Don't be too specific if you plan to use the same resume a number of times. It's better to give a general career goal. Then, in a cover letter, you can be more specific about the position in which you are interested.

Describe What You've Done Every interested employer will check your educational background and employment history carefully. It is best to present these sections in order of importance. For instance, if you've held many relevant jobs, you should list your work experience first, followed by your educational background. On the other hand, if you are just out of school with little or no work experience, it's probably best to list your educational background first and then, under employment history, to mention any part-time and summer jobs you've held or volunteer work you've done.

Under educational background, list the schools you have attended in reverse chronological order, starting with your most recent training and ending with the least recent. Employers want to know at a glance your highest qualifications. For each educational experience, include years attended, name and location of the school, and degree or certificate earned, if any. If you have advanced degrees (college and beyond), it isn't necessary to include high school and elementary school education. Don't forget to highlight any special courses you took or awards you won, if they are relevant to the kind of job you are seeking.

Chronological and Functional Resumes Information about your employment history can be presented in two ways. The most common format is the chronological resume. In a chronological resume, you summarize your work experience year by year. Begin with your current or most recent employment and then work backward. For each job, list the name and location of the company for which you worked, the years you were employed, and the position or positions you held. The order in which you present these facts will depend on what you are trying to emphasize. If you want to call attention to the type or level of job you held, for example, you should put the job title first. Regardless of the order

you choose, be consistent. Summer employment or part-time work should be identified as such. If you held a job for less than a year, specify months in the dates of employment.

It is important to include a brief description of the responsibilities you had in each job. This often reveals more about your abilities than the job title. Remember, too, that you do not have to mention the names of former supervisors or how much you earned. You can discuss these points during the interview or explain them on an application form.

The functional resume, on the other hand, emphasizes what you can do rather than what you have done. It is useful for people who have large gaps in their work history or who have relevant skills that would not be properly highlighted in a chronological listing of jobs. The functional resume concentrates on qualifications—such as familiarity with particular equipment, organizational skills, or managerial experience. Specific jobs may be mentioned, but they are not the primary focus of this type of resume.

Explain Special Skills You may wish to include a third section called "Related Skills," "Professional Qualifications," or "Related Qualifications." This is useful if there are points you want to highlight that do not apply directly to educational background or work experience. Be sure these points are relevant to the kind of work you are seeking. This section is most effective if you can mention any special recognition, awards, or other evidence of excellence. It is also useful to mention if you are willing to relocate or can work unusual hours.

Have References Available Employers may also want to know whom they can contact to find out more about you. At the start of your job search, you should ask three or four people if you may use them as references. If you haven't seen these people for a while, you may want to send them a copy of your resume and let them know what kind of position you're seeking. Your references should be the kind of people your potential employer will respect, and they should be able to comment favorably on your abilities, personality, and work habits. You should indicate whether these people are personal references or former work supervisors. Avoid using any relatives. You can list the names and addresses of your references at the end of your resume or in a cover letter. Or, you can simply write, "References available upon request." Just be sure you have their names, addresses, and phone numbers ready if you are asked.

Present Yourself Concisely Tips for making your resume concise include using phrases instead of sentences and omitting unnecessary words. When

RYAN RADVIK

391 Macarthy Drive
Malvern, PA 12345
(555) 123-5678
Rradvik@email.com391

November 5, 2005

Ms. Amy Liebowitz
Postmaster
Malvern Central Post Office
Malvern, PA 12345

Dear Ms. Liebowitz:

As I mentioned during our telephone conversation this morning, I am interested in employment as a letter carrier with the Malvern Central Post Office.

I am accustomed to outdoor work because two of my previous positions have involved this type of work. I have a valid driver's license and a good driving record. I am available to work any shift.

I enclose my resume as requested. I would be grateful if you would send me the application form you mentioned. I have arranged to take the postal service employee's exam this month.

Thank you for explaining the application process to me. I look forward to receiving the material.

Sincerely yours,

Ryan Radvik

Enclosure

DOROTHY LEHMAN

Apartment 8
989 Cameron Boulevard
Arlington, VA 12345
(555) 123-4567
dlehman@email.com

January 12, 2005

Mr. Joseph Delgado
Director of Library Services
Middlesex Township
62 Marlboro Avenue
Richmond, VA 12347

Dear Mr. Delgado:

Rita Spalding, reference librarian at Middlesex Public Library, mentioned that she will be retiring in February. I am interested in applying for her position.

I have experience in school and university libraries and am familiar with the major classification systems. I have worked extensively with automated catalog equipment and on-line reference systems. I am familiar with the county interlibrary loan system and with the community programs run at Middlesex and other local libraries.

I enclose my resume. Since Ms. Spalding has just announced her retirement, perhaps you would let me know how you will be conducting the search for her successor. I am available at any time for an interview and can be reached at my home.

Sincerely yours,

Dorothy Lehman

Dorothy Lehman

Enclosure

appropriate, start a phrase with a verb, such as "maintained" or "coordinated." There is no need to say "I"—that is obvious and repetitive.

Present Yourself Well Employment counselors often recommend that resumes be no longer than one page because employers won't take the time to read a second page. If you've held many positions related to your occupation, go on to the second page, but don't include beginning or irrelevant jobs. If you have a lot of work experience, limit the education section to just the essentials.

You should also concentrate on the appearance of your resume. A traditional resume should be printed on a good grade of 8½" x 11" white paper. Consult a resume preparation guide for specific information about the best ways to format a resume that will be processed by e-mail or other electronic means. If you don't have access to a computer and printer, you can pay someone to type your resume, but it is up to you to read it carefully and ensure that it is error-free. Be sure that it is neatly typed with adequate margins. The data should be spaced and indented so that each item stands out. This enables a busy executive or personnel director to see at a glance the facts of greatest interest.

These suggestions for writing a resume are not hard-and-fast rules. Resumes may be adapted to special situations. For example, people with a variety of work experience often prepare several versions of their resumes and use the experience that's most relevant when applying for a particular job.

If this is your first resume, show it to someone else, perhaps a guidance counselor, for constructive advice. Make sure there are no spelling or punctuation mistakes anywhere on the page. No matter what, be truthful while emphasizing your assets. You can do that by showing the abilities, skills, and specific interests that qualify you for a particular job. Don't mention any weaknesses or deficiencies in your training. Do mention job-related aptitudes that showed up in previous employment or in school. Don't make things up; everything that's in your resume can, and often will, be checked.

Writing Cover Letters

Whenever you send your resume to a prospective employer, whether it's on paper or in e-mail form, you should send a cover letter with it. This is true whether you are writing to apply for a specific job or just to find out if there are any openings.

A good cover letter should be neat, brief, and well written, with no more than three or four short paragraphs. Since you may use your resume for a variety of job openings, your cover letter should be very specific. Your goal is to get the person who reads it

to think that you are an ideal candidate for a particular job. If at all possible, send the letter to a specific person—either the personnel director or the person for whom you would be working. If necessary, call the company and ask to whom you should address the letter.

Start your letter by explaining why you are writing. Say that you are inquiring about possible job openings at the company, that you are responding to an advertisement in a particular publication, or that someone recommended that you should write. (Use the person's name if you have received permission to do so.) Let your letter lead into your resume. Use it to call attention to your qualifications. Add information that shows why you are well suited for that specific job.

Completing the Application Form

Many employers ask job applicants to fill out an application form. This form usually duplicates much of the information on your resume, but it may ask some additional questions. Give complete answers to all questions except those that are discriminatory. If a question doesn't apply to you, put a dash next to it.

You may be given the application form when you arrive for an interview, or it may be sent to your home. When filling it out, print neatly in ink. Follow the instructions carefully. For instance, if the form asks you to put down your last name first, do so.

The most important sections of an application form are the education and work histories. As in your resume, many applications request that you write these in reverse chronological order, with the most recent experience first. Unlike your resume, however, the application form may request information about your earnings on previous jobs. It may also ask what rate of pay you are seeking on the job you are applying for.

Be prepared to answer these and other topics not addressed on your resume. Look at the sample application form, and make note of the kinds of questions that you are likely to be asked—for example, your Social Security number, the names of previous supervisors, your salary, and your reason for leaving. If necessary, carry notes on such topics with you to an interview. You have a responsibility to tell prospective employers what they need to know to make an informed decision.

Neatness Counts Think before you write on an application form so you avoid crossing things out. An employer's opinion of you may be influenced just by the general appearance of your application form. A neat, detailed form may indicate an orderly

1. Always print neatly in blue or black ink. When completing an application at home, type it, if possible.

2. Read the application carefully *before* you start to fill it out. Follow instructions precisely. Use standard abbreviations.

3. If you aren't applying for a specific job, indicate the kind of work you're willing to do.

4. You don't have to commit to a specific rate of pay. Write "open" or "negotiable" if you are uncertain.

5. Traffic violations and so on do not belong here. Nor do offenses for which you were charged but not convicted.

6. If a question doesn't apply to you, write "NA" (for not applicable) or put a dash through the space.

7. Take notes along to remind you of school names, addresses, and dates.

8. If you're short on "real" employment, mention jobs such as babysitting, lawn mowing, or any occasional work.

9. Your references should be people who can be objective about you, such as former employers, teachers, and community leaders.

10. Under the heading "Reason for Leaving," a simple answer will do. Avoid saying "better pay"—even if it's so.

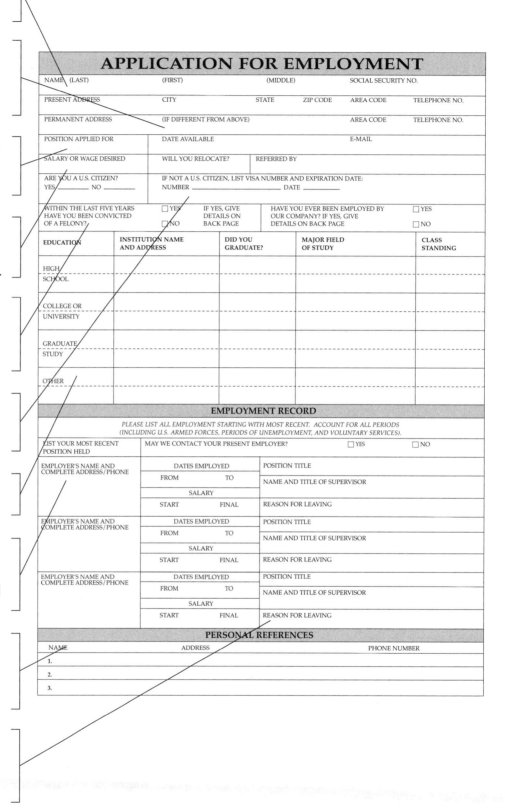

APPLICATION FOR EMPLOYMENT

NAME (LAST)	(FIRST)	(MIDDLE)		SOCIAL SECURITY NO.	
PRESENT ADDRESS	CITY	STATE	ZIP CODE	AREA CODE	TELEPHONE NO.
PERMANENT ADDRESS	(IF DIFFERENT FROM ABOVE)			AREA CODE	TELEPHONE NO.
POSITION APPLIED FOR	DATE AVAILABLE			E-MAIL	
SALARY OR WAGE DESIRED	WILL YOU RELOCATE?	REFERRED BY			
ARE YOU A U.S. CITIZEN? YES_____ NO_____	IF NOT A U.S. CITIZEN, LIST VISA NUMBER AND EXPIRATION DATE: NUMBER _____ DATE _____				

WITHIN THE LAST FIVE YEARS HAVE YOU BEEN CONVICTED OF A FELONY? ☐ YES ☐ NO — IF YES, GIVE DETAILS ON BACK PAGE — HAVE YOU EVER BEEN EMPLOYED BY OUR COMPANY? IF YES, GIVE DETAILS ON BACK PAGE ☐ YES ☐ NO

EDUCATION	INSTITUTION NAME AND ADDRESS	DID YOU GRADUATE?	MAJOR FIELD OF STUDY	CLASS STANDING
HIGH SCHOOL				
COLLEGE OR UNIVERSITY				
GRADUATE STUDY				
OTHER				

EMPLOYMENT RECORD

PLEASE LIST ALL EMPLOYMENT STARTING WITH MOST RECENT. ACCOUNT FOR ALL PERIODS (INCLUDING U.S. ARMED FORCES, PERIODS OF UNEMPLOYMENT, AND VOLUNTARY SERVICES).

LIST YOUR MOST RECENT POSITION HELD — MAY WE CONTACT YOUR PRESENT EMPLOYER? ☐ YES ☐ NO

EMPLOYER'S NAME AND COMPLETE ADDRESS/PHONE	DATES EMPLOYED	POSITION TITLE
	FROM TO	NAME AND TITLE OF SUPERVISOR
	SALARY	
	START FINAL	REASON FOR LEAVING
EMPLOYER'S NAME AND COMPLETE ADDRESS/PHONE	DATES EMPLOYED	POSITION TITLE
	FROM TO	NAME AND TITLE OF SUPERVISOR
	SALARY	
	START FINAL	REASON FOR LEAVING
EMPLOYER'S NAME AND COMPLETE ADDRESS/PHONE	DATES EMPLOYED	POSITION TITLE
	FROM TO	NAME AND TITLE OF SUPERVISOR
	SALARY	
	START FINAL	REASON FOR LEAVING

PERSONAL REFERENCES

NAME	ADDRESS	PHONE NUMBER
1.		
2.		
3.		

mind and the ability to think clearly, follow instructions, and organize information.

Know Your Rights Under federal and some state laws, an employer cannot demand that you answer any questions about race, color, creed, national origin, ancestry, sex, marital status, age (with certain exceptions), number of dependents, property, car ownership (unless needed for the job), or arrest record. Refer to the information on job discrimination in this essay for more information about your rights.

PRESENTING YOURSELF IN AN INTERVIEW

If your qualifications, as presented in your resume, cover letter, and application, are a strong match for the requirements of the job, you may be invited to a job interview. On the basis of this meeting, the prospective employer will decide whether or not to hire you, and you will decide whether or not you want the job.

Prepare in Advance

Before an interview, there are a number of things you can do to prepare. Begin by giving thought to why you want the job and what you have to offer. Then review your resume and any lists you made when you were evaluating yourself so that you can keep your qualifications firmly in mind.

Learn as much as you can about the organization. Check with friends who work there, read company brochures, search the Internet, or devise other information-gathering strategies. Showing that you know something about the company and what it does will indicate your interest and demonstrate that you are a well-informed job candidate.

Try to anticipate some of the questions an interviewer may ask and think about how you would answer. For example, you may be asked: Will you work overtime when necessary? Are you ready to go to night school to improve some of your skills? Preparing answers in advance will make the process easier for you. It is also wise to prepare any questions you may have about the company or the position for which you are applying. The more information you have, the better you can evaluate both the company and the job.

Employers may want you to demonstrate specific skills for some jobs. An applicant for a job in a lumber mill or a mine, for example, might be required to demonstrate mechanical ability. Prospective technicians might be expected to demonstrate mathematical skills.

On the appointed day, dress neatly and in a style appropriate for the job you're seeking. When in doubt, it's safer to dress on the conservative side, wearing a shirt and tie rather than a turtleneck or wearing a dress or blouse and skirt rather than pants and a T-shirt. Be on time. Find out in advance exactly where the company is located and how to get there. Allow extra time in case you get lost, get caught in a traffic jam, can't find a parking spot, or encounter another type of delay.

Maintain a Balance

When your appointment begins, remember that a good interview is largely a matter of balance. Don't undersell yourself by sitting back silently, but don't oversell yourself by talking nonstop about how wonderful you are. Answer all questions directly and simply, and let the interviewer take the lead.

Instead of saying, "I'm reliable and hardworking," give the interviewer an example. Allow the interviewer to draw conclusions from your example.

It's natural to be nervous before and during a job interview. However, you need to try to relax and be yourself. You may even enjoy the conversation. Your chances of being hired and being happy if you get the job are better if the employer likes you as you are.

Avoid discussing money until the employer brings it up or until you are offered the job. Employers usually know in advance what they are willing to pay. If you are the one to begin a discussion about the salary you want, you may set an amount that's either too low or too high.

Be prepared to ask questions, but don't force them on your interviewer. Part of the purpose of the interview is for you to evaluate the company while you are being evaluated. For instance, you might want to ask about the company's training programs and its policy on promotions.

Don't stay too long. Most business people have busy schedules. It is likely that the interviewer will let you know when it's time for the interview to end.

Don't expect a definite answer at the first interview. Employers usually thank you for coming and say that you will be notified shortly. Most employers want to interview all the applicants before they make a hiring decision. If the position is offered at the time of the interview, you can ask for a little time to think about it. If the interviewer tells you that you are not suitable for the job, try to be polite. Say, "I'm sorry, but thank you for taking the time to meet with me." After all, the company may have the right job for you next week.

Follow Up after the Interview

If the job sounds interesting and you would like to be considered for it, say so as you leave. Follow up after the interview by writing a brief thank-you note to the employer. Express your continued interest in the position and thank the interviewer for taking the time to meet with you.

It's a good idea to make some notes and evaluations of the interview while it is still fresh in your mind. Write down the important facts about the job—the duties, salary, promotion prospects, and so on, which will help you make a decision should you be offered the job. Also evaluate your own performance in the interview. List the things you wish you had said and things you wish you had not said, which will help you prepare for future interviews.

Finally, don't hesitate to contact your interviewer if you haven't heard from the company after a week or two (unless you were told it would be longer). Write a brief note or make a phone call in which you ask when a decision might be reached. Making such an effort will show the employer that you are genuinely interested in the job. Your call will remind the interviewer about you and could work to your advantage.

TAKE CHARGE

Job hunting is primarily a matter of organizing a well-planned campaign. Scan the classified ads, search through online job banks, watch for trends in local industry that might be reported in the news, and check with people you know in the field. Take the initiative. Send out carefully crafted resumes and letters. Respond to ads. Finally, in an interview, state your qualifications and experience in a straightforward and confident manner.

TRADE AND PROFESSIONAL JOURNALS

The following is a list of some of the major journals in the fields of public and community services. These journals can keep you up to date with what is happening in your field of interest and can lead you to jobs through their classified advertising sections.

Armed Services

Armed Forces Journal International, Defense News Media Group, 6883 Commercial Drive, Springfield, VA 22159.
http://www.afji.com

Legal Work

ABA Journal, 321 N. Clark Street, Chicago, IL 60610.
http://www.abanet.org/journal/redesign/home.html
Trial, Association of Trial Lawyers of America, 1050 31st Street NW, Washington, DC 20007-4499.
http://www.atla.org/Publications/Tier3/TRIAL.aspx

Public, Civil, and Social Services

Academe, American Association of University Professors, 1012 Fourteenth Street NW, Suite 500, Washington, DC 20005-3465.
http://www.aaup.org/publications/Academe/index.htm
American City and County, 6151 Powers Ferry Road, Suite 200, Atlanta, GA 30339.
http://www.americancityandcounty.com
American Libraries, 50 East Huron Street, Chicago, IL 60611-2795.
http://www.ala.org/alonline
American School Board Journal, 1680 Duke Street, Alexandria, VA 22314.
http://www.asbj.com
American Sociological Review, University of Pennsylvania, Department of Sociology, 3718 Locust Walk, Philadelphia, PA 19104-6299.
http://www2.asanet.org/journals/asr
Monitor on Psychology, American Psychological Association, 750 First Street, NE, Washington, DC 20002-4242.
http://www.apa.org/monitor
Associations Now, American Society of Association Executives, 1575 I Street NW, Washington, DC 20005.
http://www.asaecenter.org/publicationsresources/
Child Welfare, 440 First Street, NW, Third Floor, Washington, DC 20001-2085.
http://www.cwla.org
Christian Century, 104 South Michigan, Suite 700, Chicago, IL 60603.
http://www.christiancentury.org
Chronicle of Higher Education, 1255 Twenty-third Street, NW, Suite 700, Washington, DC 20037.
http://chronicle.com
Community College Journal, One Dupont Circle NW, Washington, DC 20036.
http://www.aacc.nche.edu
Corrections Today, American Correctional Association, 4380 Forbes Boulevard, Lanham, MD 20706-4322.
http://www.corrections.com/aca
Environmental Science and Technology, P.O. Box 182426, Columbus, OH, 43218-2426.
http://pubs.acs.org/hotartcl/est/est.html

Journal of Career Planning and Employment, 62 Highland Avenue, Bethlehem, PA 18017.
http://www.naceweb.org/info_public/journal.htm

Law Library Journal, 53 West Jackson Boulevard, Suite 940, Chicago, IL 60604.
http://www.aallnet.org/products/pub_journal.asp

Library Journal, 360 Park Avenue South, New York, NY 10010.
http://www.libraryjournal.com

Public Administration Review, University of Colorado at Denver, 1380 Lawrence Street, Suite 500, Campus Box 142, P.O. Box 173364, Denver, CO 80217-3364.
http://www.blackwellpublishing.com/

Science and Children, National Science Teachers Association, 1840 Wilson Boulevard, Arlington, VA 22201-3000.
http://www.nsta.org/elementaryschool#journal

Social Service Review, School of Social Service Administration, University of Chicago, 969 E. 60th Street, Chicago, IL 60637.
http://www.journals.uchicago.edu/SSR

Armed Services Career

Definition and Nature of the Work

The armed services—the U.S. Army, the Air Force, the Marine Corps, the Navy, and the Coast Guard—offer jobs in the United States and abroad that are comparable to hundreds of civilian positions. The jobs range from postal clerk and helicopter repairer to court reporter and dental hygienist. In each area of expertise, military personnel receive classroom and field training and are encouraged to advance to the limits of their capabilities.

Those who join the armed services, whatever their jobs may be, are trained to be professional soldiers. They must accept a life of discipline and order that is different from civilian life. The military has its own rules for proper behavior, its own courts for adjudication of wrongdoing, and its own requirements for advancement. Those who enlist should have a strong desire to serve their country in both peacetime and war.

In a field such as Maneuver Combat Arms, enlistees learn to operate and maintain weapons, vehicles, and other equipment. Beginners may be trained for jobs such as rifleman or ammunition handler. With experience and ability, they may be assigned to more difficult positions, such as armor reconnaissance specialist.

In the field of medicine, beginning military personnel help care for patients, treating minor cuts and wounds, serving meals, and transporting patients within a medical center. Those who had training prior to enlistment, such as registered nurses, are assigned similar jobs in the military. Those who have no previous training may learn to be X-ray technicians or physical therapy specialists.

Education and Training
Varies—see profile

Salary
Varies—see profile

Employment Outlook
Good

The armed services offer a wide variety of careers for those who want to enter military service. (© Hans Halberstadt/Corbis.)

Some enlisted personnel are assigned to office work, typing correspondence, processing orders, or budgeting. Experienced personnel and officers have more complex and more responsible duties, such as supervising other personnel.

While some people spend their entire careers in the armed services, others enlist for three to six years, become well trained in their fields, and return to civilian life with valuable experience. Still others stay in the military for twenty years, retire with pensions, and then obtain civilian jobs.

Education and Training Requirements

Military service is now entirely voluntary, although in an emergency Congress can reactivate the draft. To enlist, applicants must be at least seventeen years of age. U.S. Air Force personnel must enter active duty before their twenty-eighth birthday; other branches of the armed services require that enlistees be no older than thirty-five. After taking aptitude tests, enlistees may enter any field for which they qualify and for which the service has need. If they are interested only in a specific training program and do not qualify, they are free to change their minds about enlisting. Some jobs are open only to those who have completed high school.

Military personnel can enlist for three or more years of active duty. Those who wish to enlist for six years of reserve duty must serve at least four months of that time on active duty. Some enlistees may be qualified to apply for Officer Candidate School (OCS) training. College students can join the Reserve Officers Training Corps (ROTC) and begin training while in school. The program provides a monthly allowance. Full-tuition scholarships are also available. When ROTC students graduate and are commissioned as officers, they must serve on active duty for two years.

Some individuals join the military by entering one of the service academies—the Air Force Academy in Colorado Springs, CO; the Coast Guard Academy in New London, CT; the army's Military Academy in West Point, NY; or the Naval Academy in Annapolis, MD. Applicants must be nominated by a member of Congress or have a family affiliation with the military. While at the academy, their tuition and expenses are paid. After graduating, they must serve on active duty for five years.

Enlistees get classroom education as well as on-the-job training. They may participate in off-duty programs ranging from correspondence courses to classes at military bases or local civilian schools. Training continues throughout their military service.

Getting the Job

Each branch of the military service has its own recruiting operation, with recruiters working from local offices, and provides publications that describe career opportunities and military life. High school and college placement offices and state employment offices may also have some of these brochures.

Advancement Possibilities and Employment Outlook

There are many possibilities for advancement in the armed services. Those who work hard and show leadership abilities are given additional training to prepare them for advanced positions. Almost all who enlist are rapidly promoted to higher pay grades.

The military has more than 1.4 million people on active duty and about 1.2 million in the reserves. Depending on its needs, it may limit the number of positions in certain areas of expertise. However, job turnover in some fields can be high, so opportunities usually exist for anyone who wants to enter military service.

Working Conditions

Members of the armed services must be willing to accept orders from superiors without question. In combat zones, they may work long hours with very little sleep and no time off. They may be stationed on the front lines of battle, where they may be killed or seriously injured. In noncombat situations, they usually face work conditions similar to those in the private sector, including a forty-hour workweek.

Living quarters for military personnel vary from barracks at training camps and trenches in war zones to comfortable apartments at military bases.

Earnings and Benefits

Salaries vary according to length of service, type of job, and level of performance. Beginning personnel earn about $11,000 per year. High-ranking officers with many years of service can earn more than $100,000 per year.

Although their salaries are somewhat lower than those received by civilians doing similar jobs, military personnel receive other benefits that raise their total compensation. Besides education and training, they receive free meals and living quarters when they reside on a military base or an allowance for food and lodging when they live off the base. They get a uniform allowance, free medical and dental care, thirty days of paid vacation each year, life insurance, and retirement with a pension after twenty years of service. Military personnel receive special pay for hazardous duty. Some recruits may be offered an enlistment bonus.

Where to Go for More Information

U.S. Air Force
(800) 423-8723
http://www.airforce.com

U.S. Army and Reserves Recruiting Services
1307 Third Ave.
Fort Knox, KY 40121-2725
(800) USA-ARMY
http://www.goarmy.com

U.S. Marine Corp
2008 Elliot Rd.
Quantico, VA 22134-5030
(800) 627-4637
http://www.usmc.mil

U.S. Navy Recruiting Services
4015 Wilson Blvd.
Arlington, VA 22203-1991
(800) 872-6289
http://www.navy.com

U.S. Coast Guard Recruiting
4200 Wilson Blvd., Ste. 450
Arlington, VA 22203
(877) 669-8724
http://www.uscg.mil

Building Custodian

Definition and Nature of the Work

Building custodians, or janitors, wash and wax floors, vacuum carpets, and clean bathrooms. They make minor repairs, such as replacing lightbulbs and fixing leaky faucets; kill insects and rodents; and collect and discard trash. Some custodians clear snow from sidewalks and mow lawns. A few collect rent and enforce building management rules. Generally, their work does not require special skills.

Many custodians work during the day, when buildings are occupied, making repairs that cannot wait, such as unclogging drains in public bathrooms. Others work only at night so they do not disturb a building's occupants. Many work for janitorial service firms and clean a number of different buildings.

Custodians' tools include floor-waxing machines, carpet sweepers, pliers, and screwdrivers. They often use chemicals to wash floors and clean carpets and bathrooms.

Education and Training
On-the-job training

Salary
Median—$23,414 per year

Employment Outlook
Good

Building custodians, or janitors, clean and maintain buildings such as schools, theaters, hospitals, office buildings, and factories. (© Darren Modricker/ Corbis.)

Education and Training Requirements

While there are no educational requirements for the job, high school shop courses that teach how to make simple repairs are useful. Custodians must be able to do simple arithmetic. Many employers require good character references.

Building custodians generally learn under the supervision of an experienced worker. They start by cleaning and, after gaining experience, take on repairs and more complex duties.

Getting the Job

Job seekers can apply directly to schools, manufacturing plants, and companies that manage apartment and office buildings. Janitorial service firms are usually listed in the Yellow Pages. State employment offices, federal civil service offices, newspaper classified ads, and job banks on the Internet are other sources of job information.

Advancement Possibilities and Employment Outlook

Advancement for custodians often means moving to a larger building or company that offers a higher rate of pay. In large buildings that employ several custodians they can advance to the position of supervisor. Those with administrative ability sometimes start their own cleaning and maintenance services.

The employment outlook for building custodians is good through 2014. Most of the job growth is expected to be in janitorial service firms. New buildings are being constructed every day, and more custodians will be needed to maintain them. However, improvements in cleaning equipment and chemical compounds can make cleaning easier and faster, reducing the total number of workers required.

Working Conditions

Building custodians generally work between forty and forty-eight hours a week, mostly indoors, although snow removal and grounds maintenance require outdoor work. Janitors may be scheduled for day or night shifts, depending on the individual job.

Most building custodians have a variety of duties with relatively little pressure. They may have to move furniture and other heavy objects and work with dirty, greasy machinery. They may get minor cuts, bruises, and burns from handling chemicals.

Custodians must be able to get along well with others, be courteous to other employees and occupants of the building, and be honest and trustworthy.

Earnings and Benefits

In 2004 the median salary for building custodians was $23,414 per year. For a senior custodian, or building custodian supervisor, the median salary was $26,918 per year. Benefits usually included paid sick leave and vacations, life and health insurance, and pension plans. Custodians who work for apartment buildings are often provided housing at no charge. Many custodians are members of labor unions.

Where to Go for More Information

National Education Association
1201 Sixteenth St. NW
Washington, DC 20036-3290
(202) 833-4000
http://www.nea.org

Service Employees International Union
1313 L St. NW
Washington, DC 20005
(202) 898-3200
http://www.seiu.org

Day Care Worker

Definition and Nature of the Work

Workers in day care centers help preschool children in their educational and personal growth. Under a director's supervision, they provide all the necessary primary care for infants and independent and group activities for toddlers and older children. Through games and exercises, they help children develop self-esteem, curiosity, imagination, physical skills, and speech. Workers also oversee the children's health and nutrition, sometimes having the children participate in the preparation of breakfast and lunch.

Some day care centers are nonprofit organizations operated or subsidized by community or government agencies, while others are privately owned. Many corporations run day care centers for the children of their employees. Children's parents may assist staff members.

Education and Training Requirements

Day care workers must have high school diplomas and know how to make children feel secure. Some form of on-the-job training is usually required. Many workers enroll in formal programs that include courses in education, nutrition, psychology, and speech. Some two-year colleges offer associate's degrees in preschool or early childhood education.

Workers interested in advancement to administrative positions need bachelor's degrees. Some centers require teaching certification for higher-level positions.

Getting the Job

Job seekers can apply directly to day care centers. State departments of education often have information about state-run centers. School placement offices, newspaper classified ads, and job banks on the Internet are other sources of employment information.

Education and Training
High school and on-the-job training

Salary
Average—$9.76 per hour

Employment Outlook
Very good

Day care workers tend to the needs of preschool children at a day care center. They use a variety of games and exercises to aid a child's growth.
(© Jacques M. Chenet/Corbis.)

Advancement Possibilities and Employment Outlook

Day care workers usually start as staff assistants. After a period of training, they take responsibility for the care of a group of children. With extensive experience, they may advance to supervisor. Workers with college degrees in early childhood development or related fields may start at positions with more responsibility.

The job outlook is very good through 2014. Turnover in the field is high. In addition, increases in the number of children under age five and in the number of women of childbearing age entering the labor force are expected over the next decade, creating a demand for day care.

Working Conditions

Many day care centers are open twelve hours each day, with staff working eight-hour shifts. Usually a worker is in charge of a group of six to twelve children. Some centers are in modern buildings specially designed for day care, while others are in remodeled homes or older buildings. Some are on the premises of factories or corporations where the children's parents are employed.

Earnings and Benefits

Earnings and benefits of day care workers vary according to education, experience, and the type of day care center. In 2004 the average wage was $9.76 per hour. Benefits ranged from minimal to average when compared with other professions.

Where to Go for More Information

National Association for the Education of
    Young Children
1313 L St. NW, Ste. 500
Washington, DC 20005
(800) 424-2460
http://www.naeyc.org

National Association of Child Care
    Resources and Referral Agencies
3101 Wilson Blvd., Ste. 350
Arlington, VA 22201
(703) 341-4100
http://www.naccrra.org

National Child Care Association
2025 M St. NW, Ste. 800
Washington, DC 20036-3309
(800) 543-7161
http://www.nccanet.org

Electric Power Service Worker

Education and Training
None

Salary
Median—$16.60 to $25.27 per hour

Employment Outlook
Poor

Definition and Nature of the Work

Electric companies employ many people to help their customers. Service representatives, who work in offices, deal directly with the public by telephone or in person. They take orders for service, explain rates and billing procedures, and handle complaints. Meter installers and repairers work in customers' homes and businesses, installing, testing, and repairing equipment.

In regions that are not heavily populated, a power company may have one person, a district representative, perform all service jobs. If major repairs are necessary, the district representative may contact the central office to have a skilled meter repairer sent to the customer's home or business.

Education and Training Requirements

Employers generally prefer to hire high school graduates. Service representatives often have some college education, but it is not required. Meter installers and repairers need a basic knowledge of electricity. Vocational school courses and high school classes, such as shop, are useful.

Beginning workers are trained on the job by experienced workers. Training periods vary with the size and location of the company, but can last up to four years for meter installers and repairers. Some power companies are owned by municipalities, so workers may be required to pass civil service exams.

Getting the Job

Job seekers can apply directly to local power companies. School placement offices, civil service commissions, newspaper classified ads, and job banks on the Internet are other sources of job information.

Advancement Possibilities and Employment Outlook

Experienced, diligent service workers have many opportunities for advancement. Service representatives may be promoted to supervisory positions, while meter installers and repairers can move on to larger companies and work with more complicated equipment. Workers who have civil service jobs may need to take additional exams to advance.

The number of jobs for service workers is expected to decline through 2014. Although electrical power is essential, opportunities for employment may be limited by improved technology, energy-conserving appliances and policies, and a more competitive regulatory environment.

Working Conditions

Although conditions vary by location, most service workers are on the job forty hours a week. Service representatives work in offices, usually with other representatives. Meter installers and repairers do most of their work at the homes and businesses of customers. District representatives usually drive great distances to serve a large area by themselves.

Earnings and Benefits

Earnings vary according to employees' experience and the company's location. In 2004 the median salary for service representatives was $16.60 per hour. The median wage of meter installers and repairers was $25.17 per hour. District representatives, who drive great distances to cover larger areas, may make more. Benefits generally included paid holidays and vacations and health insurance.

Where to Go for More Information

International Brotherhood of Electrical
  Workers
900 Seventh St. NW
Washington, DC 20001
(202) 833-7000
http://www.ibew.org

Utility Workers Union of America
815 Sixteenth St. NW
Washington, DC 20006
(202) 974-8200
http://www.uwua.net

Electric Power Transmission and Distribution Worker

Definition and Nature of the Work

Power transmission and distribution workers move electricity from generating plants to homes, offices, and factories. One group of workers controls the flow of energy, while another group installs and maintains the power lines and other transmission and distribution equipment.

Load dispatchers work in control rooms of generating plants, usually with several assistants. Watching gauges and other equipment, they make sure the amount of electricity produced matches the amount customers need at any given time. When adjustments are necessary, dispatchers tell other power plant workers to start or shut down generators. Dispatchers throw switches to route the current to specific areas where there is demand. Substation operators, who work in smaller, regional relay stations, control the flow of electricity in specific ar-

Education and Training
Varies—see profile

Salary
Median—$23.61 per hour

Employment Outlook
Poor

Line installers and repairers install cables to service new electric customers and repair broken or unsafe electrical lines. (© Roger Ball/Corbis.)

eas. Some substation operators work alone, maintaining the equipment as well as directing the energy flow.

The lines that send electric power from generating plants to customers are installed and maintained by line installers and repairers. For example, when a new housing development is built, installers place cables underground or on poles and connect them to the houses. The same work crews usually repair broken or unsafe lines. Line installers and repairers are assisted by ground helpers and cable splicers. Ground helpers, or laborers, dig the holes into which poles are placed. They may also hold wires and tools for installers. Cable splicers secure new connections between cables and repair old connections to prevent fires. Some splicers also inspect cables to make sure they are in good condition. Troubleshooters are line installers and repairers who work in emergency situations, repairing and replacing equipment to restore service.

Education and Training Requirements

Job applicants must have high school diplomas or the equivalent. Some vocational and technical schools, working with local power companies, offer one-year certificate programs that emphasize hands-on fieldwork. Two-year associate degree programs, where available, include courses in electricity, electronics, fiber optics, and microwave transmission. Graduates of these programs get special consideration from employers.

Power companies train most of their employees on the job, with experienced workers teaching beginners. Classroom instruction may be provided for new workers and for workers seeking advancement. The classes cover the fundamental laws of electricity, safety rules, and how to read blueprints.

High school classes related to electricity, mechanical drawing, and shop can be helpful to beginning workers.

Getting the Job

Job seekers can apply directly to power companies. School placement offices, civil service commissions, newspaper classified ads, and job banks on the Internet are other sources of employment information.

Advancement Possibilities and Employment Outlook

Chances for advancement are good for efficient, reliable workers. With about four years of experience, ground helpers may be promoted to cable splicers or line installers and repairers. Assistants at substations often become substation operators after three to seven years. Substation operators with seven to ten years of experience may become load dispatchers.

The job market for this field is expected to grow more slowly than the average for all occupations through 2014. The demand for electricity is increasing, but the demand for additional workers may be offset somewhat by mechanization. Nationwide, only a few thousand new positions are expected to open each year for transmission and distribution workers.

Working Conditions

Working conditions vary. Load dispatchers and substation operators work inside in comfortable surroundings forty hours a week. Rotating shifts, including weekend and evening work, may be required. Installation workers usually work during the day, forty hours a week. Maintenance workers and troubleshooters work day or night, in all kinds of weather. Rotating shifts and overtime are fairly common.

Earnings and Benefits

Wages vary with the jobs and their location. In 2004 the median salary for all transmission and distribution workers was $23.61 per hour, with the most experienced workers earning more than $32.54 per hour. Benefits generally include medical and accident insurance, life insurance, and paid holidays and vacations. Union workers often receive retirement plans.

Where to Go for More Information

Edison Electric Institute
701 Pennsylvania Ave. NW
Washington, DC 20004-2696
(202) 508-5000
http://www.eei.org

International Brotherhood of Electrical
   Workers
900 Seventh St. NW
Washington, DC 20001
(202) 833-7000
http://www.ibew.org

Utility Workers Union of America
815 Sixteenth St. NW
Washington, DC 20006
(202) 974-8200
http://www.uwua.net

Firefighter

Definition and Nature of the Work

Firefighters protect life and property from fires. Called first responders, they are usually the first emergency personnel at traffic accidents or explosions and may be called upon to put out fires or treat injuries.

Firefighters are organized in companies under commanding officers. All have specific tasks. Tillers, for instance, guide the part of the fire truck that carries long ladders. Hose operators connect the hoses to fire hydrants, while pump operators make sure the water gets through the hoses to the blaze. Once at a fire, they use axes to break down walls or windows so they can evacuate people trapped by flames and other obstacles. Between alarms, firefighters maintain equipment so it is in good working order. Most firefighters work for city or community governments, although some work for private companies. Volunteer firefighters have other full-time jobs and fight fires only when they are called.

In large cities, firefighters may work on special squads that require advanced training. Rescue squads take first-aid equipment to fires and help the injured until ambulances arrive. They also may be called for injuries and accidents not

Education and Training
High school plus training

Salary
Median—$18.43 per hour

Employment Outlook
Very good

Firefighters are organized into companies. Each member of the company has a special task. (Photograph by Kelly A. Quin. Thomson Gale. Reproduced by permission.)

caused by fire, such as heart attacks. Marine squads specialize in water rescues, while hazardous material, or "haz mat," squads handle gases, poisons, and other chemical substances that cause fire, explosions, and injuries.

Fire inspectors and fire-science specialists work to prevent fires. Fire inspectors usually work for fire departments, checking buildings to see that fire escapes, automatic fire alarms, and sprinkler systems are in good condition. Fire-science specialists not only inspect buildings, but also help plan fire prevention and suggest equipment for fighting fires. Some work for insurance companies, setting insurance rates, investigating arson, and helping claims adjusters determine compensation due those who were injured or lost property because of fires.

Education and Training Requirements

Prospective firefighters must be at least eighteen years old and high school graduates to take the fire exam. In recent years, most applicants have had a few years of college or completed two- or four-year programs in fire science at community colleges or universities. Experienced firefighters sometimes take these courses to prepare for promotion. These courses are also useful for those preparing for jobs as fire-science specialists.

The firefighter exam includes a written section; tests of strength, physical stamina, and agility; and a medical examination, including a drug screening. Applicants with the highest scores undergo several weeks of formal training at an academy. Some fire departments offer apprenticeship programs that last three or four years. Experienced firefighters go on practice drills to maintain their skills.

Firefighters must also be certified as emergency medical technicians (EMTs). Most departments provide this training at the academy, but others prefer that trainees have EMT certification before they take the firefighter's exam.

Getting the Job

Job seekers should apply to take the firefighter's exam, a civil service test. Local fire departments usually have Web sites that provide specific qualifications for jobs available. Other sources of employment information include union offices, state employment services, school placement offices, newspaper classified ads, and job banks on the Internet.

Advancement Possibilities and Employment Outlook

Firefighters are usually promoted from within the department. They advance to higher ranks by passing civil service tests and being recommended by supervisors. Advanced ranks include captain, battalion chief, and fire chief.

About 353,000 firefighters are employed in the United States. Some growth should occur in this field as paid positions replace volunteer positions. The employment outlook is very good through 2014, although applicants should expect stiff competition. Most openings occur when experienced workers retire or leave the occupation.

Working Conditions

Firefighters work under extremely dangerous conditions, risking their own lives to save others. They must have courage and stamina as well as great physical strength, for they often carry heavy and bulky equipment. Despite the dangers, firefighters take satisfaction from providing an important public service.

Because fire protection is provided around the clock, firefighters work in shifts, which vary by community. Some work eight-hour day shifts or fourteen-hour night shifts. Others work for twenty-four hours and then receive equal time off. Firefighters may be required to live at the fire station for days at a time. They must be able to work as part of a team and follow orders. Many firefighters belong to labor unions.

Earnings and Benefits

Salaries vary by location and years of experience. In 2004 the median salary for firefighters was $18.43 per hour. The lowest ten percent earned less than $9.71 per hour, and the top ten percent earned more than $29.21 per hour. The median salary for fire inspectors was $46,340 per year.

Firefighters generally receive paid sick days and vacations and medical and liability insurance. They are usually permitted to retire at half pay when they are fifty years old and have served for twenty-five years. Firefighters who are unable to work because of injury on the job may retire at any age.

Where to Go for More Information

International Association of Fire Fighters
1750 New York Ave. NW
Washington, DC 20006-5395
(202) 737-8484
http://www.iaff.org

National Fire Protection Association
PO Box 9101
1 Batterymarch Park
Quincy, MA 02169-7471
(617) 770-3000
http://www.nfpa.org

U.S. Fire Administration
16825 S. Seton Ave.
Emmitsburg, MD 21727
(301) 447-1000
http://www.usfa.fema.gov

Geriatric Aide

Definition and Nature of the Work

Geriatric aides offer personal care and assistance to elderly people who no longer have the health, strength, or resources to be completely self-sufficient. They work in nursing homes, adult day care centers, specialized recreation programs, health care facilities, and private homes.

Some geriatric aides help medical personnel care for patients who are ill, disabled, or medically fragile. Duties may include feeding, dressing, and bathing the patients, as well as providing physical therapy. The older adults they serve range from critically ill patients who need constant attention to relatively healthy individuals who require only social activities, transportation, or companionship.

Education and Training
On-the-job training

Salary
Median—$8.47 to $9.11 per hour

Employment Outlook
Very good

Geriatric aides assist elderly people in a variety of settings, including nursing homes, adult day care centers, specialized recreation programs, health care facilities, and private homes. (© Martha Tabor/Working Images Photographs. Reproduced by permission.)

Education and Training Requirements

Many geriatric aide positions have no educational requirements, although high school diplomas are often preferred. On-the-job training is usually provided. Many colleges now offer two- or four-year degrees in gerontology. Courses in first-aid, cardiopulmonary resuscitation (CPR), biology, psychology, health care, and sociology are useful.

Getting the Job

Job seekers can apply directly to nursing homes or public agencies serving the elderly. Newsletters and other publications in the geriatric field may have job listings. School placement offices, state employment services, newspaper classified ads, and job banks on the Internet are other sources of employment information.

Advancement Possibilities and Employment Outlook

Aides who pursue higher education may advance to professional positions in the field, becoming geriatric nurses, therapists, or counselors. Others may obtain additional training and become medical assistants.

Employment of geriatric aides is expected to grow faster than the average for all occupations through 2014. The elderly population is increasing, and many in this age group may require assistance. In addition, many families want to contain costs by moving patients out of hospitals and nursing care facilities to keep them at home with geriatric aides.

Working Conditions

At facilities that offer around-the-clock care, night and weekend work is usually required. In addition, aides may be on call for emergencies. The job may be strenuous if patients need to be lifted and stressful if they are failing mentally or physically. Patience, sensitivity, and good judgment are essential.

Earnings and Benefits

In 2004 the median hourly wage for geriatric aides ranged from $8.47 to $9.11, depending on experience, type of facility, and geographic location. Experienced workers earned $12.32 per hour or more, with the highest pay going to workers in nursing homes.

Some facilities offer health insurance, retirement plans, and holiday and vacation pay. Overtime is frequently available.

Where to Go for More Information

American Association for Homecare
625 Slaters La., Ste. 200
Alexandria, VA 22314-1171
(703) 836-6263
http://www.aahomecare.org

American Geriatrics Society
350 Fifth Ave., Ste. 801
New York, NY 10118
(212) 308-1414
http://www.americangeriatrics.org

National Council on the Aging
300 D St. SW, Ste. 801
Washington, DC 20024
(202) 479-1200
http://www.ncoa.org

Highway Maintenance Worker

Definition and Nature of the Work

Highway maintenance workers keep state, county, and city highways and roads in safe condition. They repair guardrails and snow fences; put up stop signs; paint dividing lines between traffic lanes; and fix potholes caused by weather or heavy traffic. When it snows, maintenance workers drive trucks and tractors with snowplows and blowers to clear the roads. After storms, they remove trees that have fallen across the road. Specific tasks vary with the location of the roads they maintain.

Education and Training Requirements

A high school education is preferred. A doctor's health certificate and a driver's license are often required. An applicant who wants to work in a large city or on state highways must take a civil service examination, which tests a worker's ability to read, write, and follow directions. Many small towns and cities do not give the written tests. A beginner is trained on the job by more experienced workers.

Some highway maintenance workers take courses to acquire special skills, such as tree climbing and tree cutting. Their employers may pay their tuition.

Getting the Job

Job seekers can apply directly to the town or county administrator or to the state highway commission. Civil service commissions, state employment services, school placement offices, newspaper classified ads, and job banks on the Internet are other sources of employment leads.

Advancement Possibilities and Employment Outlook

Highway maintenance workers can advance from the first grade of laborer to senior maintenance worker to other supervisory positions. Some workers go on to become highway inspectors.

Education and Training
High school plus on-the-job training

Salary
Median—$14.21 per hour

Employment Outlook
Very good

Employment of highway maintenance workers is expected to grower faster than the average for all occupations through 2014. More new roads are being built throughout the country, requiring more maintenance workers. Job openings also occur when workers retire or leave the occupation.

Where to Go for More Information

American Federation of State, County, and
   Municipal Employees
1625 L St. NW
Washington, DC 20036-5687
(202) 429-1000
http://www.afscme.org

International Brotherhood of Teamsters
25 Louisiana Ave. NW
Washington, DC 20001-2198
(202) 624-6800
http://www.teamster.org

National Asphalt Pavement Association
5100 Forbes Blvd.
Lanham, MD 20706
(888) 468-6499
http://www.hotmix.org

Working Conditions

Highway maintenance workers need to be in good health and have physical stamina. They work outdoors in snow, sleet, rain, and summer heat. Heavy snowfall and rain often require them to work at night to clear roads for morning commuters. They work as part of a team and can enjoy the companionship of other workers.

Earnings and Benefits

In 2004 the median wage for highway maintenance workers was $14.21 per hour. They are paid with tax money, so their earnings depend on the size and wealth of the community, county, or state in which they work. Wages are highest in large cities and for specialized work.

All highway maintenance workers receive health insurance, workers' compensation, and paid vacations and holidays. Many highway maintenance workers belong to unions.

Institutional Housekeeper

Education and Training
On-the-job training

Salary
Median—$16,900 per year

Employment Outlook
Good

Definition and Nature of the Work

Institutional housekeepers clean the interiors of hotels, hospitals, school dormitories, and government residences. The size of the institution determines the number of workers on the housekeeping staff and the range of duties that individual housekeepers perform. While hotel housekeepers may only clean and straighten guest rooms, workers at a government residence such as an embassy often serve at banquets and walk dogs.

Institutional housekeepers clean floors and windows, make beds, wash dishes, and take care of indoor plants. Head housekeepers coordinate the housekeeping staff, the building maintenance staff, kitchen workers, and doorkeepers. They may also order linen and cleaning supplies and act as the liaison between management and the housekeeping staff.

Education and Training Requirements

Some employers prefer housekeepers to have high school diplomas. However, experience and a sense of responsibility are often more important than formal qualifications. Foreign language skills and the ability to deal with people can be useful.

Most housekeepers are trained on the job by experienced workers. Some vocational schools, community colleges, and unions offer training programs in housekeeping. These courses may help secure promotion to supervisory positions.

Getting the Job

In large cities, employment agencies specialize in finding jobs for institutional housekeepers. Job seekers can also apply directly to hotels and hospitals. State employment services, newspaper classified ads, and job banks on the Internet are other sources of employment information.

Advancement Possibilities and Employment Outlook

Housekeepers usually advance by getting jobs at institutions that offer better working conditions and higher wages. Some become supervisors or start their own housekeeping businesses.

The employment outlook is as good as the average for all occupations through 2014. Housekeeping has a high turnover rate.

Working Conditions

Housekeepers may lift and carry heavy objects while cleaning or stand for long periods. Working hours vary. Most housekeepers begin work before breakfast and finish after the rooms and halls are clean and tidy. Others work later shifts. Some may have accommodations provided.

Earnings and Benefits

In 2004 the median salary for institutional housekeepers was $16,900 per year. The most experienced workers earned more than $20,570 per year. Supervisors earned a median annual salary of $29,510. Most institutional housekeepers received limited health insurance, retirement plans, and vacation benefits.

Where to Go for More Information

Service Employees International Union
1313 L St. NW
Washington, DC 20005
(202) 898-3200
http://www.seiu.org

International Executive Housekeepers
    Association, Inc.
1001 Eastwind Dr., Ste. 301
Westerville, OH 43081-3361
(800) 200-6342
http://www.ieha.org

Postal Service Worker

Education and Training
High school plus on-the-job training

Salary
Varies—see profile

Employment Outlook
Poor

Definition and Nature of the Work

More than six hundred thousand postal workers are employed in the United States. They sort, distribute, and deliver mail; sell stamps and money orders; and figure postal rates for boxes and large envelopes. They also collect postage-due fees and obtain signed receipts for registered, certified, and insured mail. Most are postal clerks, who work indoors handling the bulk of the mail, or letter carriers, who work outdoors delivering mail to the correct address.

In large cities postal clerks may have specialized tasks. Distribution clerks unload the mail from trucks and sort it into rough categories—parcel post, magazines, letters, and foreign mail. They have to memorize distribution "schemes" according to geographic areas. Window clerks weigh mail, sell stamps and other products, answer questions from the public, and listen to complaints. In small towns postal clerks are responsible for all of these duties.

Letter carriers may have residential, business, parcel post, or rural routes, delivering mail on foot or in carts, small trucks, or cars. They arrive at the post office early in the morning to sort the mail for their routes.

Supervisors, who oversee the work of postal clerks and letter carriers, are usually employed at post offices with large staffs. Postmasters have complete responsibility for the work at the post offices they manage.

Education and Training Requirements

All postal workers must be citizens of the United States, have high school diplomas or the equivalent, and be at least eighteen years of age. They are tested for speed and accuracy in checking names and numbers and for their ability to memorize mail distribution procedures. Letter carriers and postal clerks must also be able to carry thirty-five-pound shoulder bags and lift seventy-pound mailbags. Many jobs require driver's licenses and road tests. All postal workers must pass drug screening.

Most jobs in the postal service fall into one of two categories. Postal clerks work indoors handling the mail. Letter carriers work outdoors delivering the mail. (© LWA-Dann Tardif/Corbis.)

Postal workers get on-the-job training. Clerks and letter carriers usually train as substitutes until vacancies occur in their offices or departments. Beginning clerks learn postal regulations and practice sorting for speed and accuracy. In large towns and cities they are taught how to run sorting machines. Letter carriers usually work inside the post office for a while to learn postal procedures.

Getting the Job

Job seekers can get applications and testing schedules at local post offices. Appointments to postal jobs are made from the three highest scores on each test. Candidates who are not appointed may be selected at a later time.

Advancement Possibilities and Employment Outlook

Large post offices that employ supervisors offer the most opportunities for promotion. The usual path for advancement is from top-level clerk to supervisor to postmaster. Supervisors' and postmasters' jobs require experience, education, and examinations.

Postal workers with seniority may receive preferred assignments, such as day shifts. Whenever preferred assignments open up, requests are made by written bid. The jobs go to the qualified bidders with the longest service.

Employment in the postal service is expected to decline somewhat through 2014. Although thousands of jobs open each year as workers retire or leave the service, each job gets many applicants and competition is strong. Automation is eliminating many jobs as well.

Working Conditions

Many post office buildings are modern, comfortable places to work, and a major effort is being made to replace or modernize the others. Postal employees often work in groups or teams and have fairly secure jobs because the ups and downs of business cycles do not affect them. However, many jobs require strenuous lifting and moving of mail. Letter carriers need good health and physical stamina to work outdoors in all kinds of weather. Postal clerks sometimes face periods of stress when large loads of mail need to be dispatched quickly. Many postal workers belong to labor unions.

Earnings and Benefits

Salaries and benefits vary with workers' experience and the location of the post office. In 2004 the median salary of mail carriers was $44,450 per year, with the most experienced carriers earning more than $54,240 per year. The median salary for postal clerks was $40,950 per year, with the top ten percent making more than $50,510 per year. The median annual salary for sorters, processors, and machine operators was $39,430.

Postal workers receive time and a half for overtime and premium pay on holidays. Benefits include pension plans and health and life insurance. Paid vacations range from thirteen days for the first three years to twenty-six days after fifteen years of service. Paid sick leave can be accumulated over several years.

Where to Go for More Information

U.S. Postal Service
475 L'Enfant Plaza SW
Washington, DC 20206-0001
(800) 275-8777
http://www.usps.com

American Postal Workers Union
1300 L St. NW
Washington, DC 20005
(202) 842-4200
http://www.apwu.org

National Association of Letter Carriers
100 Indiana Ave. NW
Washington, DC 20001-2144
(202) 393-4695
http://www.nalc.org

National Rural Letter Carriers Association
1630 Duke St.
Alexandria, VA 22314-3465
(703) 684-5545
http://www.nrlca.org

Power Plant Worker

Education and Training
High school plus on-the-job training

Salary
Median—$52,530 per year

Employment Outlook
Poor

Definition and Nature of the Work

Power plants produce electricity by drawing energy from such natural resources as oil, coal, falling water, and radioactive ore. They are located throughout the country, usually near population centers where energy needs are highest.

The jobs of power plant workers vary from plant to plant, depending on the type of fuel used and the age of the equipment. However, some jobs are central to nearly all power plants. Boiler operators, for instance, heat water until it becomes steam, which moves the turbines that generate electricity. They read gauges, meters, and thermometers to determine the right amount of steam. In large power plants they sometimes operate more than one boiler. Turbine operators monitor the speed and temperature at which the turbines are spinning. They also shut down the turbines when less electricity is needed and start them again when demand increases. Turbine operators often have helpers and junior operators working with them. Switchboard operators regulate the voltage and amount of electricity that flows out of the power plant. They take orders over the telephone from load dispatchers, who monitor the needs of customers in the system. The switchboard operators tell turbine operators when to start or shut down the turbines. In some modern plants, all the meters, dials, and gauges are centralized so that one operator, working with assistants, can do the work of boiler, turbine, and switchboard operators.

Nuclear power plants have their own technology and require several specialized workers. However, some jobs in nuclear power plants are much like jobs in conventional plants. For instance, nuclear reactor operators do a job similar to that of boiler operators.

Whether plants are new or old, operators are supervised by watch engineers, who ensure that each worker does what is necessary to keep the electricity flowing. Watch engineers report to superintendents, who take final responsibility for all work done in their plants.

Power plant workers are employed by plants that produce electricity by burning oil or coal, by using falling water, or by drawing on radioactive ores. (© Richard Hamilton Smith/Corbis.)

Education and Training Requirements

Many employers prefer applicants with high school diplomas or the equivalent. High school classes that may be useful include algebra, science, and shop. Experience in other power plants or with the navy's nuclear propulsion plants can be a plus in getting hired. Most operators start as cleanup workers or helpers and move up to positions as junior or assistant operators. Four to eight years of on-the-job training may be required before workers are considered fully qualified as boiler, turbine, or switchboard operators.

Nuclear reactor operators must pass Nuclear Regulatory Commission (NRC) exams. Once they get their licenses, they are required to pass annual practical plant-operation exams and biennial written exams administered by their employers.

Getting the Job

Job seekers can apply directly to power plants. Openings are rarely advertised because companies get more applications than they have positions available.

Advancement Possibilities and Employment Outlook

Boiler operators or turbine operators may be promoted to assistant switchboard operators and then to switchboard operators. Switchboard operators must have five to ten years of experience before becoming watch engineers.

Employment in this field is expected to decline through 2014. In response to deregulation and increasing competition, the industry has restructured its companies, eliminating many jobs.

Working Conditions

Most power plants are clean, safe places to work, although controversy lingers over the danger and effects of radiation leaks at nuclear power plants. The equipment can be noisy. Boiler and turbine operators spend most of their time on their feet, while switchboard operators usually sit in front of monitoring equipment.

Eight-hour days and forty-hour weeks are standard, but because electricity is produced around the clock, rotating shifts are required. Plant operators usually receive extra pay for night, weekend, and holiday work. Overtime may be necessary in emergencies. Many operators belong to labor unions.

Earnings and Benefits

Salaries for operators depend on seniority, which jobs they do, and where they work. In 2004 the median salary of all power plant workers was $52,530 per year. Median salaries at nuclear power plants were higher, with reactor operators earning $64,090 per year.

Benefits generally include paid vacations and holidays, health insurance, and retirement plans.

Where to Go for More Information

Edison Electric Institute
701 Pennsylvania Ave. NW
Washington, DC 20004-2696
(202) 508-5000
http://www.eei.org

International Brotherhood of Electrical Workers
900 Seventh St. NW
Washington, DC 20001
(202) 833-7000
http://www.ibew.org

National Association of Power Engineers
1 Springfield St.
Chicopee, MA 01013
(413) 592-6273
http://www.powerengineers.com

Nuclear Regulatory Commission
Washington, DC 20555
(800) 368-5642
http://www.nrc.gov

Refuse Worker

Education and Training
High school plus on-the-job training

Salary
Median—$13.87 per hour

Employment Outlook
Poor

Definition and Nature of the Work

Refuse workers remove waste material from industrial plants, businesses, and private homes and take it to disposal sites. Some workers, the refuse collectors, can be heard on city streets, often at night. Crews of collectors pick up garbage and put it into trucks with built-in compacting devices. When the trucks are full, the drivers take the refuse away. Incinerator operators, who work at disposal sites, control and maintain the equipment that burns the garbage. They direct other workers who feed the refuse into furnaces and remove the ashes afterward. Landfill operators dump refuse into specially designed pits—often using cranes and other heavy equipment—and cover it with earth.

Refuse workers may be employed by cities or towns or by privately owned disposal services. The private companies may have many trucks and crews that operate in a number of municipalities. Incinerator and landfill operators may work for a single municipality or for a centrally located waste disposal area that provides service to several cities and towns.

Education and Training Requirements

Applicants with high school or vocational school education are preferred. They may also qualify by passing civil service examinations or other oral or written tests. Because refuse workers must be strong, doctors' health certificates are required. Truck drivers must have driver's licenses. Beginners are trained on the job by experienced workers.

Many training requirements are standardized by the U.S. Occupational Safety and Health Administration. Operators are evaluated at least once every three years and receive additional training when new procedures and regulations are developed.

A refuse collector dumps garbage and other waste material into a truck before it is transported to a disposal area. (© David H. Wells/Corbis.)

For crane operators and those working with specialized loads, training and apprenticeship programs are offered by the International Union of Industrial Engineers and the National Commission for the Certification of Crane Operators. Some employers may require crane operators to be certified, and twelve states have laws requiring crane operators to be licensed.

Getting the Job

Job seekers can apply directly to city or town administrators, state public utility commissions, or private disposal services. Those who intend to apply for government jobs should take civil service examinations.

Advancement Possibilities and Employment Outlook

Refuse collectors usually start as laborers. Later they may become truck drivers or supervisors, usually after passing written tests or civil service examinations. Most incinerator and landfill operators have civil service jobs and must take additional examinations for advancement.

Employment in this field is expected to grow more slowly than the average for all jobs through 2014. Technological advancement in equipment, such as automated storage and retrieval systems and conveyors, has allowed operators to raise productivity and eliminate jobs. However, an increased emphasis on recycling waste materials may create new jobs for refuse workers.

Working Conditions

Refuse workers are outdoors most of the day, lifting heavy containers, driving trucks, and operating heavy equipment, which can be stressful to the body. Although the work can be physically demanding and dangerous, safety procedures have decreased the risk of accident or injury. Refuse workers usually are on the job forty hours a week, although overtime may be required. Many refuse workers belong to labor unions.

Earnings and Benefits

The earnings of refuse workers vary greatly, depending on geographic location and the specific task that is performed. Differences in union scales also affect earnings.

In 2004 the median wage for refuse collectors was $13.87 per hour, with supervisors earning $18.40 per hour. Industrial truck and tractor operators earned $12.78 per hour, and crane and tower operators received $17.99 per hour.

The benefits that are available to most refuse workers include paid holidays and vacations, medical and hospital insurance, workers' compensation, and retirement plans.

Where to Go for More Information

American Federation of State, County, and
  Municipal Employees
1625 L St. NW
Washington, DC 20036
(202) 429-1000
http://www.afscme.org

International Brotherhood of Teamsters
25 Louisiana Ave. NW
Washington, DC 20001-2198
(202) 624-6800
http://www.teamster.org

Solid Waste Association of North America
PO Box 7219
Silver Spring, MD 20907-7219
(800) 467-9262
http://www.swana.org

Security Guard

Education and Training
High school plus training

Salary
Median—$20,320 per year

Employment Outlook
Good

Definition and Nature of the Work

Security guards protect people and property from robberies, fires, and other damage. They work in banks, museums, nightclubs, government offices, stores, factories, and office buildings. They are employed by the companies they protect, by building management companies, and by private agencies that provide security services.

The duties of security guards vary according to the size of the building they guard, the number of guards who share the work, and the kind of security system used. In large operations guards generally work under security directors, while in smaller establishments they may work alone. Guards patrol buildings and grounds on foot, in cars, or on motor scooters. They may work with trained dogs that alert them to intruders.

Guards check windows, lights, doors, fire extinguishers, and sprinkler and alarm systems. Sometimes they answer telephones at night, run elevators, control who enters buildings, and check packages of those entering and leaving to prevent theft.

Some guards work with electronic alarm systems, monitoring closed-circuit television screens in a central station. If they see unusual activity, they send a runner to investigate. Such systems are often used on loading platforms of warehouses, factories, railroads, and ports where material or equipment is being prepared for shipment. Guards also protect people carrying jewels or large sums of money. Security guards summon police officers and firefighters when necessary. They may carry guns.

A security guard at a central station communicates with other guards in the building to ensure that all areas are properly secured. (© Martha Tabor/ Working Images Photographs. Reproduced by permission.)

Education and Training Requirements

Employers generally prefer applicants with high school education or the equivalent. Several states require that guards be licensed, which involves passing a background check and completing classroom training in such subjects as property rights, emergency procedures, and detention of suspected criminals. Drug testing often is required.

Previous training in police or military police work is useful. Many employers train guards on the job. Others provide several weeks of formal classroom work, covering alarm systems and first aid and emergency procedures. Armed guards undergo rigorous training in firearm safety, weapons retention, and laws covering the use of force.

Getting the Job

Job seekers can apply directly to businesses and protective agencies. Those who apply for jobs with government agencies must pass civil service examinations. Part-time or temporary work, such as guarding department stores during holiday periods, can often lead to permanent jobs. Employment agencies, state employment services, newspaper classified ads, and job banks on the Internet may offer employment leads.

Most employers require that guards be bonded, or insured. Bonding companies investigate the background and character of security guards, which protects employers against dishonest and unreliable workers.

Advancement Possibilities and Employment Outlook

With experience, guards can advance to supervisory positions. Opportunities are best in government agencies, where promotion is based on civil service examinations. In small companies advancement may be limited. Experienced professionals sometimes open their own security agencies.

Employment is expected to grow as fast as the average for all jobs through 2014. New positions will be created because of an increased desire for security. Openings will also occur as experienced guards retire or leave the field. Security agencies are expected to provide most of the new jobs.

Working Conditions

Security guards are on their feet much of the time. Small companies may need guards only for an eight-hour shift at night, while large institutions and companies may need security around the clock. Guards generally rotate shifts.

Security work may be very dangerous, so guards often wear uniforms and bulletproof vests. Some employers provide uniforms or a uniform allowance. Many guards belong to labor unions.

Earnings and Benefits

Earnings vary with experience, location, and duties. In 2004 the median salary of security guards was $20,320 per year. Experienced guards earned more than $33,270 per year. Benefits generally include paid vacations and holidays, health insurance, and retirement plans. Government guards get benefits similar to those received by other government workers.

Where to Go for More Information

American Federation of State, County, and
   Municipal Employees
1625 L St. NW
Washington, DC 20036-5687
(202) 429-1000
http://www.afscme.org

American Society for Industrial Security
1625 Prince St.
Alexandria, VA 22314-2818
(703) 519-6200
http://www.asisonline.org

Information Systems Security Association
7044 S. Thirteenth St.
Oak Creek, WI 53154
(414) 908-4949
http://www.issa.org

Border Patrol Agent

Education and Training
College and training

Salary
Average—$55,000 per year

Employment Outlook
Good

Definition and Nature of the Work

Border patrol agents, who are federal law enforcement officers, make sure that laws are observed when goods or people enter the United States. They work at ports of entry and all along the border to prevent smuggling and the entrance of illegal aliens.

One of their chief duties is covert surveillance along the border, using electronic sensors, infrared scopes, low-light television systems, and aircraft. They also conduct traffic and transportation checks at ports of entry; arrest aliens who live in this country illegally; and make suggestions to the courts about immigration matters, including applications for citizenship.

Education and Training Requirements

Applicants, who must be younger than thirty-seven years of age, need either college degrees or enough education and experience to demonstrate they can make decisions and handle stressful situations. They also must pass written examinations that assess their logical reasoning and ability to speak Spanish (or their ability to learn Spanish). After passing the examinations, applicants undergo in-depth interviews that evaluate their interpersonal skills, judgment, and problem-solving abilities. Prospective agents must undergo drug tests, medical screenings, and comprehensive background checks. Applicants must also have valid driver's licenses.

Border patrol agents work at border crossings to check the identification papers of people entering the United States from a foreign country.
(© FRED GREAVES/Reuters/Corbis.)

Those who pass the examinations are required to take classes at the Border Patrol Academy in Artesia, New Mexico. During the nineteen-week training program, agents-in-training study immigration and nationality law, criminal law and statutory authority, behavioral science, Spanish, Border Patrol operations, firearm safety, and motor-vehicle operation.

Getting the Job

The U.S. Customs and Border Protection Web site lists job opportunities and the application requirements for each position.

Advancement Possibilities and Employment Outlook

New agents may be promoted after a probationary period lasting about six months. They may be promoted again at the end of their third year of service. Some agents advance to supervisory positions or transfer to other jobs in immigration and naturalization.

Each year between one hundred and two hundred job openings occur, depending largely on government funding for the patrol. Because the number of people entering the country illegally is increasing, opportunities for border patrol agents many increase as well.

Working Conditions

Border patrol agents often work outdoors along international borders. They may be sent on temporary assignments on short notice and be permanently reassigned to any duty location. Like all law-enforcement personnel, agents must be responsible and able to act quickly. They are required to be proficient in the use of and carry firearms. Agents work forty hours a week, usually in rotating shifts, plus overtime. Agents are subject to random drug testing.

Earnings and Benefits

Earnings depend on years of service. In 2004 the average wage for experienced agents was $55,000 per year. All agents received Administratively Uncontrollable Overtime based on the number of unscheduled hours of overtime worked each week. Almost all employees received the maximum amount, about twenty-five percent of base pay.

Agents receive paid vacations; health, long-term care, and life insurance; pensions; and other benefits given to federal employees.

Where to Go for More Information

U.S. Citizenship and Immigration Service
425 I St. NW
Washington, DC 20536
(202) 514-2000
http://www.uscis.gov

U.S. Customs and Border Protection
1300 Pennsylvania Ave. NW
Washington, DC 20229
(202) 354-1000
http://www.cbp.gov

Correctional Officer

Correctional officers guard inmates inside and outside the prison, counsel them on prison rules, and listen to their complaints and needs. *(Damian Dovarganes/ AFP/Getty Images.)*

Definition and Nature of the Work

Correctional officers guard inmates inside and outside local, state, and federal prisons. They counsel individuals and groups on prison rules and listen to their complaints and needs.

Inside prisons, they escort inmates from their cells to dining rooms, classrooms, hospitals, chapels, and work areas. They stand guard over recreational activities, watching for possible disturbances. Sometimes they search prisoners for forbidden articles. Officers also patrol buildings and grounds, checking locks, windows, bars, and gates to see that they cannot be used by prisoners to escape.

Other officers escort inmates outside prison boundaries, taking them to jobs in the community or on court-ordered trips. They bring back escapees and those who have violated parole. Correctional officers may watch over people who have been arrested and are waiting to strand trial. They are trained in the use of guns, handcuffs, and other restraint equipment.

Education and Training Requirements

Age requirements vary. Some correctional systems expect applicants to be eighteen years old, while others require them to be twenty-one. At the state level, high school education is either required or preferred. The Federal Bureau of Prisons prefers that applicants have bachelor's degrees; it may accept three years of full-time experience in counseling and supervision of individuals or a combination of college study and counseling work.

Most correctional systems require written examinations that determine applicants' reading level and ability to follow directions. Some give civil service tests and psychological examinations. Applicants at all levels must undergo rigorous physical examinations. They cannot have been convicted of any felony.

Training periods last from one to six months, depending on the size of the prison. The training, which may take place in the department of correction, an academy, or in the prison itself, includes courses in the principles, practices, terminology, and rules of modern correctional methods. Personal defense, physical restraint of prisoners, and the use of guns are also studied. Many prisons require that officers practice their rifle skills at regular intervals.

Certification at different levels is offered through the American Correctional Association. Candidates must pass examinations that measure their knowledge of the field.

High school courses in government and communications are useful for those interested in the field. Many two-year colleges offer associate degrees in correctional science, which can be helpful in gaining employment. The programs include classes on crime and delinquency, administration of justice, the court system, psychology, and sociology.

Getting the Job

Local and state prisons offer more job opportunities than federal prisons. Job seekers can apply directly to state or county correctional institutions or state and local civil service commissions. State employment services may list job openings for correctional officers. Those who want jobs in the federal prison system should take the necessary civil service tests.

Advancement Possibilities and Employment Outlook

With experience, education, and training, qualified officers may advance to a higher rank and salary. Advancement in larger prisons is usually from correctional officer to sergeant to lieutenant to captain to deputy keeper; titles often vary.

The employment outlook for correctional officers is very good through 2014. More positions are expected as existing facilities are expanded and new prisons built to house the growing number of prisoners. Other jobs should open up as experienced workers retire or leave the field.

Working Conditions

Corrections officers usually work eight-hour shifts, which rotate. They are on call for emergencies and may work weekends and holidays. All officers wear uniforms. In large prisons they must stand inspection before their daily work begins.

The job can be stressful, especially in emergency situations. Officers may find themselves in personal danger. They must act quickly, assess situations carefully, act in accordance with regulations, and protect themselves as well as inmates and other officers.

Earnings and Benefits

Pay scales vary widely, based on the kind of job, seniority, and location. In 2004 the median salary for all correctional officers was $33,600 per year. For supervisors and managers, the median salary was $44,720 per year. Some experienced officers earned more than $54,820 per year. The median salary for all federal correctional officers was $44,700 per year. Federal officers started at $26,747 in 2005.

Correctional officers receive benefit packages that include life and health insurance, pension plans, sick leave, and paid holidays and vacations.

Where to Go for More Information

American Correctional Association
206 N. Washington St., Ste. 200
Alexandria, VA 22314
(800) 222-5646
http://www.aca.org

American Jail Association
1135 Professional Ct.
Hagerstown, MD 21740-5853
(301) 790-3930
http://www.corrections.com/aja

Federal Bureau of Prisons
320 First St. NW
Washington, DC 20534
(202) 307-3198
http://www.bop.gov

National Council on Crime and
    Delinquency
1970 Broadway, Ste. 500
Oakland, CA 94612
(510) 208-0500
http://www.nccd-crc.org

Court Clerk

Court clerks are responsible for clerical and administrative duties relating to the city, county, state, and federal court system. They keep records of all court cases.
(© Jennifer Brown/Star Ledger/Corbis.)

Definition and Nature of the Work

Court clerks are responsible for the administrative work of the city, county, state, and federal court systems. Their duties often depend on which courts they serve.

In all courts, they record and transcribe the minutes of proceedings, prepare the docket of scheduled cases, and administer the oath to jurors and witnesses. Some clerks have special duties, such as processing passports or swearing in new citizens. Clerks in the larger courts direct a staff or department and spend much of their time reviewing legal papers and conferring with lawyers and judges on court matters.

Assistant court clerks, or deputy clerks, prepare reports and court forms, such as petitions and warrants, and process court decisions for publication. They may impanel jurors and provide information on court procedures.

Education and Training Requirements

Applicants must have high school diplomas or the equivalent, although two years of college or business school may be required. Bachelor's degrees are preferred, and many federal court clerks have master's degrees or law degrees. Candidates should be skilled in word processing, bookkeeping, business and personnel management, accounting, and budgeting.

English skills are essential, and knowledge of foreign languages can be helpful in some areas of the United States. Discretion, good judgment, and integrity are crucial.

Getting the Job

Job seekers can apply directly to local, state, and federal court offices. School placement offices may have information about job openings.

Advancement Possibilities and Employment Outlook

Advancement depends on experience, skill in handling responsibilities, additional education, and test performance. Assistant or deputy court clerks can become chief deputy clerks or court clerks. Clerks can also advance by moving from city or county courts to state or federal courts. Some court clerks become legal aides, parole or probation officers, or lawyers.

The job outlook for court clerks is very good through 2014. Because the judicial system is becoming more complex, court clerks are needed to keep the courts running efficiently.

Working Conditions

Although their offices and courtrooms are comfortable and well lit, court clerks often find their work stressful because of the exacting nature of their duties and the strict time limits in which they must accomplish them. They work with computers, stenotype and copy machines, microfilm, and card indexes.

Earnings and Benefits

Salaries for court clerks vary according to the type and size of the court, the responsibilities involved, and the experience and level of education attained. In 2004 the median salary was $27,300 per year. Most clerks receive benefits such as health insurance, paid holidays and vacations, and retirement plans.

Where to Go for More Information

National Association for Court
   Management
300 Newport Ave.
Williamsburg, VA 23185-4147
(757) 259-1841
http://www.nacmnet.org

National Court Reporters Association
8224 Old Courthouse Rd.
Vienna, VA 22182-3808
(800) 272-6272
http://www.verbatimreporters.com

Court Reporter

Definition and Nature of the Work

Court reporters create verbatim transcripts of legal proceedings, speeches, meetings, and even conversations. They use several methods to ensure that the spoken word is accurately recorded.

Some court reporters use stenotype machines. When they press multiple keys on the machine at the same time, it records combinations of letters that represent sounds, words, or phrases. The combinations are recorded electronically and displayed as text. This process is known as computer-aided transcription.

Stenotype machines are also used in real-time court reporting. Reporters type in text that appears instantly as real-time captions on display screens. Called Communication Access Realtime Translation, this process is primarily used in courtroom settings, although it is also used for closed-captioning of television programs for the hearing impaired. Reporters that specialize in this type of work are called stenocaptioners. They may be employed by television and cable stations, sporting events, and a variety of other businesses.

When court reporters use voice writing, they repeat the court testimony directly into voice silencers, which are hand-held masks containing microphones. The masks prevent their voices from being heard in courtrooms. Some reporters then create written transcripts after the proceedings. Others utilize speech-recognition technology to create transcripts in real time.

Court reporters who use stenographic or voice-writing methods must also create and maintain the dictionary the computer uses to translate their keystrokes. The dictionary contains parts of words, entire words, or specific terminology common in the type of reporting they do. After the proceedings are complete, stenotypists and voice writers must carefully review their transcripts to check for misspellings and grammatical errors. They also create storage and retrieval procedures for their stenographic notes and voice files.

Some workers use audio or digital recording systems. During court proceedings, reporters take notes to indicate speakers and other relevant issues and monitor the recording sessions. Once the proceedings have ended, the reporters review the tapes and make accurate transcripts.

Education and Training
High school plus training

Salary
Median—$42,920 per year

Employment Outlook
Good

Education and Training Requirements

A high school diploma or its equivalent is required to become a court reporter. About one hundred sixty vocational and technical schools and community colleges provide instruction in the different methods of court reporting. Becoming a voice writer usually takes less than a year of training, while electronic reporting skills can be learned on the job. Training for stenotypists takes thirty-three months and involves instruction in both computer-aided transcription and real-time reporting. A stenotypist should be able to capture two hundred twenty-five words per minute, which is the federal requirement for court reporting.

Some states require a court reporter to pass state examinations to obtain Certified Court Reporter designation. The National Court Reporters Association administers an examination for certification as a Registered Professional Reporter. Other levels of certification are available. Some states require a court reporter to be a notary public.

A number of states require a voice writer to have a license, which requires testing, or to be certified by the National Verbatim Reporters Association. The organization offers three levels of certification: Certified Verbatim Reporter, Certificate of Merit, and Real-time Verbatim Reporter. Earning all three types of certification is equivalent to being licensed. Once certified, a reporter must take courses to retain that status.

An electronic reporter may also be certified. The American Association of Electronic Reporters and Transcribers offers three types of certification: Certified Electronic Court Reporter; Certified Electronic Court Transcriber; and Certified Electronic Court Reporter and Transcriber. Although certification is voluntary, a growing number of employers are requiring it.

Where to Go for More Information

American Association of Electronic
  Reporters and Transcribers
23812 Rock Circle
Bothell, WA 98021-8573
(800) 233-5306
http://www.aeert.org

National Court Reporters Association
8224 Old Courthouse Rd.
Vienna, VA 22182-3808
(800) 272-6272
http://www.verbatimreporters.com

National Verbatim Reporters Association
207 Third Ave.
Hattiesburg, MS 39401
(610) 582-4345
http://www.nvra.org

U.S. Court Reporters Association
4731 N. Western Ave.
Chicago, IL 60625-2012
(800) 628-2730
http://www.uscra.org

Getting the Job

School placement offices or state employment services can help graduates find jobs. Another path to employment is working with freelance reporters who have many clients.

Applicants for jobs as court reporters in federal agencies must take civil service examinations. Licensing or certification may be necessary for state courts or agencies.

Advancement Possibilities and Employment Outlook

Court reporters may advance to administrative or management work. They may also become consultants or instructors.

Employment of court reporters is expected to increase as fast as the average for all occupations through 2014. Business and government expansion should result in more hearings, trials, and conferences that must be recorded. Growth of court-reporting services, however, will be affected by federal and state budgets. Demand for real-time closed-captioning services is strong, particularly in television, classrooms, and business settings, and should provide many job opportunities.

Working Conditions

Most court reporters work forty-hour weeks, usually in comfortable settings such as lawyers' offices or courtrooms.

Freelance reporters may work evenings and weekends or be on call for last-minute jobs. They may do some of their work at home.

Court reporters risk repetitive stress injuries such as carpal tunnel syndrome. Sitting in the same position for long periods can strain the back, neck, eyes, and wrists. The job can be both stressful and tedious.

Earnings and Benefits

Salaries vary by type of reporting job, experience, and location. Some reporters earn base salaries and per-page fees for transcripts, while others are paid by the job.

In 2004 the median salary for court reporters was $42,920 per year. The most experienced reporters earned more than $80,300 per year. Freelance reporters usually earned less, depending on their skills, the availability of work, and the region of the country.

Most salaried court reporters receive paid holidays and vacations, health insurance, and retirement plans. Freelance reporters must provide their own benefits.

Crime Laboratory Technician

Definition and Nature of the Work

Crime laboratory technicians, also called forensic science technicians or police science technicians, help solve crimes. They use scientific laboratory methods to analyze evidence found at crime scenes or accidents. Their findings often determine the guilt of criminals or the innocence of those falsely accused.

Education and Training
Two-year or four-year college

Salary
Median—$21.16 per hour

Employment Outlook
Very good

Crime lab technicians work closely with agents of the Federal Bureau of Investigation and with state and local police officers. Sometimes the evidence from crime scenes is collected by detectives or other police officers and delivered to the crime laboratory. At other times technicians gather the evidence themselves.

Crime lab technicians usually specialize. Ballistics technicians examine bullets and match them to guns. Chemical and physical analysis technicians may examine a chip of paint from an automobile or a piece of glass found in a victim's clothes. They also examine hair, soil, blood, narcotics, biological tissues and fluids, and poisons. Often, they specialize in DNA analysis. Documents technicians analyze handwriting on blackmail notes and anonymous letters, as well as the paper on which the handwriting exists. Instruments technicians match marks found on victims to the tools thought to have been used by the suspects, such as crowbars or rocks. Fingerprint technicians analyze fingerprints, footprints, and tire treads, while photography technicians take pictures of crime scenes. Polygraph technicians give lie detector tests and interpret the results.

Technicians use many kinds of equipment, including microscopes, infrared photography, ultraviolet light, X-ray machines, and spectrographs. The machinery enlarges tiny fragments, discovers hidden stains, or reveals the history of victims' lives—even their dental work. Most technicians have some knowledge of all the tools used in the lab.

A crime laboratory technician uses a scientific laboratory method to dust for fingerprints at the scene of a crime. This evidence may be used by FBI agents or police officers to solve the crime. (© Ed Kashi/Corbis.)

Education and Training Requirements

Many crime laboratories now require bachelor's degrees in forensic science or crime technology, which cover scientific crime detection, investigative photography, fingerprint science, criminal investigation and evidence, criminal law, and court procedures. There are several well-regarded two-year programs in the field, but the trend is toward more advanced courses of study. High school courses that are good preparation for this kind of work include mathematics, biology, chemistry, and physics.

Getting the Job

Job seekers can apply directly to any police department that has a crime laboratory. College placement offices and state employment offices may have information about job openings. Many employers prefer to hire those who have taken civil service tests.

Advancement Possibilities and Employment Outlook

Crime lab technicians advance by taking civil service examinations that require knowledge of the newest techniques in the field. They can advance through several ranks to supervisory positions.

The number of jobs for crime laboratory technicians is expected to increase faster than the average for all jobs through 2014. Job seekers with four-year degrees in forensic science will have more opportunities than those with two-year degrees.

Working Conditions

Technicians' work is precise and methodical, and their labs are usually clean, well-lit places to work. They get satisfaction from preparing scientific evidence for court cases and in knowing that their work brings criminals to justice. Sometimes technicians present the evidence in court themselves.

Earnings and Benefits

Salaries of crime lab technicians vary with the employer and the workers' experience. In 2004 the median salary for all crime lab technicians was $21.16 per hour. Salaries increase when technicians advance from one civil service rank to another. Health and life insurance, paid vacations, holidays, and sick leave are provided by all law enforcement agencies that employ crime lab technicians.

Customs Worker

Definition and Nature of the Work

Customs workers enforce the laws governing the import and export of goods. Most of these laws are designed to protect citizens' health and to raise revenues for the federal government. Some tariff laws protect selected businesses from foreign competition. Occasionally, under congressional order, customs workers enforce boycotts of certain nations' goods for political reasons.

Customs workers often specialize. Inspectors, for instance, look for banned or taxable items in tourists' belongings and in the cargo of ships and planes. For example, they check baggage to see whether travelers are smuggling narcotics. They also make sure that tourists declare the true value of goods they are bringing into the country and collect taxes, or duties, when the value of the goods exceeds certain limits.

Import specialists classify goods that companies plan to sell in the United States, issue customs documents, and decide how much duty importers must pay. Because a wide variety of merchandise crosses U.S. borders, import specialists often become expert in one or two fields of goods, such as antiques or machinery. Customs agents are investigators who search for evidence of suspected violations of the law.

Education and Training Requirements

Most customs workers must be at least twenty-one years old and be U.S. citizens. All customs workers must have high school diplomas, or the equivalent, and some additional education or experience. High school course work in foreign languages, English, and history may be useful. College-level courses in foreign languages and business are also helpful. Because a majority of customs work involves interpreting and enforcing the law, some knowledge of legal affairs is valuable.

Customs inspectors and import specialists generally need either bachelor's degrees or three years of experience relating to customs control. They may also be required to pass civil service examinations. Customs agents usually have bachelor's degrees or prior law enforcement experience, including several years of experience in criminal investigation.

Education and Training
College plus training

Salary
Median—$49,736 per year

Employment Outlook
Good

At an airport, a customs inspector goes through tourists' bags to check for banned or taxable items. (© Martha Tabor/Working Images Photographs. Reproduced by permission.)

Getting the Job

Job seekers can contact their local Federal Information Center or civil service office. State employment services, school placement offices, newspaper classified ads, and job sites on the Internet may also provide employment information.

Advancement Possibilities and Employment Outlook

Government employees have many opportunities to work their way up through the ranks to supervisory or management jobs. Years of experience usually qualify workers for high-level office jobs.

The employment outlook for customs workers is favorable. The great volume of goods being imported and exported, as well as increased efforts against smuggling and terrorism, are expected to result in a slight increase in the number of job openings through 2014.

Working Conditions

Customs personnel usually work in rotating shifts because ports and borders operate twenty-four hours a day. Most customs workers have forty-hour workweeks and receive extra pay for overtime. They often work outside in all kinds of weather.

Agents should be accurate judges of character and be both alert and observant. Their work may be dangerous. Most jobs are located along U.S. borders, in airports, and near large cities.

Earnings and Benefits

Customs workers have civil service ratings, so their earnings vary according to their grade and rank. In 2004 the median salary for import specialists, inspectors, and customs agents was $49,736 per year. Wages increase as responsibilities increase. Benefits include paid vacations, sick leave, health insurance, and retirement plans.

Where to Go for More Information

National Customs Brokers and Forwarders
  Association of America
1200 Eighteenth St. NW, Ste. 901
Washington, DC 20036
(202) 466-0222
http://www.ncbfaa.org

U.S. Customs and Border Protection
1300 Pennsylvania Ave. NW
Washington, DC 20229
(202) 354-1000
http://www.customs.ustreas.gov

Detective

Definition and Nature of the Work

Detectives investigate, prevent, and solve crimes against people and property. Many work for police departments, while others are employed by business and industry. Detectives use modern techniques and tools, including computers and elaborate communications systems, to prevent and solve crimes ranging from shoplifting to mass murder.

Police detectives observe criminals' actions, develop sources of information, and assist in the arrest of criminals. They often work undercover. Dressed in civilian clothes while on duty, they go to places that a suspect is known to frequent so they get to know the suspect's habits and actions. For example, detectives assigned to a gambling case might spend time at a suspect's favorite bar, posing as other gamblers and trying to learn as much as possible about the case. The detectives might also find informers in the neighborhood who have information about the suspect. Having gathered enough evidence against the suspect, the detectives can make the arrest with the help of police reinforcements.

Some detectives work for private detective agencies or individual clients. They are often former police officers, although some are trained by the private agencies themselves. Because they are not part of the police force, they have no power to make arrests. Private investigators gather information from police sources, interview witnesses, and observe suspects. Lawyers and other companies hire investigators to gather information for court trials and to investigate fraud, the passing of bad checks, and other matters. Many insurance companies hire private detectives to investigate insurance claims. Parents may hire them to locate missing children.

Some private detectives work as bodyguards for people who are in personal danger. Store detectives guard against customer shoplifting and employee theft, while bouncers ensure that order is maintained in restaurants, nightclubs, and other places of entertainment. House detectives, or hotel detectives, protect patrons from disturbances and evict troublemakers.

Education and Training Requirements

High school diplomas, or the equivalent, are required for both police and private detectives. High school courses in English, science, math, social science, and physical education provide good preparation for the field. Foreign languages, journalism, and typing are also helpful. An increasing number of police departments require a year or two of college coursework, including classes in police science, criminology, and law.

Police detectives start as police officers. Applicants for positions as police officers usually must be at least twenty-one years old, meet certain height and weight requirements, and be in good physical condition. After they have demonstrated that they have the skills necessary for detective work, they may be assigned to detective duty on a probationary basis. Some police departments require that detectives pass an exam.

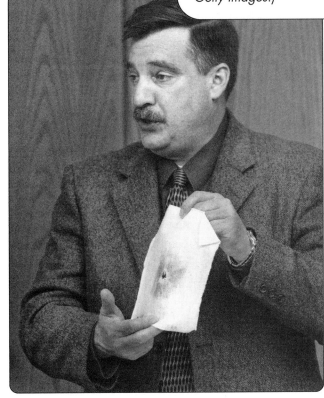

Many detectives work for police departments, investigating criminals' actions, gathering facts for cases, observing suspects, and assisting in arrests. *(Frank H. Conlon/ Getty Images News/ Getty Images.)*

Most police detectives are trained for six weeks to several months, depending on the program. Those who successfully complete the training program will probably be assigned to detective work permanently. They may be required to take refresher courses periodically to update their skills and techniques.

Because many private detectives are former police detectives, their education and training requirements are similar to those of police detectives. Private detectives also learn skills on the job from experienced private detectives.

In some states, private detectives must be licensed and participate in specially designed training programs. Each state requires a firearm permit.

Getting the Job

Job seekers can apply directly to police departments to take the police department entrance exam. Private detectives with credentials can apply to detective agencies, hotels, restaurants, law firms, manufacturing firms, and department stores.

Advancement Possibilities and Employment Outlook

Skilled and experienced police detectives can advance to chief of detectives or chief of police. Private detectives can advance to senior positions in detective agencies or become supervisors of security or detective staffs in private companies. Good detectives can start their own detective agencies.

The employment outlook for detectives is very good. Although job opportunities in police forces will be limited, openings in the private investigation field will grow faster than the average for all jobs through 2014. Companies, hotels, and restaurants increasingly use private detectives to protect their own and their customers' property. Investigators who specialize in Internet crimes, such as identity theft, spamming, e-mail harassment, and illegal downloading of copyrighted materials, will have many job opportunities.

Working Conditions

Detectives' work may be exciting and dangerous or routine and safe, depending on their assignments. Police detectives investigating narcotics smugglers may be exposed to the threat of physical violence or death. On the other hand, private detectives working as security guards may only check employee identification cards and handle routine complaints. The work of most detectives falls between these two extremes.

Detectives often work irregular hours, including nights and weekends. Although they may have to work more than forty hours a week on certain cases, they are generally given time off to compensate for their overtime.

Where to Go for More Information

National Association of Legal Investigators
908 Twenty-first St.
Sacramento, CA 95814-3118
(916) 441-5522
http://www.nalionline.org

National Association of Police Officers
750 First St. NE, Ste. 920
Washington, DC 20002
(202) 842-4420
http://www.napo.org

Earnings and Benefits

Salaries for detectives vary widely and depend on experience, location, and the responsibilities of the job. In 2004 the median salary of police detectives was $53,990 per year, with the top ten percent earning more than $86,010 per year. The median salary of private detectives was $32,110 per year. The most experienced, successful private detectives earned more than $58,470 per year.

Detectives may receive benefits such as paid sick leave and vacations, life and health insurance, and pensions. Detectives who run their own agencies must provide their own benefits.

Federal Government Worker

Definition and Nature of the Work

The federal government employs about 1.9 million civilians in the United States and abroad. Many hold jobs similar to those in private industry, such as secretaries, lawyers, physicians, biologists, truck drivers, and painters. Others have jobs exclusive to the government: postal service worker, internal revenue agent, or border patrol agent. Most work for agencies of the executive branch, printing money, caring for disabled veterans, forecasting weather, and cataloging documents. A smaller number are employed by the legislative and judicial branches of government, working as pages, court stenographers, and clerks. The government also employs mechanics, maintenance workers, chauffeurs, food service workers, plumbers, truck drivers, and countless other workers of various skills.

About one of every eight federal government employees works in Washington, DC. The rest work in all fifty states and in foreign countries.

Education and Training Requirements

A high school education is sufficient for some jobs, but others require bachelor's, master's, or doctoral degrees. Applicants for jobs in the United States must be at least sixteen years old. For overseas jobs the minimum age is twenty.

Most applicants take competitive examinations administered by the Office of Personnel Management. The tests measure applicants' ability to do particular jobs or their ability to learn to do the jobs. Some government agencies have developed their own testing and merit systems. They include the Federal Bureau of Investigation, the Foreign Service of the Department of State, the Atomic Energy Commission, and the Tennessee Valley Authority.

Federal employees usually receive training on the job or in facilities outside government. Apprenticeship programs exist for certain trade workers, and work-study programs and summer programs are available for college students.

Getting the Job

All native-born and naturalized U.S. citizens may take civil service examinations. Announcements for the exams and job openings and application forms may be obtained from local branches of the Federal Information Center.

Once applicants have taken an exam they will be notified whether they are eligible for certain government jobs. When an opening occurs in a federal agency, the agency chooses from the applicants who had the three top scores. Applicants not selected may be considered for later vacancies. Applicants can also expect to be interviewed. Some jobs are not filled by examination, but according to training and experience.

Federal government workers are employed by all branches of the federal government. Some work in Washington, DC, whereas others work in individual states or in foreign countries. (© Rob Lewine/Corbis.)

Advancement Possibilities and Employment Outlook

Skilled workers can move up within an agency or be promoted to a job in another agency. Promotion is sometimes based on additional civil service examinations. Little overall growth in the number of federal jobs is expected through 2014. Most openings will occur when experienced workers retire or leave government service.

Working Conditions

Federal government workers generally have set workweeks, although overtime may be required. Employees have a great deal of job security.

Earnings and Benefits

The majority of federally employed workers are paid according to a system called the General Schedule. Each job is assigned a grade level according to the difficulty of the work and the training and experience required. In 2005 the starting salary for workers in the lowest grade, GS-1, was $16,016 per year. Most high school graduates with no related work experience started at GS-2, with a salary of $18,007 per year. Those with bachelor's degrees generally started at grade GS-5 or grade GS-7, depending on their academic record. In 2005 starting salaries for those positions were $24,677 and $30,567 per year, respectively. Those in the highest grade, GS-15, earned between $89,625 and $116,517 per year.

Skilled workers, manual laborers, and service workers are paid according to the Wage Board schedule, which is based on prevailing rates for similar jobs in private industry. Wages vary by geographic location.

Federal government workers receive many benefits, including paid vacations, holidays, sick leave, low-cost life and health insurance, and retirement plans.

Where to Go for More Information

American Federation of Government
  Employees
80 F St. NW
Washington, DC 20001-1528
(202) 737-8700
http://www.afge.org

Federally Employed Women
1666 K St. NW, Ste. 440
Washington, DC 20006
(202) 898-0994
http://www.few.org

National Federation of Federal Employees
1016 Sixteenth St. NW, Ste. 300
Washington, DC 20036
(202) 862-4400
http://www.nffe.org

Institutional Child Care Worker

Education and Training
High school plus training

Salary
Median—$13.19 per hour

Employment Outlook
Very good

Definition and Nature of the Work

Hundreds of thousands of children live in institutions. Some need settings other than their homes because of emotional problems or physical and mental disabilities. Abandoned children and those whose parents are unable to give them proper care may be placed in institutions by courts or social service agencies. Most of them are placed there until foster homes can be provided. Children who live in institutions are usually between the ages of six and eighteen.

Workers at these institutions, which are run by both government agencies and private charities, usually provide primary care and guidance for groups of five to fifteen children of the same age. Sometimes a husband and wife team acts as house parents, living with the children in cottages on the institutions' grounds. They give the children some of the affection ordinarily provided by actual parents and see that they are fed, clothed, and in good health. They also rehabilitate the children using programs designed by medical doctors, psychologists, and other specialists. Mentally handicapped children, for instance, are taught how to get along with other people by living and learning in groups. Some of these children are trained for jobs and return to live with their families. Children with cerebral palsy, epilepsy, and sight and hearing difficulties receive therapy.

Education and Training Requirements

Child care workers must have high school diplomas, or the equivalent. Grades are not as important as an interest in children and desire for further training. Many two-year colleges offer associate-degree programs, with courses covering child and adolescent development, child care techniques, English, social science, health, and physical education. Students are supervised working with children in several types of institutions.

At some state and charitable institutions, workers may be employed part time while they attend college at no cost. Many institutions provide special seminars and workshops that help workers learn care techniques.

Getting the Job

Job seekers who do fieldwork during college programs can develop contacts for future employment. College placement offices and state mental health agencies can provide referrals. Volunteer work with children and jobs at summer camps are assets for beginning child care workers.

Advancement Possibilities and Employment Outlook

Experienced child care workers who are graduates of two-year college programs may become supervisors of several child care units. Some child care workers earn bachelor's degrees in psychology or social work to advance in the field. A few colleges have four-year programs in child care for those who wish to become institution administrators.

The employment outlook for institutional child care workers is very good through 2014. Both men and women are needed as house parents and for a variety of other child care duties.

Working Conditions

Child care workers usually work eight-hour shifts, forty hours a week. In smaller communities and rural areas they may have longer workweeks. Shifts may rotate, and workers may be on call twenty-four hours in case of emergencies.

Child care workers must enjoy children and have a great deal of patience. They need an understanding of the problems institutionalized children face and the cultural and economic conditions from which many of the children come.

Earnings and Benefits

Salaries vary greatly, depending on location, experience, and education. In 2004 the median wage for institutional child care workers was $13.19 per hour. Untrained child care workers may earn less.

Public institutions usually pay higher salaries than charitable institutions. Nearly all institutions offer child care workers pension plans, health insurance, paid vacations and holidays, and sick leave.

Where to Go for More Information

Administration for Children and Families
371 L'Enfant Promenade SW
Washington, DC 20447
(800) 424-2246
http://www.acf.hhs.gov

Council for Exceptional Children
1110 N. Glebe Rd., Ste. 300
Arlington, VA 22201
(888) 232-7733
http://www.cec.sped.org

Orphan Foundation of America
21351 Gentry Dr., Unit 130
Sterling, VA 20166
(571) 203-0270
http://www.orphan.org

Legal Assistant, Corporate

Definition and Nature of the Work

As laws grow more complex and legal services more expensive, many companies are relying on corporate legal assistants to handle tasks that do not require lawyers' expertise. Working under the supervision of a corporate attorney, assistants research background material, index and summarize documents, and help prepare financial statements and tax returns. They may also prepare employee contracts, stock option plans, and mortgages.

Legal assistants have extensive knowledge of Internet databases and computer software packages that are specifically designed for legal research. If they are working on large antitrust cases, for example, they can analyze, store, and retrieve thousands of documents by computer, decreasing the amount of paper they must handle and the time it takes to do the work.

Corporate legal assistants, who are also called corporate paralegals or legal technicians, work for banks, insurance companies, manufacturers, and many other types of businesses. Some are employed by companies that design legal research software, working as market analysts, sales representatives, and systems programmers.

Education and Training Requirements

Many companies require that legal assistants have specialized training in business law, legal procedures, and terminology. Formal paralegal training programs range from two-year programs to four-year and postgraduate programs. Most programs generally require that applicants have high school diplomas. The four-year programs often require entrance examinations. Bachelor's degrees and high scores on standardized legal aptitude tests are usually required for paralegal programs offered by law schools. Legal assistants who plan to work in business should, in addition, take courses in business law, personnel management, finance, and database research.

Some legal assistants enter programs that lead to certification in paralegal studies. Applicants must have bachelor's degrees plus one year of experience as a legal assistant or high school diplomas plus seven years of experience. Since 1976 the National Association of Legal Assistants has sponsored a certification examination that measures knowledge of federal law and procedures.

Many businesses require that their corporate legal assistants have specialized training in business law and in legal procedures and terminology. (© Lew Long/Corbis.)

Getting the Job

Placement offices of business schools and legal training programs often post recruiting bulletins and job openings, and paralegal associations maintain job banks or referral services. Employment agencies, state employment services, newspaper classified ads, and job banks on the Internet may offer job leads. Job seekers can also apply directly to companies that hire legal assistants.

Advancement Possibilities and Employment Outlook

Because law is so important to business practices, legal assistants often get promoted to administrative positions of increased responsibility. Some legal assistants advance by going to law school.

The employment of corporate legal assistants is expected to grow faster than the average for all jobs through 2014, with demand highest in insurance companies, estate and trust departments of large banks, and real estate companies. The growth of prepaid legal plans may require more legal assistants as well.

Working Conditions

People employed as corporate legal assistants may have to handle confidential business information, so the ability to use discretion is important. Most corporate legal assistants work in offices or law libraries. Overtime may be required.

Earnings and Benefits

Salaries vary, depending on education, training, experience, and type of employer. In 2004 the median salary for corporate legal assistants was $39,130 per year. The most experienced assistants earned more than $61,390 per year. Benefits generally include paid holidays and vacations, health and life insurance, and pension plans.

Where to Go for More Information

American Bar Association
321 N. Clark St.
Chicago, IL 60610
(312) 988-5000
http://www.abanet.org

National Association of Legal Assistants
1516 S. Boston Ave., Ste. 200
Tulsa, OK 74119-4013
(918) 587-6828
http://www.nala.org

Paralegal Aide

Definition and Nature of the Work

Paralegal aides help lawyers prepare for hearings, trials, and corporate meetings. They research public documents, records, and law books; investigate the validity of wills and income tax returns; get information from clients; and organize and analyze data. They are trained to use computerized legal research systems.

Paralegal aides work under the supervision of a lawyer, a senior paralegal, or a senior legal assistant. Their work differs from that of legal secretaries, who focus primarily on the clerical functions in law offices, such as typing and filing. Private law firms are the largest employers of paralegal aides. Others are employed by judges and government agencies.

Education and Training Requirements

Paralegal aides must have some knowledge of law, legal procedures, and legal terminology. More than eight hundred paralegal training programs operate nationwide; many are approved by the American Bar Association. Most programs can be completed in two years and require high school diplomas for admission. Other programs are offered by four-year colleges, universities, and business and law schools. Those offered by law schools usually require bachelor's degrees and high scores on entrance examinations. Training time may vary from a few months for a special course to four years or more.

Education and Training
Varies—see profile

Salary
Median—$39,130 per year

Employment Outlook
Very good

Getting the Job

Job seekers can apply directly to law firms or register with their school placement offices, which often receive requests for paralegal aides from law firms. Paralegal associations maintain job banks and can provide listings of private and public employers. Applicants for paralegal positions with the government should take the necessary civil service test.

Advancement Possibilities and Employment Outlook

Advancement depends on the individual law firm; moving from a small law firm to a larger one may provide the best opportunities. In a large law firm, a paralegal aide may progress from researching minor legal matters to handling tasks of greater responsibility. Experienced aides may also be promoted to supervisory positions. Some paralegal aides enter law school.

The employment outlook for paralegal aides is very good through the year 2014. The demand for legal services continues to grow, and well-trained paralegal aides are needed to perform many tasks that ease the workloads of lawyers. The best opportunities will be for graduates of formal paralegal programs.

Working Conditions

Paralegal aides must be mature and responsible people. Their work requires intelligence, analytical ability, and discretion. They usually work in comfortable, well-lit offices or law libraries. Sometimes they may attend court proceedings.

Most paralegal aides work full time, usually forty hours a week. Overtime may be necessary. Some paralegals work part time while they are training to be lawyers.

Earnings and Benefits

Earnings for paralegal aides depend on education, experience, employer, and location. In 2004 the median salary for paralegals was $39,130 per year. Benefits usually included paid vacations and holidays, life and health insurance, and retirement plans.

Where to Go for More Information

American Bar Association
321 N. Clark St.
Chicago, IL 60610
(312) 988-5000
http://www.abanet.org

National Federation of Paralegal
   Associations
PO Box 2016
Edmonds, WA 98020
(425) 967-0045
http://www.paralegals.org

Police Officer

Education and Training
High school plus training

Salary
Median—$45,210 per year

Employment Outlook
Good

Definition and Nature of the Work

Police officers protect the lives and property of citizens. They maintain order, catch lawbreakers, and work to prevent crimes. In small towns they perform many duties. Larger cities have a more structured division of responsibility. Police officers may patrol the streets on foot or in squad cars; control traffic; or work as detectives investigating crimes. At the police station officers may be assigned to work in the crime laboratory or the records department. All officers file reports of incidents, and many testify at trials and hearings.

Police officers are supervised by senior officers. The chain of command is modeled after that of the armed services. In larger cities sergeants, lieutenants, and captains direct the work of squads or companies of officers. Ranking officers

generally report to police chiefs or commissioners. In small towns the chief of police may be the only ranking officer.

Education and Training Requirements

Many police departments require that applicants be high school graduates; an increasing number expect some college education. Applicants usually must be at least twenty-one years of age and U.S. citizens. In many communities, applicants must meet minimum requirements for height, weight, eyesight, and hearing.

Because most police departments fall under civil service regulations, applicants must pass written tests that measure their analytical skills. Rigorous physical examinations and background checks are also required. Senior officers screen applicants.

New recruits often participate in formal classroom training in police academies. After graduating they continue to train on the job with experienced officers for three to twelve months. In small communities there may be no formal training program. Officers are usually encouraged to continue their education by taking college courses in criminal justice.

Getting the Job

Those who want to be police officers must first take the civil service test. Many departments allow high school graduates and college students studying criminal justice to start out as cadets or trainees while still in their teens. If they meet all the requirements, cadets may be appointed to regular police work when they turn twenty-one.

Advancement Possibilities and Employment Outlook

For promotion to higher rank, officers must take civil service tests. Good work records and special honors help officers get ahead. Police officers who have investigation abilities may advance to detective. Other positions include sergeant, lieutenant, captain, and inspector.

The employment of police officers is expected to grow as fast the average for all jobs through 2014. Openings will depend on government funding and the number of experienced officers who retire or leave the profession. Competition for jobs will be stiff. The best opportunities will be found in urban areas.

Working Conditions

Police work can be dangerous and stressful. Officers often deal with violent criminals and may be injured or killed. They must make quick decisions while on duty, yet be tactful and patient with people who are in trouble or have been victims of terrible crimes and abuse.

Police protection is provided twenty-four hours a day, so officers may work outdoors in all kinds of weather. Work shifts are usually rotated; however, officers are on call at all times for emergencies. Overtime may be required. Most police departments provide uniforms or uniform allowances. Many officers belong to labor unions.

Earnings and Benefits

Earnings vary, depending on location. In 2004 the median salary for police officers was $45,210 per year. As officers advanced through the ranks, wages increased. The average minimum salary for police sergeants was $49,895 per year, while the average minimum for lieutenants was $56,115 per year.

Benefits include paid health and life insurance, sick days, and vacations. Many officers are covered by pension plans that allow them to retire at half their pay after twenty or twenty-five years of service.

Where to Go for More Information

The Federal Officer's Coalition of the Fraternal Order of Police
PO Box 2681
Vineland, NJ 08362-2681
http://www.fed-fop.org

National Association of Police Organizations
750 First St. NE, Ste. 920
Washington, DC, 20002
(202) 842-4420
http://www.napo.org

National Fraternal Order of Police
1410 Donelson Pike, Ste. A-17
Nashville, TN 37217-2933
(800) 451-2711
http://www.grandlodgefop.org

State Police Officer

Education and Training
High school plus training

Salary
Median—$23.55 per hour

Employment Outlook
Good

Definition and Nature of the Work

State police officers, or troopers, patrol and enforce laws on highways, issuing traffic tickets, investigating accidents, and administering first aid. They also help motorists by radioing for automobile mechanics and by giving directions and tourist information. Sometimes they check the weight of commercial vehicles and give the public information about highway safety.

Some specialize, conducting fingerprint classification, analyzing microscopic evidence, and piloting police aircraft. Others work in special units such as the mounted police or canine corps. In areas that do not have regular police forces, troopers help city or county police investigate crimes. However, most of their work is restricted to highway matters.

Education and Training Requirements

Most states require troopers to have high school diplomas or the equivalent. Courses in English, social science, government, chemistry, and physics are good preparation for the job.

All states provide formal training, usually lasting several months, that covers state laws, procedures for accident investigation, and traffic control. Recruits are also taught how to use guns, administer first aid, and handle cars at very high speeds.

Many officers continue their education while on the job, particularly if they are interested in advancing to higher positions. Several two- and four-year colleges offer courses in criminology and police science.

Getting the Job

To become a state trooper, you must be a U.S. citizen. In most states, you must be at least twenty-one years old and meet height, weight, and eyesight requirements. You will be selected on the basis of your score on a civil service exam, a personal interview with an officer, and an investigation of your character.

In some states you can become a cadet when you graduate from high school. You will receive a salary while you attend classes to learn about police work. If you are successful at nonenforcement duties, you may become a trooper at age twenty-one.

Advancement Possibilities and Employment Outlook

New recruits, who usually start as privates, are required to serve probationary periods lasting from six months to three years. Examinations are necessary to advance in rank to corporal, sergeant, first sergeant, lieutenant, and captain. State police officers who show administrative ability may become commissioners or directors.

The number of job openings for state police officers is expected to grow as fast as the average through 2014. Some openings will occur when experienced officers retire or leave the force. Stiff competition is expected in many states.

Working Conditions

Police protection is provided twenty-four hours a day, so troopers usually work rotating shifts, including weekends and holidays. Overtime is often required, because troopers are on call at all times for emergencies.

Troopers spend most of their time driving police cars and are exposed to all types of weather. Like other police officers, they may deal with dangerous and stressful situations and risk their lives in the line of duty. However, the job can also be rewarding, for they aid stranded motorists and prevent accidents. At all times they must be tactful, patient, and alert.

Earnings and Benefits

Salaries vary from state to state. In 2004 the median wage for state patrol officers was $23.55 per hour. Earnings increase with advancement to higher ranks.

Most states provide uniforms or uniform allowances. Benefits usually include paid vacations, sick leave, health and life insurance, and pension plans.

Where to Go for More Information

National Association of Police
    Organizations
750 First St. NE, Ste. 920
Washington, DC, 20002
(202) 842-4420
http://www.napo.org

National Fraternal Order of Police
1410 Donelson Pike, Ste. A-17
Nashville, TN 37217-2933
(615) 399-0999
http://www.grandlodgefop.org

Teacher Assistant

Definition and Nature of the Work

Teacher assistants provide clerical and instructional support in classrooms, allowing certified teachers to devote more time to lesson planning and teaching. They work under the guidance and supervision of teachers or school administrators.

Some assistants provide noninstructional support. Their tasks are largely housekeeping: putting the classroom in order; passing out paper, pencils, and textbooks; and preparing bulletin boards. They also take attendance, update health records, monitor study halls and playgrounds, and supervise children as they board and leave school buses.

Technical assistants are in charge of audiovisual equipment. They set up television sets, film projectors, tape recorders, and stereo systems and operate them during lessons.

Instructional assistants help teach classes. For example, assistants who play the piano may participate in music instruction. Those who can draw help in art classes. Assistants who have some college training may correct tests or help teach reading, math, spelling, and social studies.

Teacher assistants may be employed in preschool classrooms, in elementary schools, or in junior and senior high schools. Most work in the earlier grades.

Education and Training Requirements

Teacher assistants have a wide range of educational backgrounds. Requirements vary, depending on the duties to be performed, the grade level, and the type of school district. High school diplomas are required; many schools prefer candidates with some college background.

Some two-year colleges offer associate degree programs for teacher assistants. Courses cover educational psychology, the history of education, and teaching

A teacher assistant demonstrates to preschool children how to paint an art project. (© Jose Luis Pelaez, Inc./Corbis.)

methods for English, biology, math, art, and music. Some states have instituted certification procedures for teacher assistants.

Many schools that employ teacher assistants provide one- or two-week training courses, which detail the tasks to be performed, the schools' educational policies, and methods for helping children at different age levels and with different learning capabilities. Most schools provide additional training throughout the school year.

Getting the Job

Job seekers can apply directly to the administration offices of school districts. State employment services, newspaper classified ads, and job banks on the Internet are other sources of employment information. Applicants can expect to be interviewed by either classroom teachers or school administrators.

Advancement Possibilities and Employment Outlook

Higher earnings and more responsibility usually come with increased experience. Some teacher assistants advance by taking college courses that lead to bachelor's degrees. Once they have degrees, they can take examinations to be certified as teachers.

The employment of teacher assistants is expected to grow as fast as the average for all jobs through 2014. As elementary and secondary school enrollments increase, so should the demand for teacher assistants. Increasing numbers of students who speak English as a second language, as well as rising enrollments of students with disabilities, may also spur job growth. However, the job outlook is heavily dependent on the economy and the funds available for hiring. Some school districts receive government grants to finance the hiring of teacher assistants.

Working Conditions

About forty percent of teacher assistants work part time. Many of those who are employed full time work fewer than forty hours per week. Some assist teachers during the summer, but most have to find other jobs. Teacher assistants must enjoy working with children or young people. They should communicate effectively, be patient and fair, and work well with supervising teachers, school administrators, and parents. Some teacher assistants belong to unions.

Earnings and Benefits

Salaries vary, depending on location, qualifications, and experience. In 2004 the median salary for teacher assistants was $19,410 per year. The lowest ten percent earned less than $13,010 per year, while the top ten percent earned more than $29,220 per year.

Benefits, which generally go to full-time workers, include paid holidays and vacations, medical and hospital insurance, and retirement plans.

Where to Go for More Information

American Federation of Teachers
555 New Jersey Ave. NW
Washington, DC 20001
(202) 879-4400
http://www.aft.org

National Education Association
1201 Sixteenth St. NW
Washington, DC 20036
(202) 833-4000
http://www.nea.org

Teacher, Vocational Education

Definition and Nature of the Work

Vocational education teachers have personal experience in skill-based occupations, such as cosmetology, commercial art, electronics, and plumbing. In the classroom, they help students develop those same skills. Also called career and technical education teachers, they work in public or private high schools, in community colleges, or in privately owned trade schools. They may also work in special teaching facilities run by noneducational organizations such as labor unions.

Some teachers specialize in one subject, while others teach a variety of subjects. In addition to teaching the skills and evaluating students' knowledge and performance, vocational teachers sometimes place students in actual work settings and monitor their progress.

Education and Training Requirements

Education and training requirements for this field vary by state and subject. Most teachers need bachelor's degrees, plus three years of work experience in their specialties. Some specialties require licenses or certification. Many teachers, especially those who are in rapidly changing technological fields, continue their own education throughout their careers.

Getting the Job

Jobs seekers can apply directly to vocational and technical schools. Industry journals, school placement offices, state employment services, newspaper classified ads, and job listings on the Internet are all sources of employment information. Some teachers break into the field as teaching assistants in vocational programs, dividing their time between teaching and working in the industry. Assistant positions usually go to vocational program graduates who place at or near the top of their classes.

A vocational education teacher works with students in an automotive body shop classroom. (© Martha Tabor/ Working Images Photographs. Reproduced by permission.)

Advancement Possibilities and Employment Outlook

Vocational education teachers may advance to supervisory or administrative positions, but such promotions often require additional education.

Employment is expected to grow as participation in adult education increases. Workers who must switch careers or who need to keep abreast of technological changes will spur this growth. Opportunities should be best for part-time positions and in fields such as computer technology, automotive mechanics, and medical technology.

Working Conditions

The hours are fairly regular, but teachers usually have to prepare lessons and grade tests on their own time. Most teachers work the conventional school year and do not work during the summer months.

Most vocational teachers do not encounter behavioral and social problems in the classroom, because their students are there by choice, are highly motivated to learn, and often bring years of experience to the classroom. However, they may teach students with very different levels of development or few study skills.

Earnings and Benefits

In 2004 the median salary for vocational education teachers was $45,830 per year. Experienced teachers earned more than $53,810 per year.

Benefits generally include vacations, sick pay, and health and life insurance. Some employers may offer tuition reimbursement programs for employees who wish to attend college.

Where to Go for More Information

Association for Career and Technical
 Education
1410 King St.
Alexandria, VA 22314
(800) 826-9972
http://www.acteonline.org

International Vocational Education and
 Training Association
186 Wedgewood Dr.
Mahtomedi, MN 55115
(651) 770-6719
http://www.iveta.org

Youth Organization Worker

Definition and Nature of the Work

The YMCA down the street, the Girl Scout troop that meets in the church basement, and the teen center just opened in the municipal building are all led by youth organization workers. These workers are employed by many different organizations, but all share the same goal: helping young people enjoy themselves and grow to be responsible adults.

Youth organization workers are employed full time or part time, as salaried employees or as volunteers. In large organizations, such as Hillel and the Boy Scouts of America, both full-time and part-time workers are employed. Full-time workers manage organizations on a daily basis. Executive directors raise funds, develop new programs, balance budgets, plan for new buildings, and supervise other workers. Activity directors plan specific programs for youths and organize other workers to help run them.

Education and Training
Varies—see profile

Salary
Average—$16,000 to
$18,000 per year

Employment Outlook
Fair

A youth organization worker plays chess with teenagers at a program sponsored by the city's department of recreation. (© Martha Tabor/Working Images Photographs. Reproduced by permission.)

Education and Training Requirements

Most youth organization jobs require at least high school education. Most full-time activity directors have associate degrees or bachelor's degrees, while executive directors usually have bachelor's degrees.

High school courses in English, math, science, and social studies are useful, as are college classes in sociology, child psychology, recreation, public speaking, art, music, and physical education. Many youth organization workers earn degrees in recreation with emphasis on youth work. Volunteer work for youth agencies—day camp counselor, municipal recreation helper, or aide in a church organization—can be a good credential for employment.

Getting the Job

Job seekers can apply directly to any youth agency or to the national or regional headquarters of such organizations as the Girl Scouts of America or the YMCA. School placement offices may have information about job openings.

Advancement Possibilities and Employment Outlook

Most workers begin their careers as assistants to activity or recreation directors. With experience and training, they may be promoted to administrative positions.

While most communities need youth organization workers, employment depends on the funds available, which are usually provided through private grants and charitable donations.

Working Conditions

Working conditions vary. Some employees are on the job forty hours each week, while others work mainly at night and on weekends. Most spend a good deal of time outdoors.

Youth organization workers generally must be in good physical condition because much of the work involves supervising recreation programs for youngsters. They must be patient, kind, and able to communicate with all kinds of people. Above all, they must enjoy working with young people.

Earnings and Benefits

Earnings depend on location, duties, education, and experience. Average salaries for full-time youth organization workers with bachelor's degrees range from $16,000 to $18,000 per year.

Full-time workers generally receive paid sick leave and vacations and life and health insurance.

Where to Go for More Information

American Alliance for Health, Physical
    Education, Recreation, and Dance
1900 Association Dr.
Reston, VA 20191
(800) 213-7193
http://www.aahperd.org

National Community Education Association
3929 Old Lee Hwy., Ste. 91-A
Alexandria, VA 22030-2401
(703) 359-8973
http://www.ncea.com

Adult Education Worker

Education and Training
College

Salary
Median—$14.85 per hour

Employment Outlook
Very good

Definition and Nature of the Work

Adult education workers usually teach evening classes at public high schools. Most of their students are older than eighteen—too old for regular high school. Others work for community colleges, private and religious organizations, and community groups.

Goals and subjects vary by school. Most offer basic adult education courses, which provide instruction in reading, writing, mathematics, and often English as a second language. Success in these courses can lead to general equivalency diplomas (GED), which are comparable to high school diplomas.

Continuing education is generally intended for people who have completed their basic education. Courses range from specific skills, such as typing and flower arranging, to more academic subjects, including literature, history, and Bible interpretation.

Education and Training Requirements

Most basic education workers need only bachelor's degrees, but those who teach in public high schools may need teacher certification. Administrators may need

Adult education workers teach a specific skill, such as computer use, to adults in the community. (© Tom Stewart/Corbis.)

teaching experience and master's degrees or doctorates in community education and administration.

Continuing education programs, by contrast, need workers with specific skills. Schools that need ceramics teachers are likely to hire experienced potters.

Getting the Job

If you have a specific skill you would like to teach, write to your local school board and propose a course. If you are interested in teaching basic education, you can apply directly to the superintendent of schools. Openings are sometimes listed in local newspapers, in job banks on the Internet, and with state employment services.

Advancement Possibilities and Employment Outlook

Continuing education teachers usually begin by working part time. They may decide to pursue teaching on a full-time basis or become program administrators. Advancement to other kinds of teaching positions may require additional education and certification. Basic education workers can also become administrators.

The job outlook is very good. Many schools that want to put their facilities to best use are offering evening classes. More employers are demanding higher levels of academic skill, which may increase enrollment in classes that teach reading, writing, mathematics, and GED preparation. Participation in continuing education depends entirely on marketing and the number of adults interested in classes for personal enrichment.

Working Conditions

Many adult education workers teach one or two courses a week, usually in addition to their full-time jobs. They are most likely to teach in the evening because their students work during the daytime.

Classes, ranging from three to sixty students, usually last from one to three hours and meet one to five times a week. Classes are most often held in public high schools and community colleges or at the facilities of community organizations. Some are conducted in prisons and private homes.

Earnings and Benefits

Workers are often paid by the hour, and their wages vary by school, state, or private sponsor. In 2004 the median salary for adult education workers was $14.85 per hour. Part-time workers get few, if any, benefits.

Where to Go for More Information

American Association for Adult and
　Continuing Education
10111 Martin Luther King Jr. Hwy., Ste.
　200C
Bowie, MD 20720
(301) 459-6261
http://www.aaace.org

National Community Education Association
3929 Old Lee Hwy., Ste. 91-A
Fairfax, VA 22030-2401
(703) 359-8973
http://www.ncea.com

National Education Association
1201 Sixteenth St. NW
Washington, DC 20036
(202) 833-4000
http://www.nea.org

City Manager

Education and Training
College

Salary
Median—$88,695 per year

Employment Outlook
Fair

Definition and Nature of the Work

City managers are professional administrators who try to make city governments operate with the efficiency of successful businesses. However, they are not authorized to take action on their own. Their work is directed by elected officials, such as mayors and city councils, who hire them.

For example, a city council may direct its city manager to cut the costs of tax collection. After considering alternatives, the city manager decides to replace the existing method of billing taxes with a new computerized system. Before the plan can be put into action, however, the manager must present it to the city council for approval. Only after getting the council's okay can the manager hire the computer specialists to make the switch.

City managers prepare budgets, hire administrative officers, oversee record keeping, and supervise the heads of such departments as law enforcement, fire protection, and sanitation. Because many cities employ great numbers of unionized teachers, police officers, firefighters, and refuse workers, city managers are usually involved in labor relations and contract negotiations. They often meet with business and community groups to explain city policies and hear citizens' demands.

City managers must be familiar with all aspects of government and public works. They cannot, however, take sides publicly in political disputes.

Most city managers are employed by governments of small and medium-size cities—generally those with populations of ten thousand to five hundred thousand people. Smaller cities may have only a city manager and one administrative assistant. In larger cities a manager may have an assistant manager for each department, such as transportation or education.

City managers take direction from and report to city council members on a broad range of issues, including budgets, record keeping, labor relations, and city policies. (© Martha Tabor/Working Images Photographs. Reproduced by permission.)

Education and Training Requirements

City managers must have college degrees. Courses in economics, sociology, statistics, urban planning, political science, finance, and management may prove essential. However, most city councils and mayors prefer to hire individuals who have master's degrees in public administration.

Some graduate programs in the field require internships, lasting from six to twelve months, that give students practical experience that may help them find jobs. Most recent graduates start as administrative assistants or assistant city managers and gain more responsibility with experience.

Getting the Job

Internships often lead to permanent jobs after graduation. College placement offices, professional organizations, and government journals may list job openings for city managers, assistant city managers, or administrative assistants. Job seekers may also apply directly to city managers' offices.

Advancement Possibilities and Employment Outlook

Some city managers advance by taking jobs in larger cities in which the management problems are more complex and the work is more challenging. Others use their expertise in related fields, such as higher education.

As more cities employ managers, qualified people will be needed in greater numbers. However, the number of qualified applicants is increasing, so competition will be stiff through 2014. In some geographical areas, budgetary constraints may limit the number of new hires in this field. Applicants with master's degrees will have the best opportunities.

Working Conditions

City managers work long hours and must be available when crises develop—and work as long as it takes to solve problems. They work under pressure from elected officials, civic groups, and labor unions. Although the job is stressful, they get satisfaction when policies are implemented and they know they have positively affected the lives of many people.

While city managers spend most of their time in offices, they are in constant contact with the public and with others in government. Sometimes they travel to meetings and conferences.

Earnings and Benefits

Salaries vary, depending on the size of the city, region of the country, and the amount of responsibility. In 2004 the median salary for city managers was $88,695 per year. Benefits include health and life insurance, vacations, and pension plans.

Where to Go for More Information

American Society for Public Administration
1301 Pennsylvania Ave. NW, Ste. 840
Washington, DC 20004
(202) 393-7878
http://www.aspanet.org

International City/County Management
   Association
777 North Capitol St. NE, Ste. 500
Washington, DC 20002-4201
(202) 289-4262
http://www.icma.org

National League of Cities
1301 Pennsylvania Ave. NW, Ste. 550
Washington, DC 20004
(202) 626-3000
http://www.nlc.org

College Student Personnel Worker

A college admissions officer is a type of college student personnel worker who interviews applicants to the college and determines whether the college will admit them. (© Martha Tabor/ Working Images Photographs. Reproduced by permission.)

Definition and Nature of the Work

College student personnel workers, a group that can include dozens of employees, make sure that school policies are carried out and that students understand how those policies affect their education. Through daily interaction, they gather student opinion and interpret it for top administrators. They also coordinate and supervise departments that provide extracurricular activities.

Workers and their roles vary by school. Deans of students, for example, usually supervise the administrative staff and assist college presidents in planning policies. They also determine how policies, both academic and nonacademic, are working and whether they need to be altered or explained and implemented in more effective ways. College admissions officers evaluate applicants to see if they will be admitted. Besides examining credentials, they determine if the school can meet the applicants' needs and if the applicants would add special talents and interests to the college community. Registrars keep records of all student grades and transcripts, while financial aid officers help students obtain scholarships and government loans.

Many personnel workers provide counseling. College placement workers help students determine their educational and career goals and, after graduation, place them in jobs. Sometimes they administer occupational interest tests and set up job fairs and interviews with corporate recruiters. Foreign student advisers help international students adjust to their new environment both academically and socially, while other counselors help students who are experiencing emotional difficulties.

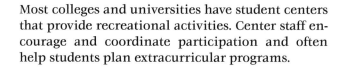

Most colleges and universities have student centers that provide recreational activities. Center staff encourage and coordinate participation and often help students plan extracurricular programs.

Education and Training Requirements

College student personnel workers generally have at least bachelor's degrees. Courses in administration, educational psychology, and student personnel work can prove helpful. Workers with little or no experience usually start as assistants. People with graduate training in counseling or psychology generally work in counseling jobs. Higher administrative jobs often require doctorates as well as several years of experience in higher education.

Getting the Job

College placement offices may know about job openings. Professional associations and journals, private employment agencies, newspaper classified ads, and job sites on the Internet are other sources of employment leads.

Advancement Possibilities and Employment Outlook

Student personnel offices at large universities often have many staff members. With experience assistants may become department heads. With additional education they may qualify for such top-level jobs as dean of students or college president. College administrators sometimes go on to government posts.

Employment of college student personnel workers is expected to grow about as fast as the average for all jobs through 2014. While some schools may have to reduce their staffs because of funding, other schools foresee increased enrollments that will require the same number or additional personnel to service students' needs. Some openings regularly occur when experienced workers retire or leave the field.

Working Conditions

College student personnel workers usually have comfortable offices. Their jobs involve regular contact with students, so they must enjoy working with people. Work can be stressful, especially when semesters begin and end. Most college student personnel workers are on the job at least forty hours per week. Top-level positions require many extra hours for consultations, meetings, and attendance at college functions. Some staff members combine their administrative duties with teaching.

Earnings and Benefits

Salaries vary by institution and specific job. In 2004 median salaries ranged from $45,636 for directors of student activities to $75,245 per year for deans of students. Registrars were paid $61,953, while financial aid officers earned $48,448.

Benefits include vacations, health insurance, retirement plans, tuition wavers for dependents, and, at some schools, paid sabbaticals.

Where to Go for More Information

American Association of Collegiate
  Registrars and Admission Officers
1 Dupont Circle NW, Ste. 520
Washington, DC, 20036
(202) 293-9161
http://www.aacrao.org

American College Counseling Association
5999 Stevenson Ave.
Alexandria, VA 22304-3300
(800) 473-2329
http://www.collegecounseling.org

National Association for College
  Admission Counseling
1631 Prince St.
Alexandria, VA 22314-2818
(703) 836-2222
http://www.nacacnet.org

National Association of Student Financial
  Aid Administrators
1129 Twentieth St. NW, Ste. 400
Washington, DC 20036-3453
(202) 785-0453
http://www.nasfaa.org

Criminologist

Definition and Nature of the Work

Criminologists study the social and psychological conditions that cause crime, the criminals themselves, and methods of rehabilitation. One branch of criminology, called criminalistics, develops scientific ways to detect and solve crime. All criminologists work toward the same ends: to ensure that laws are just and practical, to protect society, and to help criminals reenter society as useful citizens.

Criminologists study data about crimes, arrests, and convictions to determine the social background from which most criminals come. They ask—and attempt to answer—such questions as "Are most criminals poor?" and "Why do some members of a social class commit crimes?" Their answers may lead to changes in social conditions so crime can be diminished.

Education and Training
Advanced degree

Salary
Varies—see profile

Employment Outlook
Poor

Criminologists study data about crimes, arrests, and convictions to learn about criminal actions and to suggest practical methods for controlling and rehabilitating criminals. (© Martha Tabor/Working Images Photographs. Reproduced by permission.)

Some criminologists study the criminals themselves, examining their personal histories to reveal incidents that may have influenced them. The conclusions they draw can suggest ways to help at-risk individuals before they turn to crime.

Other criminologists study the history and theories of crime and the nature of the criminal justice system. For instance, they investigate the effects that arrest and conviction have on criminals. Their studies may suggest ways to impede the influence hardened criminals have on people sent to prison for minor crimes They may also determine that certain punishments do not prevent crime.

Criminologists interested in crime detection develop scientific methods, such as lie detector tests and fingerprinting, to study clues. When crimes are committed, these and other techniques are used by crime laboratory technicians to try to identify the criminals.

Criminologists are employed as teachers and researchers at colleges and universities, as administrators of large social agencies or prisons, and as directors of crime prevention projects. A few criminologists put their theoretical knowledge to practical use as police commissioners.

Education and Training Requirements

Applicants need master's or doctoral degrees in subjects related to criminology, such as juvenile delinquency, abnormal psychology, and statistics.

Getting the Job

Job seekers can apply directly to agencies or colleges that hire professionals in the field. School placement services and professional organizations are other sources of employment information.

Advancement Possibilities and Employment Outlook

Advancement in the field of criminology depends on education and experience. Doctoral degrees are generally required for professors, directors of research departments, administrators of large social agencies or crime prevention projects, and police commissioners.

Comparatively few positions exist for criminologists. The number of new jobs in the field depends entirely on public funding for crime prevention projects and agencies.

Working Conditions

Criminologists in social agencies generally work in offices. Those involved in casework may counsel or interview criminals in prisons, while professionals in the field of criminalistics work in laboratories. Administrators, such as police commissioners, usually have high-profile jobs and must respond to the public's concerns about crime. Criminologists generally work more than forty hours per week.

Earnings and Benefits

Salaries of criminologists vary according to the responsibilities of their jobs and the size of the population served. Both training and experience affect their earnings. Beginning criminologists earn about $28,000 per year, while those with experience can earn up to $50,000 per year. Police commissioners, prison administrators, and others who administer public or private agencies or crime prevention projects earn higher salaries. Those who work as consultants on special projects are paid on a fee basis. Retirement plans, health insurance, and paid holidays and vacations are generally available.

Where to Go for More Information

American Board of Criminalistics
PO Box 1123
Wausau, WI 54402-1123
http://www.criminalistics.com

American Society of Criminology
13142 Kinnear Rd.
Columbus, OH 43212-1156
(614) 292-9207
http://www.asc41.com

International Association for the Study of
    Organized Crime
PO Box 50484
Washington, DC 20091-0484
http://www.iasoc.ne

FBI Special Agent

Definition and Nature of the Work

Federal Bureau of Investigation (FBI) special agents investigate violations of U.S. laws and report their findings to the office of the attorney general. They investigate crimes such as kidnapping, extortion, espionage, bank robbery, fraud, and sabotage. To carry out their jobs, they talk to witnesses, observe the activities of their suspects, do research, and participate in raids.

Because their work is strictly investigative, special agents do not express opinions about the guilt or innocence of suspects. These decisions are left to lawyers employed by the federal government. If agents testify in court, they relay the information they have gathered. Much of their work is confidential, so they are not allowed to discuss it with outsiders, including members of their families. On assignments they may have to carry firearms.

Agents work from field offices located in the United States and Puerto Rico and from the national headquarters in Washington, DC. To uncover facts, they use the crime detection laboratory in Washington, where experts analyze blood, paint, and fragments that agents find at the scenes of crimes. They also use a fingerprint database.

Education and Training
College plus training

Salary
Varies—see profile

Employment Outlook
Fair

Some federal crimes, such as tax evasion and counterfeiting, are investigated by other agencies. However, FBI agents may be called in for assistance. FBI agents also run character and security checks on many employees of the government.

Education and Training Requirements

To become an FBI special agent, you must be a graduate of a state-accredited law school or be a college graduate with a major in accounting. You may also qualify if you have a bachelor's degree in any discipline, with fluency in a foreign language that is especially useful to the bureau; a bachelor's degree in any discipline plus three years of full-time work experience; or an advanced degree plus two years of work experience.

Applicants must be citizens of the United States, between the ages of twenty-three and thirty-seven, and in good physical condition. Excellent eyesight and hearing are essential. Background and character are investigated thoroughly. Applicants must pass physical, written, and oral examinations, which are similar to those required for employment by the federal civil service.

During the first year, which is probationary, agents receive sixteen weeks of intensive training in Washington, DC, and at the FBI Academy in Quantico, VA. They learn self-defense, FBI rules and methods, fingerprinting, criminal law, and weapons use. At the end of their training, they are assigned to one of the field offices for the remainder of the year, after which they are given permanent assignments.

Getting the Job

If you are interested in getting a job as a special agent, write to the director of the FBI. In addition to sending a resume and cover letter, request information on vacancies, requirements, and employment applications.

Advancement Possibilities and Employment Outlook

Special agents are eligible for periodic salary increases. After demonstrating ability and proving that they are capable of assuming more responsibilities, agents may be promoted to supervisory or administrative positions.

Openings are limited. The rate of turnover in the FBI is very low. Each year some agents are hired because of expansion, but most people working as agents remain in their positions until retirement.

Working Conditions

FBI special agents must be ready for assignments in all places at all times. They are subject to call twenty-four hours a day. Because agents generally put in many extra hours, they are compensated with an annual bonus in a fixed amount.

The work can be both exciting and dangerous. Agents work alone or in small groups. Agents who can accept the responsibilities of the job find it a rewarding career. The work is seldom routine.

Where to Go for More Information

Federal Bureau of Investigation
J. Edgar Hoover Building
935 Pennsylvania Ave. NW
Washington, DC 20535-0001
(202) 324-3000
http://www.fbi.gov

Earnings and Benefits

In 2004 beginning special agents received a base salary of $42,548 per year, but they could earn $53,185 per year with overtime pay. Experienced agents who had advanced to field assignments that were nonsupervisory received a base salary of $64,478 per year. Overtime brought their total wage to $80,597 per year. Supervisory agents earned $76,193 or more per year. Benefits include paid holidays and vacations, medical insurance, and retirement plans.

Foreign Service Worker

Definition and Nature of the Work

Foreign service workers represent the United States in countries with which the nation has diplomatic relations. The foreign service, a branch of the U.S. State Department, includes officers and reserve officers as well as support staff members and specialists.

Foreign service officers interpret U.S. foreign policy to the governments of their host countries and help foster friendly political and trade relations. They make periodic reports to their supervisors at the State Department on political activities, market conditions, public opinion, and other important matters. Sometimes foreign service officers help negotiate treaties and agreements that protect U.S. shipping, economic, and legal interests. Foreign service officers help ensure the welfare of Americans visiting or residing in foreign countries.

Foreign service officers can specialize in one of four areas of service: administrative, consular, commercial-economic, or political. However, most workers are knowledgeable in more than one field.

Officers with administrative duties plan, develop, and direct the operations of their offices. They are in charge of their posts' expenses and budgets, the acquisition and maintenance of government property, and the supervision of personnel. Consular officers assist Americans with problems they face in foreign countries, issue passports and visas to Americans abroad, and help foreigners who want to visit the United States obtain visas. Commercial-economic officers promote U.S. business in foreign countries, analyze and report on foreign economic trends, and negotiate commercial and economic agreements. Political officers interpret U.S. foreign policy to other governments, promote understanding between the United States and foreign countries, and negotiate agreements.

This American foreign service officer serves as a liaison to the governments of Africa and helps to foster friendly political and trade relations. (© Martha Tabor/Working Images Photographs. Reproduced by permission.)

Foreign service reserve officers perform similar tasks on a temporary basis. They work where they are needed most. Reserve officers usually have special skills that the department needs in such fields as agriculture, labor, economics, and finance.

Foreign service staff members provide the support needed to operate State Department offices in other countries. Workers include secretaries, nurses, communications and records assistants, and specialists in budget and fiscal problems.

Education and Training Requirements

Education requirements vary with the level of the job. Foreign service officers must be at least twenty-one years old and U.S. citizens. Applicants must pass written examinations to be eligible for appointment. Although there is no formal requirement that applicants have college degrees, many candidates have bachelor's and postgraduate degrees.

Candidates for appointment do not have to be fluent in foreign languages. After being hired, however, they must develop professional competence in at least one foreign language before the end of the four-year probationary period.

Education and training requirements for foreign service support staff and specialists vary as well. Secretaries must type forty words per minute, take dictation at eighty words per minute, and have three to five years of experience in clerical, secretarial, or administrative work. Education beyond high school may be substituted for part of the required experience. Communications and records assistants need at least eighteen months of experience in the field. They are also required to pass qualifying tests in typing, clerical, and verbal abilities. Staff employed as diplomatic couriers, or mail carriers, generally are college graduates who have had military experience. All applicants and their dependents must pass comprehensive medical examinations.

Getting the Job

Applicants must apply directly to the U.S. Department of State. Foreign service officers must take competitive written and oral examinations. The written tests assess applicants' general intelligence, problem-solving abilities, writing skills, and knowledge of history, government, geography, commerce, administration, and economics. Candidates who pass the written tests take oral examinations before a board of foreign service officers. The oral examination rates verbal ability. Board members ask questions on U.S. culture, history, economics, politics, and foreign affairs. Foreign service reserve officers do not have to take competitive examinations.

Candidates accepted into the foreign service are trained to serve as workers in particular areas of the world. The training period may last two years or more, depending on the needs of the service and the officers' qualifications. The training is part of the four-year probationary appointment that newly hired candidates serve before they become commissioned officers. After several overseas assignments, foreign service officers specialize in one area and, if they wish, may return to school to expand their knowledge and skills.

Staff secretaries may take three- to four-week training courses and then be assigned overseas. Others may choose to work in Washington, DC, for one year before applying for overseas assignments.

All applicants for foreign service positions are investigated thoroughly before employment. Candidates must be loyal to the U.S. government.

Advancement Possibilities and Employment Outlook

Officers may rise through the ranks; promotions are based on ratings from superiors. Highly ranked officers may be appointed ambassadors. Staff workers are also promoted on the basis of their merit ratings. If they meet the necessary requirements, they may eventually become officers.

Positions in foreign service are highly coveted, and the field is comparatively small. As a result, competition for appointment is stiff, with applicants far outnumbering available posts.

Working Conditions

Foreign service workers travel widely and meet many people of different nationalities. Maintaining relations with other countries is highly rewarding work, and members of the foreign service take great pride in their accomplishments. However, the work is physically and mentally demanding. Workers are under pressure much of the time. They are not always sent to the countries of their choice, and living conditions in some areas are substandard. Employees are on duty at all times, and work hours are often uncertain.

Earnings and Benefits

Beginning foreign service officers with bachelor's degrees earn between $18,000 and $28,000 per year. Experienced officers with special skills can earn $30,000 or more per year. Senior officers can earn up to $100,000 per year. Support staff members often start at about $16,000 per year.

Foreign service workers receive such benefits as paid vacation and sick leave, a housing allowance if government housing is not available, and special compensation for certain types of duty.

Where to Go for More Information

American Foreign Service Association
2101 E St. NW
Washington, DC 20037
(800) 704-2372
http://www.afsa.org

Diplomatic and Consular Officers, Retired
1801 F St. NW
Washington, DC 20006-4497
(800) 344-9127
http://www.dacorbacon.org

U.S. Department of State
2201 C St. NW
Washington, DC 20520
(202) 647-4000
http://www.state.gov

Fund-Raiser

Definition and Nature of the Work

Professional fund-raisers solicit contributions from corporations and individuals for nonprofit institutions, such as hospitals, colleges and charities, and for politicians running for office. They develop fund-raising drives, organize volunteers to run them, and monitor progress every step of the way. Their most important function is marketing: they must sell the worthiness of their cause, institution, or candidate to a skeptical public. To do so, they must choose the best slogan, write the most compelling speeches and press releases, and prepare memorable videos and television commercials. They often meet with corporate officers, government officials, and community leaders to make their sales pitch.

Fund-raisers work either on a consulting basis or full time for one institution. Consultants often work for firms that specialize in offering this service; sometimes they create their own companies and oversee several small-scale fund drives at the same time. While politicians generally employ consultants for short

Education and Training
College

Salary
Median—$60,259 per year

Employment Outlook
Good

periods, many colleges and universities, large hospitals, and national charities employ full-time fund-raisers who supervise ongoing campaigns.

Besides marketing skills, fund-raisers need managerial skills to direct and inspire those who are soliciting funds and knowledge of finance and tax laws so that they can explain the tax advantages of contributions.

Education and Training Requirements

Most fund-raisers develop their skills as volunteers in fund-raising campaigns. However, most fund-raisers have at least bachelor's degrees. College preparatory courses in English, mathematics, social studies, and foreign languages are useful, as are college courses in accounting, business administration, economics, marketing, psychology, speech, and statistics. Some colleges offer courses that relate directly to fund-raising. Professional societies often hold seminars and workshops that explain the latest techniques.

Getting the Job

Job seekers can apply directly to consulting companies that raise funds and to such institutions as hospitals, colleges, and charities. Beginners may start as assistant fund-raisers. Jobs in public relations can be good training, for fund-raising is a closely related field. College placement offices, state and private employment agencies, newspaper classified ads, and job banks on the Internet may list entry-level jobs in fund-raising.

These fund-raisers are working on a mass mailing campaign to solicit money for a charity. (© Martha Tabor/Working Images Photographs. Reproduced by permission.)

Advancement Possibilities and Employment Outlook

With experience, workers may become directors of fund-raising programs. Some become the heads of consulting companies or start their own firms. Some seek more challenging positions by taking on fund-raising drives for high-profile organizations.

Employment of fund-raisers is expected to grow about as fast as the average for all jobs through 2014. In some parts of the country—where political campaigns are hotly contested, for example—employment of effective personnel may grow even faster.

Working Conditions

Fund-raisers generally work irregular hours, including nights and weekends. They travel extensively, especially when running national campaigns. They must be able to work well with all kinds of people—from college presidents to volunteers—and thrive under pressure.

Earnings and Benefits

Salaries vary with experience and the complexity of fund-raising campaigns. Those who work in northeastern states tend to earn higher salaries. In 2004, the median salary for fund-raising managers was $60,259 per year. Less experienced fund-raisers usually make from $40,000 to $50,000 per year, while those with many years of experience may earn $90,000 or more per year.

Fund-raisers employed by institutions and consulting firms usually receive paid holidays and vacations, health insurance, and pension plans. Self-employed fund-raisers must provide their own benefits.

Where to Go for More Information

American Association of Fund-Raising
  Counsel
4700 W. Lake Ave.
Glenview, IL 60025
(800) 462-2372
http://www.aafrc.org

Association of Fundraising Professionals
1101 King St., Ste. 700
Alexandria, VA 22314
(703) 684-0410
http://www.nsfre.org

Government Inspector and Examiner

Definition and Nature of the Work

Inspectors and examiners work for many government agencies, enforcing regulations that keep the public safe. Food and drug inspectors, for example, visit companies that manufacture, warehouse, or sell food and drugs to verify that their products are fresh or effective. Meat graders and grain inspectors in the U.S. Department of Agriculture check meat-handling and -labeling procedures. Agricultural quarantine inspectors keep potentially contaminated meats and produce away from good foods. At ports of entry, they keep contaminated foods from entering the country. Aviation safety officers investigate airplane accidents and review airport procedures and facilities, while construction inspectors see that buildings are erected according to approved blueprints.

Inspectors at all levels—federal, state, and local—collect taxes and enforce tax laws. In the federal government, they work for the Department of the Treasury and the Internal Revenue Service. Alcohol and tobacco tax inspectors check the quantities of liquor and tobacco that are sold and collect the proper amount of taxes. Other agencies, such as the Social Security Administration, employ claim examiners who see that people receive the correct benefits.

Some inspectors oversee the work of the agencies themselves. Their job is to make sure the agencies are run honestly and efficiently. For that reason, all agencies have budget examiners.

Education and Training Requirements

Requirements can vary by agency. In general, applicants must be U.S. citizens and at least eighteen years of age. For a number of positions, bachelor's degrees or specialized course work are required, although relevant work experience can often be substituted. All applicants must take civil service examinations.

Beginning government inspectors and examiners get on-the-job training under the guidance of experienced workers. Some employees serve probationary periods before they become permanent employees.

Education and Training
Varies—see profile

Salary
Median—$32,000 to $40,000 per year

Employment Outlook
Good

Construction inspectors ensure that buildings are erected according to code. (© Natalie Forbes/Corbis.)

Getting the Job

Applicants for government inspector and examiner positions should take the necessary civil service tests. Information about federal jobs is available from local Federal Information Centers, which are listed in the phone book. Job bulletins for state, county, and municipal governments are usually available at post offices or state and local civil service commissions.

Advancement Possibilities and Employment Outlook

Inspectors and examiners generally advance by moving up the civil service ranks. Additional civil service tests may be required for each promotion. Inspectors and examiners may become supervisors or heads of their departments.

Employment of government inspectors and examiners is expected to increase about as fast as the average for all jobs through 2014. While job opportunities may vary from agency to agency, the general need for more inspectors reflects the growing public demand for safer products and a cleaner environment. Job openings regularly occur when experienced workers retire or leave the field.

Working Conditions

Working conditions vary by agency; some inspectors and examiners may work in unpleasant conditions, coming into contact with dangerous substances and hazards. Inspectors and examiners often must travel on assignment, so their workweeks can be irregular. Overtime may be necessary. Workers are either paid extra for overtime or given the same number of hours off.

Earnings and Benefits

Earnings vary by agency, experience, and location. In 2004 the median salary for all inspectors and examiners ranged from $32,000 to $40,000 per year. Benefits include paid vacations and holidays, sick leave, health and life insurance, and retirement plans.

Where to Go for More Information

Food and Drug Administration
5600 Fishers La.
Rockville, MD 20857-0001
(888) 463-6332
http://www.fda.gov

Federal Aviation Administration
800 Independence Ave. SW
Washington, DC 20591
(866) 835-5322
http://www.faa.gov

Internal Revenue Service
1111 Constitution Ave. NW
Washington, DC 20224
(800) 829-1040
http://www.irs.gov

Internal Revenue Service Worker

Definition and Nature of the Work

Internal Revenue Service (IRS) workers collect taxes for the federal government and make sure taxpayers abide by the law. They work in the national office in Washington, DC, and in regional offices throughout the country.

IRS personnel hold a number of professional positions. Tax examiners, for instance, scrutinize the tax returns and accounting records of individual taxpayers and businesses to determine how much tax money is owed. They may question individual taxpayers or survey the accounting books of large enterprises. They also advise taxpayers on accounting methods and assist government attorneys handling tax cases.

Tax auditors are experts in IRS regulations. They examine tax returns in cases where adherence to regulations is at issue. Internal auditors examine the operations of the IRS itself. Revenue officers collect delinquent, or late, taxes, while special agents investigate cases of suspected tax fraud and advise government attorneys of their findings.

Some IRS workers are lawyers. Tax law specialists—who are employed only in Washington, DC—interpret federal tax laws, preparing informational and instructional publications for taxpayers and IRS workers. Estate tax attorneys interpret laws relating to estate and gift taxes.

Education and Training Requirements

Requirements vary, although all professional IRS workers need at least bachelor's degrees. Tax examiners, internal auditors, and special agents need expertise in accounting. Business courses are useful for tax auditors. Tax law specialists and estate tax attorneys need law degrees. All IRS workers receive both formal and on-the-job training after they are hired.

Getting the Job

Job seekers can apply directly to IRS recruitment offices, which have job listings and the requirements for all positions. Applicants may need to take federal civil service examinations.

Advancement Possibilities and Employment Outlook

IRS workers can advance with additional education and experience. Many go into administrative work. Tax examiners who get master's degrees in accounting earn higher salaries. Some go into private tax work.

The employment of federal tax examiners, revenue agents, and specialists is expected to grow more slowly than the average for all jobs through 2014. Stronger tax enforcement efforts are anticipated, but computerization and outsourcing to private-sector collection agencies may limit job opportunities.

Working Conditions

Most IRS personnel work in offices and handle a great deal of paperwork. Tax work demands care, attention to detail, and a responsible attitude.

Education and Training
College plus training

Salary
Average—$36,963 to $81,417 per year

Employment Outlook
Fair

Earnings and Benefits

Salaries vary widely, based on pay grade and type of job. In 2005 tax examiners earned an average salary of $36,963 per year, while revenue agents averaged $81,417 per year. Beginning workers earned between $21,000 and $27,000 per year, depending on their academic records and experience. Benefits include paid holidays and vacations, health and life insurance, and retirement plans.

Judge

Education and Training
Advanced degree

Salary
Median—$93,070 per year

Employment Outlook
Good

Definition and Nature of the Work

Judges preside over trials and hearings in federal, state, and local courts. They rule on the admissibility of evidence, monitor the testimony of witnesses, and settle disputes between prosecutors and defense attorneys. When standard procedures do not already exist, judges establish new rules based on their own knowledge of the law. They must ensure that all proceedings are fair and protect the legal rights of everyone involved.

Judges often conduct pretrial hearings to determine if the evidence warrants a trial. In criminal cases they must decide whether to hold defendants in jail pending trial or to set bail and other conditions for release. Judges instruct jurors about their duties and advise them of applicable laws. If defendants are found guilty, judges pronounce sentences. They determine verdicts in cases without juries.

Outside the courtroom, judges work in private offices, called chambers, where they read legal briefs and motions, research legal issues, hold hearings with lawyers, and write opinions. They also supervise their courts' administrative and clerical personnel.

Judges' duties vary depending on their jurisdictions and powers. Federal and state trial judges have jurisdiction over all cases in their systems. Administrative law judges are employed by government agencies to rule on appeals of such matters as individuals' eligibility for workers' compensation or the enforcement of health and safety regulations. Appellate court judges have the power to overrule decisions made by federal and state trial judges and administrative law judges if they find legal errors or contradictory legal precedents. Magistrates, or municipal court judges, form the majority of state court judges. Most of their work involves small-claims cases, misdemeanors, and pretrial hearings.

Education and Training Requirements

Almost all judges have law degrees and several years of legal experience. Many states permit individuals who are not lawyers to be administrative law judges and to hold limited-jurisdiction judgeships; however, law degrees are preferred. All federal and state trial and appellate court judges and federal administrative law judges must be lawyers. In addition, federal administrative law judges must pass examinations administered by the U.S. Office of Personnel Management.

Judges must ensure that court proceedings are fair and that the legal rights of all parties are protected. (© Bob Gomel/Corbis.)

Getting the Job

Judges are either appointed or elected. The president, with Senate approval, appoints federal judges for life. The various federal agencies appoint federal administrative law judges, generally for life. About half of all state judges are appointed; the other half are chosen in statewide elections. Most state and municipal judges serve fixed terms; limited-jurisdiction judges usually serve terms of four to six years, while some appellate court judges serve terms as long as fourteen years.

Advancement Possibilities and Employment Outlook

Judges advance by moving into courts that extend their jurisdictions and powers. Administrative law judges may become trial court judges and, with experience, appellate court judges. They may eventually be elected or appointed to the highest courts in their states or, in very rare cases, to the U.S. Supreme Court.

Employment opportunities for judges are expected to be about as good as the average for all jobs through 2014. Although public concerns about crime and the need for justice are likely to increase the demand for judges, cuts in government spending may slow job growth. Most job openings will be created because many judges are retiring early.

Working Conditions

Many judges work a standard forty-hour week, but about a third work more than fifty hours a week. Judges who preside over small-claims or family courts may work evening hours. Criminal arraignments may be held at any time.

Earnings and Benefits

Judges' annual salaries vary according to the type of judgeship. In 2004 the median salary for judges, magistrates, and magistrate judges was $93,070 per year. Judges on federal courts of appeals earned $171,800 per year, while district court judges had salaries of $162,100 per year. Salaries for associate justices of the U.S.

Where to Go for More Information

American Bar Association
321 N. Clark St.
Chicago, IL 60610
(312) 988-5000
http://www.abanet.org

American Judges Association
National Center for State Courts
300 Newport Ave.
Williamsburg, VA 23185-4147
(757) 259-1841
http://aja.ncsc.dni.us

Supreme Court were $199,200 per year. The chief justice of the United States was paid $208,100 per year.

The median salary of administrative law judges, adjudicators, and hearing officers was $68,930 per year, and arbitrators, mediators, and conciliators earned $54,760 per year.

Associate justices of the states' highest courts earned average salaries of $130,461 per year. State intermediate appellate court judges averaged $122,682 per year.

Benefits for most judges include health, life, and dental insurance; judicial immunity protection; expense accounts; vacation, holiday, and sick leave; and matching contributions to retirement plans.

Lawyer

Education and Training
Advanced degree

Salary
Median—$94,930 per year

Employment Outlook
Good

Definition and Nature of the Work

Lawyers serve as both advocates and advisers. As advocates, they speak for their clients in court by presenting supportive evidence. As advisers, they counsel their clients on their legal rights and obligations. Lawyers—also called attorneys and counselors—can interpret laws, apply laws to specific situations, and draft new laws.

Much of their work involves researching precedents, which are earlier interpretations of laws and the history of judicial decisions based on that law. Lawyers use precedents to support their cases in court. Many resources—from law libraries and public documents to computer databases and the Internet—are available to lawyers for research.

Many lawyers specialize. Criminal lawyers, for example, are hired by people facing prosecution for crimes. Public defenders are employed by the government to represent people who cannot afford to pay lawyers.

Some lawyers handle only civil cases, which do not involve criminal misconduct. For example, divorce and damage suits fall under civil law. Labor law concerns disputes between management and unionized workers, while patent law concerns disputes over the rights to inventions. Real estate law controls the purchase, sale, rental, and development of land and buildings. Some attorneys specialize in international law, the system of treaties and informal agreements between nations.

Some lawyers practice corporate law. They advise corporations on their rights, responsibilities, and obligations in business transactions. They may also represent the companies in government investigations and hearings.

Most lawyers have private practices that handle many kinds of legal problems. Some work for larger law firms, corporations, and government agencies. Others teach law. Some lawyers become district attorneys or judges, while many enter politics.

Education and Training Requirements

Most lawyers obtain bachelor's degrees and law school degrees. Helpful college courses include English, history, political science, economics, and social science. Those who want to be patent attorneys often major in engineering, while future tax lawyers get accounting degrees.

Occasionally, students are offered early admission to law school after two or three years of college. But most students complete college before going on to three years of law school. Good scores on the Law School Aptitude Test are required for admission. Law school courses include classes in contracts, property law, criminal law, and constitutional law. In the last two years of law school, students specialize in the areas of law in which they hope to work.

Law graduates must be admitted to the bar, or organization of lawyers, in the states in which they want to practice. In most states admission to the bar requires graduating from law school and passing bar examinations. In some states candidates are permitted to take bar examinations if they have substituted legal work experience for formal training. Those who do not attend law school must study law on their own to prepare for the examinations. In certain states graduates of "preferential" law schools may be admitted to the bar without taking the examinations. Some state bars have cooperative arrangements that allow lawyers who are members of the bar in one state to practice in another state without taking that state's bar exam.

In addition to representing clients in a court of law, lawyers draw up legal documents and handle out-of-court settlements. They spend much of their time preparing arguments and researching precedents. (© Rick Gomez/Corbis.)

Getting the Job

Law school placement offices usually help graduates find jobs. Many law firms and corporations send representatives to law schools to recruit graduating students. Part-time or summer jobs during law school sometimes lead to permanent jobs after graduation. Students with good grades and students who have worked on the law reviews published by each law school have the best chances to be hired by top law firms.

Job seekers who are interested in working for the government should take civil service tests. Many corporations, including insurance companies, banks, accounting firms, and manufacturers, employ lawyers. Newspaper classified ads and job banks on the Internet may provide other employment leads.

Advancement Possibilities and Employment Outlook

Most beginning lawyers start in salaried positions as associates in law firms or as research assistants or law clerks to experienced lawyers or judges. After several years of experience, they may become partners in their firms or set up their own practices. Some lawyers go into politics or become judges. Some become prosecutors or district attorneys.

About seven hundred and thirty-five thousand lawyers practice nationwide. The demand for lawyers is expected to grow as fast as the average for all jobs through 2014. However, many people are entering the profession, so competition for available jobs may be stiff. Lawyers who want to work for law firms will find the best opportunities in big cities, while those who are interested in setting up their own practices will find more opportunities in small towns or suburban areas.

Working Conditions

Lawyers often work long hours while preparing for court cases. Those in private practice can schedule their own workloads, while lawyers who work for law firms are assigned cases and must often work overtime to prepare for appearances in court or to draw up legal documents. All lawyers must spend some time keeping up with new laws and court decisions in their areas of interest.

Where to Go for More Information

American Bar Association
321 N. Clark St.
Chicago, IL 60610
(312) 988-5000
http://www.abanet.org

Association of Trial Lawyers of America
1050 Thirty-first St. NW
Washington, DC 20007
(800) 424-2725
http://www.atlanet.org

National Association of Women Lawyers
American Bar Center
321 N. Clark St.
Chicago, IL 60610
(312) 988-5000
http://www.abanet.org/nawl/

Earnings and Benefits

In 2004 the median salary for all lawyers was $94,930 per year. The median earnings of all state and local government lawyers ranged from $70,280 to $73,410 per year, while the median for federal government lawyers was $108,070 per year. Those who entered practice in large law firms started with salaries ranging from $34,000 to $80,000 per year.

Lawyers who start their own practices right after graduating from law school generally earn very little for the first few years. As their businesses grow, however, they can do quite well. The most experienced lawyers can earn between $130,000 and $1 million per year. Associates in law firms are paid salaries and receive raises as they take on more responsibilities. After some years of experience, they may become partners in their firms and receive percentages of the firms' profits.

Lawyers generally receive health and life insurance and pension plans. Those in private practice must make their own insurance and retirement arrangements.

Lawyer, Corporate

Education and Training
Advanced degree

Salary
Average—$50,000 to $90,000 per year

Employment Outlook
Good

Definition and Nature of the Work

Corporate lawyers advise their clients or employers on their legal rights and obligations. As advocates, they may represent companies in both criminal and civil court cases. Self-employed corporate lawyers may advise several corporate clients. Corporate lawyers may also work in-house as full-time employees of one company.

Whether serving as in-house or outside counsels, corporate lawyers are hired to keep companies out of trouble by anticipating and helping to circumvent problems. They also keep their clients up to date on new business laws and regulations. Corporate lawyers provide advice on labor relations, employee contracts, tax issues, suits against the corporation, employee injury, patents, and contracts with suppliers of raw materials.

The head of a corporation's legal department may be called the general counsel and hold vice presidential status. The counsel is supported by legal staff.

Education and Training Requirements

Bachelor's degrees and three years of law school are minimum requirements for work as corporate lawyers. All law students take core courses in corporate law, trusts, and tax and insurance law. However, those who want to specialize in corporate law should also take relevant electives, such as creditors' rights, trade regulations, commercial transactions, and trial advocacy.

To practice corporate law, graduates of law schools must be admitted to the bar, or organization of lawyers, in the states in which they want to practice. In most states, admission to the bar requires examinations.

Getting the Job

Work experience during law school will prove helpful for job hunting later. Typing briefs, working in the law school library, or searching records as a junior court clerk will give you job contacts and a firsthand view of the legal world. Many corporations send representatives to law schools to recruit graduating students. Check law journals and newspaper ads for corporate law vacancies.

Advancement Possibilities and Employment Outlook

Employment of corporate lawyers is expected to increase about as fast as the average for all jobs through 2014. Corporations are eager to protect themselves from skyrocketing damage suits, so they readily employ legal advisers. Most opportunities will be in urban areas, where most big corporations are located.

Working Conditions

Corporate lawyers are usually assigned their own offices with their own secretaries and access to legal research assistants and a legal library. They often work long hours, especially when they are preparing court cases. Lawyers who are employed by corporations with district branches may travel to various locations to investigate legal problems.

Earnings and Benefits

Average earnings for corporate lawyers range from $50,000 to $90,000 per year. With experience and specialization, general counsels can earn $100,000 or more per year. Benefits for corporate lawyers usually include retirement plans and health and life insurance. Lawyers who work independently must provide their own benefits.

Where to Go for More Information

American Bar Association
321 N. Clark St.
Chicago, IL 60610
(312) 988-5000
http://www.abanet.org

Lawyer, Public Service

Definition and Nature of the Work

Lawyers who work in public service usually specialize. Legal aid lawyers, for example, offer their services to people who cannot afford to pay for them. They give legal advice; draw up legal documents, such as contracts and wills; and represent their clients in court proceedings. Their salaries are usually paid by nonprofit organizations or governments. Legal aid lawyers may also work as consultants for public-interest organizations, such as the American Civil Liberties Union and the National Association for the Advancement of Colored People.

Many lawyers in public service work for state, federal, and local government agencies. They draft regulations to implement laws, prosecute criminals, or work as judges and magistrates in the courts. Environmental lawyers assist community groups in protecting environmental standards, often preparing injunctions against corporate activities. They are also consulted on major real-estate transactions because buyers and lenders fear they may inherit cleanup costs for previous toxic leaks or asbestos in buildings.

Education and Training Requirements

High school diplomas, bachelor's degrees, and good scores on the Law School Aptitude Test are required for admission to law school. Law school training usually takes three years and requires such courses as contracts, criminal law, and property law. The second and third years may be devoted to specialized courses about law in public service, including constitutional law, family law, and workers' compensation. Environmental lawyers should have technical familiarity with environmental science.

To practice public service law, graduates of law schools must be admitted to the bar, or organization of lawyers, in the states in which they want to practice. In most states, admission to the bar requires examinations.

Two public service lawyers consult on a case. They work as legal consultants for public interest organizations. (© Martha Tabor/Working Images Photographs. Reproduced by permission.)

Getting the Job

While still in law school, students can assist attorneys undertaking pro bono work (services donated for the public good). Many law firms and government agencies send representatives to law schools to recruit graduating students. Students with good grades and those who have worked on law reviews published by law schools have the best chances of being hired. Civil service tests are required for government jobs.

Advancement Possibilities and Employment Outlook

Most public service lawyers start as research assistants or law clerks to experienced lawyers or judges. After several years of experience, they may become district attorneys or heads of legal departments in state or federal agencies. From there, they may move to private law firms and use the expertise and contacts they have gained in the public arena.

The number of lawyers practicing environmental law has boomed in recent years and is expected to grow, largely because of renewed attention to air pollution and landfill problems. Some environmental lawyers work for private law firms that have departments specializing in environmental law. Others work for the U.S. Environmental Protection Agency or such organizations as the Sierra Club and the Natural Resources Defense Council.

Working Conditions

Public service lawyers may be required to work long hours, especially during emergency situations. Outside of working hours, lawyers must keep current with new laws and court decisions. Public service lawyers may have to travel to carry out their legal duties.

Earnings and Benefits

Lawyers may make a financial sacrifice when they accept jobs in government agencies or legal aid offices. Environmental lawyers, for example, earn only fifty-five to eighty percent of the standard $175 to $200 per hour received by other specialty lawyers. While the median salary for all lawyers was $94,930 per year in 2004, the median salary for public service lawyers specializing in environmental law was $77,500 per year. Benefits usually include health and life insurance and retirement plans.

Where to Go for More Information

American Bar Association
321 N. Clark St.
Chicago, IL 60610
(312) 988-5000
http://www.abanet.org

Equal Justice Works
National Association for Public Interest Law
2120 L St. NW, Ste. 450
Washington, DC, 20037-1541
(202) 466-3686
http://www.napil.org

Librarian, Public

Education and Training
Advanced degree

Salary
Median—$42,500 per year

Employment Outlook
Fair

Definition and Nature of the Work

Public libraries vary widely in scope and size, according to the needs and financial resources of their communities. The librarians who run these institutions select the books, books on tape, compact discs, government documents, films, audiotapes, videotapes, and Internet databases that they believe will best serve those needs and make best use of the resources available. They must know more than the newest books available; they must also understand the demographics and interests of the users of their libraries.

Large libraries offer librarians a chance to specialize. Acquisitions librarians, for instance, read reviews, examine sample copies, and order new materials for the library. Catalogers describe books according to their subject matter and assign subject headings and classification numbers for card catalogs or online catalogs. Catalogers or their helpers prepare books for filing on shelves according to the systems used by their particular libraries. The Dewey decimal and the Library of Congress classification systems are the ones most commonly used. Reference librarians deal directly with library users, helping them find specific pieces of information or directing them to useful sources. Because they handle questions in person and over the telephone, they must know a wide range of reference sources, including computerized information services and Internet databases. Reference librarians usually have a special desk in the reference or information section of the library.

Some librarians work with specific segments of the community. Children's librarians often prepare displays and conduct weekly story hours designed to interest children in books and library services. They may also offer film programs. Youth services librarians work mainly with junior and senior high school students, helping them learn to use libraries. They suggest books and other materials for pleasure, vocational guidance, and school-related projects.

Librarians in public libraries have duties ranging from selecting and ordering materials to assisting library patrons with research. *(AP Images.)*

Bookmobile librarians work from vans specially designed as mobile libraries, traveling to outlying neighborhoods that lack adequate library services. They select books according to the needs of the communities the bookmobile serves or fulfill requests from their patrons. Other community-outreach librarians may serve specific groups, such as those living in nursing homes.

Large library systems are generally administered by sizable staffs made up of specialists. Smaller libraries are staffed by two or three people who do all the specialists' jobs. Library administrators are responsible for the operation and continued funding of their libraries.

Education and Training Requirements

Librarians generally need master's degrees in library science. Graduate programs usually last one year and include a summer of study. Library schools offer courses in the history of books and printing, intellectual freedom, reference tools, and user services. Because most libraries now have automated systems, almost all library schools offer courses in information storage and retrieval, microcomputer technology, and the use of online information retrieval systems. Advanced courses may be taken in specialties such as children's or adult services; classification, cataloging, and indexing; library administration; library automation; and archives.

Some schools offer doctoral programs in library science. Doctorates are often prerequisites for top administrators in large library systems. Undergraduate study in the liberal arts, including English, foreign languages, data processing, and business, as well as part-time library work as technical or clerical assistants, may prove useful. Some graduate schools offer two-year work-study programs that enable students to get work experience while they are in school.

Getting the Job

Job seekers can apply directly to local libraries. School placement offices, private and state employment services, professional associations and journals, newspapers ads, and Internet job sites are all sources of employment leads.

Advancement Possibilities and Employment Outlook

Librarians can advance within their own library system or move to larger or more specialized libraries. Most top-level jobs are administrative and often require doctorates. Librarians with doctorates may also become teachers of library science.

Employment of librarians is expected to grow more slowly than the average for all occupations through 2014. The increased use of computerized systems and budget constraints may be crucial factors. Job seekers can anticipate stiff competitions for positions, most of which will open up when experienced workers retire or leave the field. Opportunities may be best in rural areas.

Working Conditions

Public libraries, particularly newer facilities, are generally pleasant and quiet places to work. Specific duties affect the conditions of work. For example, catalogers spend most of their day working in one place, while reference librarians move about the library helping people find information. Reference librarians work under pressure when patrons need information quickly. Most librarians work between thirty-five and forty hours per week, including some evenings and weekends.

Earnings and Benefits

Salaries of public librarians vary by location, size of library, education, and experience. In 2004 the median salary of librarians working for local governments was $42,500 per year. The average salary for federal government librarians in all positions, including supervisory and managerial, was $74,630 per year. Most public librarians can expect paid vacations of three or four weeks a year, as well as paid holidays, sick leave, health insurance, and pension plans.

Librarian, School

Education and Training
Varies—see profile

Salary
Varies—see profile

Employment Outlook
Fair

Definition and Nature of the Work

Elementary schools, junior and senior high schools, and colleges and universities all employ librarians, who select and order books, audiovisual materials, computer equipment, and other materials that support their schools' educational programs. They not only maintain their collections so students can access them easily and quickly; they also teach students how to do so.

Actual duties vary with the size of the library and the needs of the students. High school libraries are generally larger than those in elementary schools because older students need more extensive resources for research. Elementary and secondary school librarians may work alone, while librarians in colleges and universities may be members of sizable staffs that include technical assistants and clerks. In large libraries, assistants catalog new books, return books to the shelves, and repair damaged books. In small libraries these tasks are done by the librarians themselves.

Elementary school librarians teach basic library skills, often in regularly scheduled classes in the library. They may teach students how to distinguish among various kinds of books, such as fiction, nonfiction, poetry, and biography, and how to use the classification systems for finding books and other materials. They encourage use of the library for information and recreation, while making it an interesting and important part of the school day. To interest students in reading, librarians may conduct story hours for the younger students and arrange special programs for those in the higher grades.

Most students begin to learn research techniques in junior and senior high school, so secondary school librarians usually hold orientation sessions for individual classes to explain the use of card catalogs, computer databases, reference books, indexes to periodicals, and audiovisual materials. They help individual students by suggesting specific sources or ways of finding information. Sometimes librarians set up exhibits designed to make students aware of library holdings, often coordinating the exhibits with historical events or holidays.

College and university librarians work in relatively large libraries suited to the research needs of both students and faculty. Many have specialties. Librarians in technical services, for instance, order, process, and catalog new materials. Librarians in user services work closely with students and faculty, directing them to helpful sources. They often conduct bibliographic instruction classes to teach methods for library research. Online and other computer services available for reference may require that librarians have special training.

Some universities have separate libraries for the various disciplines they offer: one library for general use, one for technical and scientific subjects, and an art library that may include an extensive slide collection. Librarians who work in specialized libraries are sometimes required to have master's degrees in the subject field as well as in library science. Library administrators and head librarians supervise all library operations.

Education and Training Requirements

Depending on the state, elementary and secondary school librarians may need to be certified both as librarians and as teachers. To be certified as a school librarian, they generally must earn a bachelor's or master's degree in library science and pass written examinations.

Most college and university librarians have master's degrees in library science. Top administrative posts, however, generally go to those who have doctorates. Librarians who work in large university libraries are frequently required to have master's degrees in the subject areas of the faculties they represent as well as master's degrees in library science. Some academic libraries may also require proficiency in foreign languages. Rare book librarians may need special training, as well as additional advanced degrees. Because of the many automated systems in academic libraries, librarians should be familiar with computerized information retrieval systems and online catalogs.

Getting the Job

Job seekers can apply directly to private schools and public school boards. School placement offices, state employment services, and private employment agencies often list library openings. *The Chronicle of Higher Education* and other professional journals, library associations, newspaper ads, and Internet jobs sites may all have information about employment opportunities.

Advancement Possibilities and Employment Outlook

School librarians can advance with additional education. With advanced degrees in library science or with second-subject master's degrees, they may transfer to large college or university libraries or become library administrators. School librarians may also become teachers at library schools.

The growth of employment for librarians will be slower than the average for all jobs through 2014. However, jobs should be available because many librarians are more than forty-five years of age and eligible to retire within the next decade. Still, competition may be stiff in schools at all levels, especially those in urban areas. The increased use of computerized systems may contribute to reduced demand, and public funding for education may not allow the creation of new library positions.

Working Conditions

Libraries are generally quiet, pleasant places to work. Working hours vary with each school, but elementary and high school librarians usually work the same hours that teachers do, while college and university librarians often work thirty-five- to forty-hour weeks. Evening and weekend hours may be necessary. Some librarians are members of unions.

Earnings and Benefits

Salaries vary by school, location, education, and experience. In 2004 the median salary of elementary and secondary school librarians was $47,580 per year, while the median salary of college and university librarians was $47,830 per year. Benefits include paid holidays, health insurance, and retirement plans.

Librarian, *Special*

Education and Training
Varies—see profile

Salary
Median—$60,000 per year

Employment Outlook
Fair

Definition and Nature of the Work

Special librarians serve particular organizations and specialize in subjects that suit the needs of those organizations. They work in public institutions, such as the National Library of Medicine, as well as in private businesses, such as television stations, advertising agencies, and law firms. Some librarians work in museums with filmstrips, slides, prints, and art history books, while others work solely with medical books and periodicals in hospital libraries. They may translate material into English from foreign languages or abstract and index articles, research papers, or books. The growth of computer storage and retrieval of information has changed this field drastically. Many positions deal primarily or even exclusively with research using online databases.

Because special librarians deal with one subject in depth, they must have extensive knowledge about that particular field. Sometimes they do research for their companies and present their findings in reports to the staff. They also assist staff members who conduct research.

Special libraries may have a head librarian, who is in charge of planning the budget, hiring personnel, and handling important correspondence, and other

librarians who work in circulation or take care of subscription and book orders. In small libraries one or two staff members may handle all the duties.

Education and Training Requirements

Most employers prefer candidates with master's degrees in library science combined with extensive knowledge of specific fields. Art-museum librarians, for instance, need bachelor's degrees in art history and master's degrees in library science. Librarians in large technical libraries usually need master's degrees or doctorates in relevant fields, plus library science degrees. However, high school diplomas plus experience may be sufficient for some jobs. Writing skills and knowledge of computer operations are usually necessary.

Some graduate students take part in work-study arrangements that allow them to work while attending school. Graduate study often includes foreign-language courses, as well as the study of library procedures, database searching, information science, and library automation. Volunteer and part-time or summer work in libraries can prove useful for people who plan to become librarians.

Getting the Job

Job seekers can apply directly to companies and agencies that have special libraries. Professional organizations, such as the Special Libraries Association, often provide job listings or telephone hotlines. School placement offices, professional journals, newspaper classified ads, and job banks on the Internet are all sources of possible employment leads. Applicants for government jobs must take civil service examinations.

Advancement Possibilities and Employment Outlook

Advancement generally depends on experience and continuing education. Librarians with doctorates may advance to become head librarians or library administrators.

Through 2014 the employment outlook for special librarians is expected to be better than the outlook for most other librarians. Corporations, which do not have the budget constraints that face public libraries, are turning to librarians to analyze, evaluate, and organize information. Special librarians are especially in demand because of their abilities to search the Internet and databases.

Where to Go for More Information

American Library Association
50 E. Huron St.
Chicago, IL 60611-2795
(800) 545-2433
http://www.ala.org

American Society for Information Science
    and Technology
1320 Fenwick La., Ste. 510
Silver Spring, MD 20910
(301) 495-0900
http://www.asis.org

Special Libraries Association
331 S. Patrick St.
Alexandria, VA 22314-3501
(703) 647-4900
http://www.sla.org

Working Conditions

The atmosphere in libraries is generally pleasant and quiet. Special librarians, however, must sometimes work under considerable pressure, especially when information is needed quickly. They generally work thirty-five to forty hours per week.

Earnings and Benefits

Earnings depend on education and experience as well as on the budget limitations of the employing organization. According to a 2005 survey conducted by the Special Libraries Association, the median annual salary of special librarians was $60,000. Experienced librarians can earn more than $98,760 per year.

Librarians can expect two to four weeks of paid vacation and sick leave. Other benefits usually include health insurance and retirement plans.

Marriage and Family Counselor

Education and Training
College

Salary
Median—$38,980 per year

Employment Outlook
Very good

Definition and Nature of the Work

Marriage and family counselors provide therapy for people who wish to solve emotional conflicts. Their goal is to modify people's perceptions and behavior, improve communication, and prevent individual and family crises. Counselors work in mental health centers, clinics, hospitals, social service agencies, and private practice.

Therapy usually consists of talk sessions, lasting about an hour. Using techniques learned in classrooms and in fieldwork, counselors guide their clients through a series of conversations that reveal their clients' anger, fears, and needs. When couples are considering divorce, for instance, counselors work to uncover the underlying reasons for the divorce and discover whether reconciliation is possible.

Marriage counselors usually speak with a husband and wife at the same time, although they may have some sessions with them separately. They may also counsel groups of married couples, groups of husbands, or groups of wives. Family counselors work with entire families or with individual family members, using similar methods of therapy.

Counselors' work may vary by place of employment. Those in private practice, for example, may specialize in one or two kinds of problems. They may refer clients to other counselors if they determine that their clients' problems are outside their areas of expertise. Counselors who work in clinics may work in teams, consulting each other on appropriate therapy techniques. Some clinics employ counselors with special qualifications to take on the most difficult cases.

Education and Training Requirements

Requirements for marriage and family counselors typically include master's degrees in counseling, two years or three thousand hours of supervised clinical experience, and state-recognized exams. Counselors must adhere to ethical codes and standards and complete continuing education requirements every year. Courses in sociology, social work, psychology, and modern foreign languages are helpful.

Getting the Job

Job seekers can apply directly to local agencies, hospitals, and clinics. Those who wish to work for government agencies should take the necessary civil service tests. Many students make future job contacts while doing fieldwork for courses in social work and psychology. School placement offices, professional journals, newspaper ads, and job sites on the Internet are other sources of employment leads.

Advancement Possibilities and Employment Outlook

Marriage and family counselors can become self-employed or work as directors of departments or agencies. They can also advance by earning doctorates or by taking additional postgraduate courses. Experienced counselors may become trainers and teachers of new counselors.

The employment of marriage and family counselors is expected to grow faster than the average for all jobs through 2014. Demand for therapists should grow as more people become comfortable seeking professional help for personal and family problems. More employers are also offering employee-assistance programs that provide counseling.

Working Conditions

Counselors work in offices where they can speak with their clients in private or in groups. Working hours vary because many counselors combine part-time jobs in social service agencies with private practice. Agency work, especially in marriage counseling, often includes two or three evenings of work each week because many clients work during the day. Counselors in private practice can regulate their own schedules; they may have some evening and weekend sessions.

The work can be very demanding. Counselors must always give their complete attention to their clients' difficulties.

Earnings and Benefits

Pay scales vary considerably. Starting salaries for beginning counselors employed by public agencies or clinics range from $25,000 to $30,000 per year, depending on educational background. In 2004 the median salary of marriage and family counselors was $38,980 per year. The most experienced counselors earned more than $65,080 per year. Experienced counselors in private practice usually have the highest earnings.

Benefits for counselors employed by government agencies or other large public or private organizations usually include paid holidays and vacations, health insurance, and retirement plans.

Where to Go for More Information

American Association for Marriage and
　Family Therapy
112 S. Alfred St.
Alexandria, VA 22314
(703) 838-9808
http://www.aamft.org

American Association of Sexuality
　Educators, Counselors, and Therapists
PO Box 1960
Ashland, VA 23005-1960
(804) 752-0056
http://www.aasect.org

Parole Officer

Definition and Nature of the Work

Parole officers identify and supervise offenders who are eligible for conditional release from prison before they have completed their sentences. To merit parole, prisoners must obey prison rules, perform prison jobs well, and show progress in rehabilitation and therapy programs.

Some parole officers work inside correctional institutions, preparing reports for parole boards. They assess prisoners' lives before and during incarceration; how prisoners' families will affect their rehabilitation; and what job prospects prisoners might have if released. Based on the officers' reports and interviews with the prisoners and their families, the boards choose certain prisoners for release.

Field officers work with parolees once they have returned to their communities. They help parolees find jobs, schools, or therapy programs. For instance, former drug addicts may have to enroll in programs that help them stay off drugs. If parolees have financial problems, officers direct them to community agencies that can provide welfare benefits and other financial support. Some officers supervise halfway houses in which small groups of parolees live together to share experiences and lend each other support. Drug therapists, psychiatrists, and social workers often help with this supervision.

Parole officers visit their clients regularly to evaluate their progress. If parolees break the rules—by violating the law, for example, or by associating with bad company—officers may recommend that parole be revoked. Parole boards may send the parolees back to prison.

Most parole officers work for state parole departments; some are employed by counties or the U.S. Board of Parole. They may be assisted by parole aides or parole officer trainees.

Education and Training Requirements

Bachelor's degrees in sociology, psychology, criminology, or correctional science are preferred. In addition, many agencies, including the U.S. Board of Parole, require one or two years of work experience in correctional institutions or other social agencies or master's degrees in sociology or psychology.

Applicants must take written, oral, psychological, and physical examinations. In most states, parole officers must pass training programs and certification tests.

Getting the Job

Job seekers can contact federal, state, or county parole boards directly. They should take federal or state civil service tests, if necessary. Those who do fieldwork for college courses in social work may make contacts who can help them find jobs after graduation. College placement offices may have employment listings.

Advancement Possibilities and Employment Outlook

Qualified parole officers may advance to work as administrators, department heads, and directors of special projects or units.

Employment of parole officers is expected to grow as fast as the average for all jobs through 2014. Mandatory sentencing guidelines, which called for longer prison terms and fewer opportunities for parole, are being reconsidered in many states because of budgetary constraints and court decisions. If additional prisoners gain early release, more parole officers may be needed to supervise them. Jobs for parole officers should also open up as experienced workers retire or leave the field.

Working Conditions

Parole officers work independently, advising and evaluating parolees and finding jobs for them. The work can be stressful, for they are under pressure at all times to present parole and parolees positively to their communities. Caseloads may be heavy. Officers often work more than forty hours per week, sometimes making night or weekend appointments with parolees who work.

Earnings and Benefits

Earnings vary, depending on location and experience. In 2004 the median salary for all parole officers was $39,600 per year. The lowest ten percent earned less than $26,310 per year, and the highest ten percent earned more than $66,660 per year. Supervisors and directors often earned much more.

Most parole officers receive paid holidays and vacations, health insurance, and pension plans.

Political Consultant

Definition and Nature of the Work

Political consultants promote the election of certain candidates or the interests of certain groups. They plan campaign strategies, coordinate campaign staffs, and arrange meetings to publicize candidates or causes.

Using advertising, press releases, fund-raising drives, and other activities, political consultants introduce politicians and their ideas to the voting public. Consultants function as public relations specialists, salespeople, and managers. Their goal is to "sell" the public on the politicians they represent.

Corporate lobbyists are also political consultants, although they specialize in representing companies to federal or state government. They try to persuade officials to understand their companies' problems and to sway governmental policy or legislation. They may also help market companies' products to governmental departments. Lobbyists often discuss such issues as taxation and regulation with members of Congress and other senior officials.

Education and Training Requirements

If you are interested in becoming a political consultant, you should take college courses in political science, communication, English, and foreign languages. Other useful fields of study are economics, business, law, and sociology.

Education and Training
Advanced degree

Salary
Varies—see profile

Employment Outlook
Very good

Political consultants meet with politicians to promote the election of certain candidates or the interests of certain groups. (© Catherine Karnow/Corbis.)

Volunteer work for local politicians or interest groups will give you experience and helpful contacts. A master's degree in government or public administration may be supplemented by part-time work on a campaign staff or in a legislator's local office.

Getting the Job

Volunteer and part-time work during school and college will be a good springboard for finding full-time employment. Jobs in the personnel and public relations divisions of companies may lead to corporate lobbying positions. Many trade and professional associations have well-established lobbying offices and regularly hire new personnel.

Advancement Possibilities and Employment Outlook

As local, state, and federal political contests become more complex, candidates increasingly rely on consultants to manage their organizations. While there may be more jobs at the local level during election time, state and federal representatives often employ full-time political consultants in Washington, DC, and state capitals.

Smaller companies that cannot afford full-time lobbyists hire outside lobbyists who are experts on specific issues. Specialization has created new advancement possibilities for many political consultants who have opened their own consulting firms.

The employment outlook for political consultants is very good. However, competition will be stiff for those in beginning positions or those who are starting their own consulting firms.

Working Conditions

Political consultants work at an energetic pace, arguing for their candidates or causes. They spend a considerable amount of time on the telephone and in face-to-face contact with legislators and other officials. They must have excellent communication and interpersonal skills. During an election campaign consultants often travel ahead of the candidates, organizing meetings, interviews, and publicity. The job often requires evening and weekend work as well as extensive travel.

Earnings and Benefits

Entry-level political consultants may receive payment for out-of-pocket expenses. Starting salaries range from $26,000 to $31,000 per year. However, as word of energetic and successful strategies gets around, candidates and corporations will offer higher wages and benefits. In 2004 the median salary of corporate lobbyists was $96,825 per year.

Political consultants who work for corporations also receive health insurance, retirement plans, and vacation benefits. Self-employed consultants must arrange benefits for themselves.

Where to Go for More Information

American Association of Political
  Consultants
600 Pennsylvania Ave. SE, Ste. 300
Washington, DC 20003-6300
(202) 544-9815
http://www.theaapc.org

Probation Officer

Definition and Nature of the Work

Probation officers monitor offenders who get sentences of supervision—known as probation—instead of or in addition to jail time. They meet with offenders regularly to check their activities and to evaluate their progress. They make regular reports to the courts about the offenders' behavior. Sometimes they may arrange substance-abuse rehabilitation or job training for their clients. Officers generally work in the adult, juvenile, or family divisions of probation departments. Some officers work for state or county courts; others work in the probation office of the U.S. District Court.

Probation officers handle twenty to one hundred cases at a time, depending on the jurisdiction and the risks that offenders pose to the public. Technology allows efficient supervision: some clients are required to wear electronic devices so their location and movements can be more easily monitored, and computers and cell phones allow officers to handle their caseloads from home or on the road.

Probation officers also conduct pretrial investigations, interviewing those who have been accused of crimes, their families, and their coworkers. If they conclude that the accused are unlikely to commit other crimes, they may recommend to the courts that the offenders be placed under supervision instead of going to trial.

When they conduct presentence investigations, probation officers probe the character, background, and previous criminal records of people who have been tried and convicted. They then recommend punishment to the court: prison sentence, probation, or a combination of the two. In making their recommendations, they must consider the possible harmful effects to society if certain people are not imprisoned.

People who are arrested may be released pending trial if they pay a sum of money to the court. A portion of the money, called bail, is returned if they appear at the trial. Probation officers may make bail recommendations to the

Education and Training
College plus training

Salary
Median—$39,600 per year

Employment Outlook
Good

After interviewing each divorcing parent, this probation officer in a family division will make recommendations to the judge for custody, living, and visitation arrangements for the children. (© Martha Tabor/ Working Images Photographs. Reproduced by permission.)

courts—high, low, or no bail—depending on whether they think the accused are likely to appear at trial.

In large offices probation officers may specialize in one aspect of probation work, such as job placement. In rural districts where there are few clients, they often handle all kinds of probation matters and may work with both adult and juvenile offenders. Those who work in family divisions may make custody investigations and recommendations in divorce proceedings. Others work in halfway houses for offenders. They are often members of teams that include psychiatrists and social workers.

Education and Training Requirements

Bachelor's degrees are required, preferably with majors in sociology, psychology, or criminology. Some employers prefer to hire candidates with master's degrees in one of the behavioral sciences. In addition, candidates should have one or two years of work experience in social welfare agencies or correctional institutions. Probation officers are trained on the job by experienced officers.

Getting the Job

Most jobs in probation are at the county level. Job seekers can contact probation offices directly and take the required civil service examinations. College placement offices usually have job listings.

Advancement Possibilities and Employment Outlook

Probation officers receive promotions and salary increases by passing additional civil service tests. They may become supervisors of other probation officers, chief probation officers, or directors of probation departments.

Where to Go for More Information

American Federation of State, County, and
    Municipal Employees
1625 L St. NW
Washington, DC 20036
(202) 429-1000
http://www.afscme.org

American Probation and Parole Association
2760 Research Park Dr.
Lexington, KY 40511-8410
(859) 244-8203
http://www.appa-net.org

National Council on Crime and
    Delinquency
1970 Broadway, Ste. 500
Oakland, CA 94612
(510) 208-0500
http://www.nccd-crc.org

The employment of probation officers is expected to grow as fast as the average for all jobs through 2014. The increasing number of cases before the courts should spur demand. However, increased job opportunities for probation officers may be affected by public funding.

Working Conditions

Probation officers generally work forty hours per week, including some weekend and evening appointments. They often drive considerable distances to meet with offenders in their homes and at their jobs. The work can be physically and emotionally demanding.

Earnings and Benefits

Salaries vary widely, because county, state, and federal governments have different pay scales. In 2004 the median salary for all probation officers was $39,600 per year. The most experienced officers earned more than $66,660 per year. Benefits include paid holidays and vacations, health and life insurance, and retirement plans.

Rehabilitation Counselor

Definition and Nature of the Work

Rehabilitation counselors work with individuals who have mental, emotional, or physical handicaps, helping them to lead self-sufficient lives both at home and on the job. The counselors determine the training and support their clients need to deal with the personal, social, and vocational effects of their conditions. Rehabilitation counselors are employed by publicly funded agencies, schools, and medical facilities.

After evaluating their clients' strengths and limitations, counselors arrange for rehabilitation programs that may include medical care, occupational therapy, and job placement. To find suitable programs for their clients, counselors study medical and job histories and confer with doctors and therapists. They also talk to the clients and their families.

Education and Training Requirements

Some employers hire counselors with bachelor's degrees in rehabilitation services, counseling, psychology, or related fields. However, many employers require that counselors have master's degrees in rehabilitation counseling, counseling and guidance, or counseling psychology. The Council on Rehabilitation Education accredits graduate programs that include at least two years of study and six hundred hours of experience in supervised clinical internships. An increasing number of employers require that rehabilitation counselors be certified, which requires examinations. Standards were established by the Commission on Rehabilitation Counselor Certification.

Getting the Job

Because roughly a third of all rehabilitation counselors are employed by public service organizations, vacancies are usually listed in state and federal civil ser-

Education and Training
College plus training

Salary
Median—$27,870 per year

Employment Outlook
Very good

A rehabilitation counselor develops a program that is suited to a client's needs, interests, and capabilities. (© Martha Tabor/Working Images Photographs. Reproduced by permission.)

vice bulletins. Volunteer work in the field may provide useful contacts for permanent employment.

Advancement Possibilities and Employment Outlook

Counselors may become directors of rehabilitation programs or self-employed consultants. Employment of rehabilitation counselors is expected to grow faster than the average for all jobs through 2014. Both government and private industry are showing increased commitment to helping individuals with disabilities become members of the workforce. That commitment is likely to spur expanded employment for counselors.

Working Conditions

Counselors perform a diverse range of tasks, from preparing marketing presentations for corporations to locating voice boards to help disabled clients speak. Much of their work is in the field, visiting the homes of clients to determine their needs and meeting with business leaders to promote employment and training programs. Some counselors are assigned to the job sites of employees with disabilities to help orient them to the work environment. The job requires patience, perseverance, and initiative.

Earnings and Benefits

In 2004 the median salary for rehabilitation counselors was $27,870 per year, with the most experienced counselors earning more than $48,130 per year.

Rehabilitation counselors who are employed by government agencies or private businesses usually receive paid vacations, holidays, retirement plans, and medical insurance. Self-employed counselors must provide their own benefits.

Where to Go for More Information

American Medical Rehabilitation Providers
  Association
1710 N St. NW
Washington, DC 20036
(888) 346-4624
http://www.amrpa.org

Council on Rehabilitation Education
1835 Rohlwing Rd., Ste. E
Rolling Meadows, IL 60008
(847) 394-1785
http://www.core-rehab.org

National Rehabilitation Association
633 S. Washington St.
Alexandria, VA 22314-4109
(703) 836-0850
http://www.nationalrehab.org

Religious Vocation

Education and Training
Advanced degree

Salary
Varies—see profile

Employment Outlook
Varies—see profile

Definition and Nature of the Work

Clergy serve as spiritual leaders to the millions of Americans who follow religious faiths. Their main duties are overseeing sacred activities and nurturing their congregations. They may also participate in interfaith services and work with community leaders on nonreligious matters such as raising funds for hospitals.

Many duties of clergy are common to all denominations. They preside over religious services, conduct weddings and funerals, counsel members of their congregations, and deliver sermons. Some aspects of their work differ because of the beliefs of their individual religions. Jewish rabbis, for example, read the Torah, while Catholic priests hear confessions from parishioners.

Not all clergy work with congregations. Some priests and rabbis are teachers or scholars, while ministers may be missionaries, providing religious and social assistance to societies in other parts of the world. Chaplains serve people's spiritual needs in the armed services, hospitals, and schools.

Many people with religious vocations are not clergy. Roman Catholic nuns and brothers, who are members of religious orders, frequently work as teachers, counselors, nurses, and social workers. Lay employees—people who have no formal authorization for their religious vocations—often assist in social work and administration.

Education and Training Requirements

Educational requirements vary by faith and specific vocation. Most clergy have bachelor's degrees, but many denominations require additional theological study. Rabbis must complete four- or five-year courses of study, while preparation for the priesthood includes four years of seminary training. Many Protestant denominations require bachelor's degrees and study at theological schools, although some have no formal education requirements. All ministers, priests, and rabbis must have thorough knowledge of the rites and beliefs of their groups.

Training for religious vocations may begin in high school. Prospective priests study Latin; those interested in Jewish vocations study Hebrew. Many attend high schools and colleges with religious affiliations, although they are not required to do so.

Lay employees require the same training as those performing similar tasks without religious affiliation. For example, the educational requirements for leaders of Christian youth groups would be the same as those for secular social workers with similar responsibilities.

Members of the Christian clergy and the Jewish rabbinate constitute the majority of religious leaders in the United States. This rabbi dresses himself before conducting a religious service. (© Martha Tabor/ Working Images Photographs. Reproduced by permission.)

Getting the Job

Clergy are often "called" to their vocations; they believe they have been blessed with opportunities to serve their religions and their communities. Following their training, they are often assigned to parishes and temples. Students who are interested in religious vocations should contact their religious leaders for career counseling; many begin by working as assistants in their own congregations. Lay employees, such as social workers, generally find jobs the same way their secular counterparts do.

Advancement Possibilities and Employment Outlook

As priests, rabbis, and ministers become more experienced, they take on greater responsibilities. Priests, for instance, may be elevated in the church hierarchy, becoming bishops or cardinals. Religious teachers may advance to more prestigious colleges or seminaries, while lay workers sometimes assume top administrative jobs in religious institutions.

The employment outlook for both rabbis and Catholic priests is very favorable through 2014 because of shortages of ordained clergy. More competition is expected for Protestant ministers because of slow growth in church membership and large numbers of qualified candidates. Graduates of theological schools will have the best prospects. Social institutions with religious affiliations may provide additional opportunities.

Working Conditions

Clergy who have been called to their vocations choose lifestyles as well as careers. Priests, for instance, are not allowed to marry, while ministers and rabbis usually do. Some laypeople may have limited hours, but rabbis, priests, and ministers are usually on call twenty-four hours a day. Wherever they work—in majestic cathedrals, ghettos, jungles, or hospitals—clergy and others with religious vocations are held to strict moral standards set by their faiths and their communities.

Earnings and Benefits

Salaries and benefits vary by denomination, location, and experience. In 2004 the average salary for Catholic priests ranged from $12,936 to $15,483 per year. They also received room and board in parish rectories. Rabbis' salaries ranged from $50,000 to $100,000 per year, plus benefits. Salaries of Protestant ministers varied substantially.

Salaries differ not only among the religious groups but also within them. For example, larger, wealthier churches or temples can afford to pay their clergy more than smaller congregations can. Priests, ministers, and rabbis sometimes earn extra income by performing special services such as marriages.

School Administrator

Education and Training
Varies—see profile

Salary
Median—$68,340 per year

Employment Outlook
Fair

Definition and Nature of the Work

School administrators make public education work. They serve as administrators for the federal government or the state government; as superintendents working for local school boards; and as principals of individual schools.

Federal administrators develop academic standards and programs and allocate funds to the schools. State administrators interpret state policy governing such issues as teaching standards, school lunches, and student transportation. They run large education departments and supervise many staff members.

School superintendents head districts that are made up of several schools. The job can be small or large: district size ranges from two schools to eight hundred schools. Those who manage small districts work closely with each school and its faculty; those who are responsible for many schools have contact primarily with their assistant superintendents.

Superintendents set and administer policies on hiring and curriculum management. For example, they may decide which textbooks are used in classes. They also carry out their school boards' decisions on such matters as budgets and expansion of facilities.

School principals have responsibility for individual schools. They draw up their schools' budgets and see that policies on curriculum, teaching, and discipline are carried out. Principals are also in charge of their schools' physical maintenance. However, their most important function may be to represent the school to the community. Contact with students, parents, and their schools' neighbors is crucial to their success.

Education and Training Requirements

Educational requirements for administrators vary, although they usually combine teaching experience with training in school administration. Many administrators have had college courses in education, economics, business, and sociology.

In most cases, administrators need master's degrees in educational administra-tion plus two years of teaching experience. Although not all principals have master's degrees, most have taken courses in school administration and have worked as assistant principals for several years before advancing. Some urban school principals are required to have doctorates. School district superinten-dents are often required to have completed graduate study in educational ad-ministration, preferably at the doctoral level. Superintendents and principals must meet the specific certification requirements that are set by the states in which they are employed.

Getting the Job

Openings for school principals and superintendents are announced by local school boards and listed by state departments of education and public and pri-vate placement bureaus. Professional journals and associations may also carry listings. Those interested in working for state or federal government should take the appropriate civil service examinations. Civil service workers generally begin in middle-management positions and advance to higher government posts through experience, length of service, and additional examinations.

Advancement Possibilities and Employment Outlook

Principals may become superintendents. Superintendents may go on to more challenging jobs in larger districts or in state or federal government. The top posts in government are generally filled by appointment, although outstanding civil service workers may be chosen. Administrators on all levels may direct ex-perimental programs for agencies and private companies that create educa-tional materials.

Employment in this field is expected to grow as fast as the average for all occupations through 2014. New hires will be needed when experienced administrators retire or leave the field. Competition is likely to be stiff.

Working Conditions

School administrators generally work long hours. Principals are often expected to appear at after-school functions such as concerts or sporting events. Superintendents spend extra time attending meetings and traveling. All administrators are on call in case of emergencies. Their jobs carry pressure as well as prestige, for they are often called on to make difficult, unpopular decisions.

Earnings and Benefits

Salaries vary with education, experience, location, and size of the school or district. In 2004 the median annual salary of all elementary and secondary school administrators was $68,340 per year. Principals of public high schools averaged $82,225 per year, while elementary school principals averaged $74,060 per year. The average salary for superintendents was $77,420 per year.

School administrators can expect paid holidays and vacations of two to five weeks per year. They also receive health insurance and retirement plans.

Where to Go for More Information

American Association of School
   Administrators
801 N. Quincy St., Ste. 700
Arlington, VA 22203
(703) 528-0700
http://www.aasa.org

National Education Association
1201 Sixteenth St. NW
Washington, DC 20036
(202) 833-4000
http://www.nea.org

School Counselor

Education and Training
College plus training

Salary
Median—$45,570 per year

Employment Outlook
Very good

Definition and Nature of the Work

School counselors help students make decisions that affect their personal and academic development. Sometimes they provide drug- and alcohol-abuse rehabilitation or conflict-resolution sessions.

Often called guidance counselors, they can be found in both public and private schools, working with classroom teachers, school psychologists, school nurses, parents, and community groups. They meet with students individually or in group sessions.

Counselors who work in junior and senior high schools help students choose courses that will affect their later careers. Those who plan to learn trades, for instance, may need technical classes. If students wish to attend college, counselors advise them on both their academic and extracurricular activities. They also provide students with scholarship information, training manuals, and college catalogs.

Counselors in elementary schools work mainly with students who disrupt classrooms or have physical handicaps. They also counsel students who get into trouble in the community.

Education and Training Requirements

All states require school counselors to be certified, but certification standards vary widely and change frequently. Some states also require teaching certification.

Both public and private schools employ counselors to help students make personal and academic decisions and to work with students who are experiencing family and personal problems. *(AP Images.)*

Bachelor's degrees in psychology, education, or the liberal arts are required. Many counselors participate in college-level programs in education or psychology, studying group dynamics, human growth and development, testing, counseling, and statistics.

Getting the Job

Job seekers can apply directly to superintendents of school districts. College placement offices, professional associations and journals, private employment agencies, newspaper classified ads, and job banks on the Internet may offer employment leads. In some areas counselors are assigned to schools when they are certified.

Advancement Possibilities and Employment Outlook

School counselors are at the top of their profession. Some specialize in certain areas of guidance, such as vocational counseling. Others become supervisors or school administrators.

Employment of school counselors is expected to grow faster than the average for all jobs through 2014 because of increasing school enrollments and legislation requiring counselors in elementary schools. The increase in crisis-prevention counseling may also spur employment. However, jobs may be limited in some areas because of funding.

Working Conditions

Full-time school counselors work longer hours than teachers because they often meet with students and parents before and after school. Some counselors work part time or combine counseling with teaching duties. Generally, counselors have their own offices so they can conduct their interviews in private. Counselors must be able to relate well to all kinds of people. Patience, resourcefulness, and stability are important qualities for the job.

Earnings and Benefits

In 2004 the median salary for school counselors was $45,570 per year, with experienced counselors earning more than $72,390 per year. The median salary for elementary and secondary school counselors was $51,160 per year. Benefits include paid holidays and vacations, sick leave, health insurance, and retirement plans.

School Media Specialist

Education and Training
Advanced degree

Salary
Median—$45,900 per year

Employment Outlook
Fair

Definition and Nature of the Work

School media specialists advise teachers and administrators on the use of nonprint media, such as movies, audiotapes, filmstrips, and slide presentations. They are experts on the tools and techniques of media production and presentation. Sometimes, they develop new audiovisual materials for their schools or for publishing firms.

Those who work in individual schools help teachers plan programs for their classes. For example, they may consult with history teachers about the maps, tapes, and filmstrips available for U.S. history projects. They may also conduct workshops on the use of media in the classroom, explaining what equipment they have purchased and what is available from state and district offices. Many media specialists work in school libraries.

At the district level, they are administrators who develop policies about the use of media. They often help school superintendents make presentations of those policies to school boards. In many cases, they are in charge of their districts' school libraries as well.

Education and Training Requirements

Requirements for school media specialists vary widely from state to state and change frequently. Usually, they need master's degrees in educational media or in another field of education plus course work in media. In most states, certification and teaching experience are required.

Getting the Job

Job seekers can apply directly to school boards or districts. School placement offices, private employment agencies, professional associations and journals, newspaper classified ads, and job banks on the Internet may offer employment listings. In some areas, media specialists are assigned to posts when they are certified.

Advancement Possibilities and Employment Outlook

Specialists can advance from the school level to the district level or become heads of media for several school districts or state departments of education. Those with doctorates may become college teachers.

Little growth is anticipated in the employment of school media specialists through 2014. Opportunities in this relatively small field depend largely on retirement of experienced workers and public funding for education.

Working Conditions

Many specialists who work at schools combine media work with teaching, so their schedules follow those of other teachers. Sometimes their work involves handling heavy projection equipment. Specialists at district and state levels work less often in the actual production of programs. However, their hours may be longer because of evening meetings and conferences.

Earnings and Benefits

Salaries vary by state; they are usually similar to teachers' salaries. In 2004 the median salary for all school media specialists was $45,900 per year. District media supervisors earned slightly higher wages.

Benefits generally include paid holidays and vacations, health insurance, and pension plans. Media specialists often receive tenure during their years as full-time teachers, which protects them from being fired without exceptional cause.

Where to Go for More Information

American Association of School Librarians
50 E. Huron St.
Chicago, IL 60611
(800) 545-2433
http://www.ala.org/ala/aasl

Association for Educational
    Communications and Technology
1800 N. Stonelake Dr., Ste. 2
Bloomington, IN 47404-1517
(877) 677-2328
http://www.aect.org

National Education Association
1201 Sixteenth St. NW
Washington, DC 20036
(202) 833-4000
http://www.nea.org

Social Worker

Education and Training
Advanced degree

Salary
Median—$34,820 per year

Employment Outlook
Excellent

Definition and Nature of the Work

Social workers offer guidance and counseling to people in crisis. Their clients range from the unemployed to children who need foster homes to elderly people who have no one to care for them. They help their clients obtain government funds, education, or treatment. Often they begin legal action in cases of child abuse.

A variety of organizations hire social workers: public welfare agencies, private social service agencies, schools, hospitals, clinics, and recreation and rehabilitation centers. Many work with juvenile courts. A small number are employed as teachers or researchers.

Social workers have three techniques for solving problems. Casework requires conferences with individuals and families. They may counsel young people whose parents have died or families who have lost all their possessions in floods or other disasters. Group work brings together people who have problems in common, such as unwed mothers. Social workers help them solve those problems through discussions and well-planned activities. Community organization work usually has specific goals—finding jobs for idle high school students, for example.

Psychiatric social workers, who may work for the same agencies as other social workers, put more emphasis on psychological problems. They are usually supervised by psychiatrists or psychologists.

Education and Training Requirements

For most positions, master's degrees in social work are required, although a limited number of jobs are available for those with bachelor's degrees. Social workers who teach or do research generally hold doctorates.

Social workers usually major in sociology, psychology, or another social science and take courses in related fields, such as economics, child studies, education, and political science. Graduate study often covers human growth and development, social welfare policies, and methods of social work. Most graduate schools offer work-study programs that give students experience in agencies, hospitals, or schools.

Requirements for licensing, certification, or registration vary from state to state. Beginning social workers generally learn from experienced workers for the first few months on the job. After two years of supervised work, they may be eligible for membership in the Academy of Certified Social Workers, which is administered by the National Association of Social Workers. Membership is not required, but it is prestigious. Social workers with master's degrees may be eligible for such credentials as the Academy of Certified Social Workers (ACSW), Qualified Clinical Social Worker (QCSW), or Diplomate in Clinical Social Work (DCSW). Some health insurance providers require social workers in private practice to have these credentials.

Psychiatric social workers must have master's degrees in psychiatric social work. A good part of their graduate training is fieldwork supervised by clinical psychologists.

Getting the Job

Job seekers can apply directly to social service agencies, schools, and hospitals. School placement offices, private employment agencies, professional associations and journals, newspaper classified ads, and job banks on the Internet may offer employment listings. Social workers who wish to work for government agencies must take civil service examinations. Many students make job contacts during fieldwork for college courses.

Advancement Possibilities and Employment Outlook

Experienced social workers who have master's degrees may become senior case-workers, case supervisors, or chief social workers. They may also be promoted to administrative positions. Those holding doctorates may become university professors or researchers.

Employment of social workers is expected to grow much faster than the average for all jobs through 2014. While new positions depend on funding, openings often occur because experienced workers retire or leave the field. Competition for jobs may be stiff in major metropolitan areas.

Working Conditions

Cities, suburbs, and rural areas all need social workers in schools, hospitals, offices, agencies, jails, and courts. While social work is generally challenging and fulfilling, at times it can be quite frustrating and emotionally draining. Many people are afraid to share their problems, and some cases may be difficult to handle. Social workers must be mature, sensitive people who can deal with disappointment, frustration, and stress.

Social workers usually work thirty-five to forty hours per week, but overtime may be required to meet with clients, attend community meetings, and handle emergencies. They generally receive compensatory time off for extra hours worked.

Earnings and Benefits

Salaries vary, depending on education, experience, and location. In 2004 the median salary of all social workers was $34,820 per year. The most experienced workers earned more than $57,860 per year. Benefits generally include paid holidays and vacations, health insurance, and retirement plans.

Where to Go for More Information

American Federation of State, County, and
  Municipal Employees
1625 L St. NW
Washington, DC 20036
(202) 429-1000
http://www.afscme.org

National Association of Social Workers
750 First St. NE, Ste. 700
Washington, DC 20002-4241
(202) 408-8600
http://www.socialworkers.org

School Social Worker Association of
  America
PO Box 2072
Northlake, IL 60164
(847) 289-4642
http://www.sswaa.org

Teacher, College

Definition and Nature of the Work

Teachers at colleges and universities pass their knowledge and expertise on to the next generation of bankers, painters, chemists, and even teachers. They help their students to think critically as well as imaginatively; provide practical training; and shape their students' goals, careers, and lives. As experts in their subject fields, they also set standards for research—usually reflected in the articles and books they write—and expand the limits of scholarship and its importance in society.

Teachers work at two-year junior and community colleges, four-year colleges and universities, and professional schools. Some teach in evening and continuing-education programs. Most work in one department, such as history or music, and specialize in particular disciplines, such as U.S. history or vocal perfor-

Education and Training
Advanced degree

Salary
Average—$51,800 per year

Employment Outlook
Very good

Most college professors work in one department and may specialize in one phase of their discipline. They may also conduct research and write articles and books. (© A. Huber/U. Starke/zefa/Corbis.)

mance. They usually teach from two to four courses each semester, combining lecture and discussion. Even more of their time is spent reading student papers, correcting examinations, and advising students. Some teachers have administrative duties; for example, at a small college a physics teacher might also be the dean of students. Some college teachers work part time as consultants to educational organizations, government agencies, and corporations.

The profession has distinct ranks. Instructors are at the lowest level, with little job security and hardly any voice in what is taught and how their schools operate. Instructors almost always teach undergraduates. Assistant professors and associate professors are more experienced and may be active in their schools' administrative affairs and set the requirements for their own courses. They teach undergraduates and, at some schools, graduate students. Full professors may serve as department heads as well as teach.

Education and Training Requirements

College and university teachers must have master's degrees or doctorates. Many four-year colleges and universities expect their teachers to complete their doctorates if they wish to be promoted or, in some cases, keep their jobs.

Master's degrees generally require one to three years of study beyond bachelor's degrees, while doctorates require two to six years of study beyond master's degrees. Candidates for master's degrees are usually required to write papers and take written and oral examinations. Besides additional course work, doctoral students must take oral examinations and write book-length papers called dissertations, which are usually based on original research.

Many graduate students work as teaching assistants for at least one year. Some teach their own classes. Others lead small discussion groups or conduct laboratory classes that complement professors' lectures. Teaching assistantships provide graduate students with financial aid and college-teaching experience.

Getting the Job

Professors often help their students find jobs: because they know teachers at other colleges, they may learn about openings before they are publicly announced. Professional journals, such as *The Chronicle of Higher Education*, a weekly newspaper, list many positions. College placement offices, professional organizations, private employment agencies, newspaper classified ads, and job banks on the Internet may also provide employment leads.

Advancement Possibilities and Employment Outlook

About 1.6 million full- or part-time college teachers are employed in the United States. Depending on funding and qualifications, many of them advance at regular intervals: instructors become assistant professors, associate professors, and then full professors after many years of experience. The requirements for promotion vary from school to school; some colleges look for excellence in teaching, while others also require teachers to write extensively for publication. Teachers usually need doctorates to become associate professors.

A certain number of experienced and well-qualified teachers are given tenure, which means they cannot be dismissed without exceptional cause. Professors can also advance by accepting positions at more prestigious colleges or by becoming department heads or administrators.

Employment of college and university faculty is expected to grow faster than the average for all jobs through 2014 as student enrollments increase. However, some colleges and universities are facing financial difficulties, so many of the new hires may have part-time positions. Job growth may vary by discipline as well, because funding has forced schools to cut back or eliminate some academic programs and departments and increase class sizes. Teaching prospects are best in computer science, engineering, health science, nursing, and business. Openings also occur when experienced teachers are promoted, retire, or leave the field.

Working Conditions

Most teachers spend from twelve to sixteen hours in class each week, with their schedules changing each semester. Office hours, faculty meetings, advising, and class preparation account for thirty to forty additional hours per week. Teachers enjoy a certain degree of freedom because they can arrange their own schedules around their class times. The academic year generally runs from September through May, so teachers may use the summer months for research or other jobs.

At some colleges teachers are under considerable pressure to publish articles and books, so research may take up much of their time. Teachers with established reputations may work as visiting professors at other colleges. Many college teachers belong to labor unions.

Earnings and Benefits

In the 2004–05 school year the average salary for all college teachers was $51,800 per year. However, salaries varied widely by rank: instructors, for instance, averaged $39,899 per year, while assistant professors made $54,571 per year and full professors earned $91,548 per year. Salaries also varied by institution and geographic area. Some teachers increased their incomes considerably by writing for publication, consulting, or other employment.

Benefits also vary. Most professors receive health insurance and pension plans. Some colleges offer tenured teachers sabbatical leave. Some colleges provide housing, travel allowances, and tuition waivers for dependents.

Where to Go for More Information

American Association of Community
  Colleges
1 Dupont Circle NW
Washington, DC 20036
(202) 728-0200
http://www.aacc.nche.edu

American Association of University
  Professors
1012 Fourteenth St. NW, Ste. 500
Washington, DC 20005
(202) 737-5900
http://www.aaup.org

American Council on Education
1 Dupont Circle NW
Washington, DC 20036-1193
(202) 939-9300
http://www.acenet.edu

Teacher, Preschool, Kindergarten, and Elementary

Definition and Nature of the Work

Preschool, kindergarten, and elementary teachers instruct children from the nursery-school level through the sixth grade. They introduce children to learning and to the basic skills necessary for later education and for life.

Preschool teachers work with children who are two to four years old. They concentrate on social skills, such as sharing and communicating with others, and practical skills, such as tying their own shoes. They keep their pupils occupied with music, games, and storytelling.

Kindergarten teachers have many of the same goals. They help five-year-olds learn to play and communicate with others and introduce them to subjects they will pursue in later grades. Students play counting games to learn arithmetic and begin to read the letters on building blocks.

Teachers at the preschool and kindergarten levels have little difficulty keeping their students occupied. Their aim is to provide constructive outlets for their students' curiosity. Because young children generally attend school for only a few hours each day, teachers may have two separate classes—one in the morning and another in the afternoon.

Elementary school teachers concentrate on the basic skills their pupils will need throughout their school years: reading, writing, arithmetic, and simple concepts in science. Some work with the same group of students for the entire school day; others take a team approach, specializing in one subject, such as science or arithmetic, which they teach to several groups of students.

In some elementary schools, specialists work with small groups of students who need special attention. Bilingual teachers, for instance, concentrate on improving their students' English-language skills. They may also teach English as a second language when students have very limited exposure to it. Special education teachers work with diverse groups of students who have physical or mental handicaps. Some teachers give lessons to homebound students who are unable to attend school regularly because of health problems. They often go to students' homes to teach.

Teachers on the preschool, kindergarten, and elementary levels may attend meetings of the school board and the parent-teacher association. They also meet regularly with parents to tell them about their children's progress and to determine how students' home environments affect their development in school.

Many public elementary schools employ teachers who specialize in one subject, such as art, music, or computers. These teachers must be certified in the state in which they teach. (© Terry Wild Studio. Reproduced by permission.)

Education and Training Requirements

Teachers who work in public schools must be licensed or certified in the state in which they teach. Certification requirements vary, but usually include minimum educational standards and satisfactory performance on written examinations. In some states teachers at private and parochial schools must also be certified.

Kindergarten and elementary school teachers need bachelor's degrees, including course work in education and experience as student teachers. Some school districts require master's degrees. Preschool teachers generally need at least bachelor's degrees, plus experience in early childhood education. Teachers who work in specialized areas of education generally need the most training.

Getting the Job

Job seekers can apply directly to the superintendents of school districts. College placement offices and teachers' associations may help new graduates find positions. In some school districts, teachers are assigned to schools when they pass their certification examinations. Professional journals, newspaper classified ads, and job banks on the Internet often list openings for teachers.

Advancement Possibilities and Employment Outlook

As teachers become more experienced, they may find advancement in the form of higher pay. Some become specialists—those who work with bilingual students, for example—or advance to administrative positions such as teacher supervisors and principals. Preschool teachers may go on to teach kindergarten and elementary classes if they complete the necessary education.

Overall employment of kindergarten and elementary teachers is expected to grow as fast as the average for all jobs through 2014. While kindergarten and elementary enrollments may decline, many jobs should open when older teachers retire. Job opportunities for preschool teachers are expected to grow faster than the average as a result of high turnover in the field and the growing availability of government-funded programs.

Employment prospects vary by geographic area and specialty as well. Many inner cities, where schools are plagued by crime and overcrowding, have trouble attracting enough teachers. Efforts to recruit minority teachers may increase with the growing demand for bilingual teachers.

Working Conditions

Working conditions vary from school to school. The job can be tiring; the pace of activity is especially high in the early grades. Unruly students can make teaching difficult. However, teachers can find satisfaction by watching their students make progress and knowing that they are shaping young lives.

Although preparation periods are built into the workday, teachers often work on lesson plans and grade papers after school hours. Teachers sometimes attend late-day meetings, and parent-teacher conferences are usually scheduled in the evening.

Because the school year generally runs from September to June, teachers may have to teach summer school or find other jobs. Some spend their summers taking courses to improve their skills. Many teachers belong to labor unions.

Earnings and Benefits

Salaries vary widely, depending on location and education. In 2004 the median salary of preschool teachers was $20,980 per year, while the median earnings of kindergarten and elementary teachers ranged from $41,400 to $45,920. The most experienced teachers earned more than $71,370 per year. Private school teachers generally earn less than public school teachers.

Where to Go for More Information

American Federation of Teachers
555 New Jersey Ave. NW
Washington, DC 20001
(202) 879-4400
http://www.aft.org

National Association for the Education of
   Young Children
1313 L St. NW
Washington, DC 20005
(800) 424-2460
http://www.naeyc.org

National Education Association
1201 Sixteenth St. NW
Washington, DC 20036
(202) 833-4000
http://www.nea.org

Benefits vary, but elementary school teachers can usually expect paid holidays and vacations, health insurance, and pension plans. Benefits for most preschool teachers, however, are minimal.

Teacher, Secondary School

Education and Training
College plus training

Salary
Median—$41,400 to $45,970 per year

Employment Outlook
Good

Definition and Nature of the Work

Secondary school teachers instruct students in junior and senior high schools. They conduct classes in academic subjects, such as English and mathematics, or skills, such as mechanical drawing and woodworking. They start with the basics and add complexity to spur students' imaginations and intellects and to prepare them for advanced education and jobs as adults.

Teachers also help their colleagues plan courses that use new methods and materials and organize extracurricular activities such as sports and social groups. They work as teams that include school administrators, school counselors, and school psychologists. Their work goes beyond the classroom to include parents, parent groups, and community and governmental agencies.

Junior high school teachers instruct students in the seventh to ninth grades, while high school teachers instruct the tenth to twelfth grades. In some school districts, junior high schools have been replaced by middle or intermediate schools, which start with the fifth grade.

On most days teachers have from four to seven classes in their fields of specialization. English, mathematics, science, and history are taught in all schools and are usually taken by all students. Some teachers specialize in foreign languages, computer sciences, music, and art, which many students take as electives. Physical education teachers concentrate on improving students' strength and motor skills. They may administer physical fitness and posture tests, set up special exercise programs, and coach softball, basketball, and other sports. Some secondary school teachers work with students who have physical or mental handicaps or students who need bilingual education. Others give lessons to homebound students who are unable to attend school regularly because of health problems.

Teachers may be assigned to homeroom classes, where they take attendance and handle other school business, and study halls, where they must maintain an orderly, quiet atmosphere for study.

Education and Training Requirements

Teachers who work in public secondary schools must be certified. Requirements vary from state to state and change frequently, but usually include examinations, bachelor's degrees, student-teaching experience, and course work in education. Many states now require teachers to have or be working toward master's degrees at the time of certification. In some states private and parochial school teachers also must be certified.

Getting the Job

Job seekers can apply directly to principals of schools or superintendents of school districts. College placement offices and professional associations may help new graduates find positions. Private employment agencies, professional

Secondary school teachers generally conduct classes only in their field of interest. Academic subjects taught in secondary schools include science, English, mathematics, and history. (© Terry Wild Studio. Reproduced by permission.)

journals, newspaper classified ads, and job banks on the Internet may list openings. In some areas teachers are assigned to schools when they are certified.

Advancement Possibilities and Employment Outlook

Teachers may become heads of their departments. With experience and additional education, they may take on administrative duties as assistant principals, principals, and superintendents. Most of these positions require at least master's degrees; some require doctorates.

About 1.1 million secondary school teachers are employed in the United States. Employment is expected to grow as fast as the average for all jobs through 2014. Teachers in the natural and physical sciences, mathematics, special education, and computer science are likely to find more job opportunities than teachers in other fields.

Working Conditions

Working conditions vary by subject taught. While most teachers work with ten to thirty students per class, music teachers may work with one student at a time. Teaching is physically strenuous; most teachers stand most of the day and may suffer from voice strain. While preparation time is built into the school day, teachers often plan lessons and correct papers after school hours. Some attend school meetings or supervise extracurricular activities, such as drama productions or sports events, in the evening. Secondary school teachers usually do not work during the summer months; many use that time to get additional education or earn extra income. Most secondary school teachers belong to labor unions.

Earnings and Benefits

Teachers' salaries vary with education, length of service, and location of the school. In 2004 the median salary for secondary school teachers ranged from

$41,400 to $45,970 per year. Teachers with master's degrees or doctorates earn much more than those who have only bachelor's degrees. In some schools, teachers receive extra pay for coaching sports or supervising other extracurricular activities. Private school teachers generally earn less than public school teachers. Teachers receive paid vacations and holidays, as well as health insurance and retirement plans.

Urban and Regional Planner

Education and Training
Advanced degree

Salary
Median—$53,450 per year

Employment Outlook
Very good

Definition and Nature of the Work

Urban and regional planners determine the best uses of land and resources for homes, businesses, and recreation. They devise ways to renovate slums, expand cities, modernize transportation systems, and distribute public facilities such as schools and parks. They also find ways to attract industries to communities to create jobs. Urban planners design new communities and develop programs to revitalize and expand existing cities. Regional planners work on a much larger scale, studying the problems of states, multistate regions, and sometimes entire countries.

Planning generally begins with requests from city or state officials to develop new communities or renovate areas that are run down. Planners gather information about the economic and social climate, projected population growth or decline, and plans for industrial development. To get a cross section of public opinion, they meet with community groups, government agencies, and labor and business organizations. Future needs get as much attention as current problems. An expected increase in an area's population, for instance, will create a need for more electrical power. Planners determine how the necessary power can be generated without creating pollution or otherwise injuring the area.

Once the data are collected and studied, planners draw up proposals and submit them to planning commissions or other government officials. If the plans get approved, construction or renovation begins. Planners usually supervise the work through to completion. Projects may take many years to complete.

Most planners work for city, county, state, federal, or regional agencies. Some work for large construction companies and architectural firms. Others work as consultants or hold teaching or research positions. Planners also work for international organizations that plan projects in developing nations.

Education and Training Requirements

Most entry-level jobs in federal, state, and local government agencies require master's degrees in urban or regional planning. Some employers may consider applicants who studied related subjects, such as urban design and landscape ar-

Urban planners design new communities and develop programs for improving cities. Regional planners do the same type of work on a much larger scale for states, regions, or even entire countries. (© Martha Tabor/Working Images Photographs. Reproduced by permission.)

chitecture, or have equivalent work experience. Courses in architecture, public administration, landscape architecture, civil engineering, political science, economics, and geography offer good preparation.

With bachelor's degrees in architecture or engineering, students can usually earn master's degrees in one year. Many programs take two to three years to complete. Graduate students usually do part-time fieldwork in an office or agency, which may lead to job contacts for the future.

Getting the Job

Job seekers can apply directly to city, state, or federal agencies, which employ most urban and regional planners. They can also apply directly to private and international organizations and corporations. Applicants for government jobs must pass civil service tests and meet the necessary educational and experience requirements. School placement offices, state employment services, private employment agencies, professional associations and journals, newspaper classified ads, and job banks on the Internet are all sources of employment leads.

Advancement Possibilities and Employment Outlook

Recent graduates expand their skills on the job. Generally, they begin by working on small projects under the supervision of experienced workers. After several years of work, they can advance to project-director positions. Some choose to take on more challenging projects that offer them greater responsibility.

The job outlook for urban and regional planners is very good, with employment expected to grow faster than the average for all jobs through 2014. Because of budget constraints, state and local governments want to regulate housing, land use, and transportation as effectively and efficiently as possible. They have learned to hire the best planners to help them make decisions. Openings in private industry may grow more rapidly than those in government because they have different budgetary considerations. Opportunities will be best in more affluent, rapidly growing communities.

Working Conditions

Urban and regional planning can be highly rewarding work. Planners find satisfaction not only in knowing that they help others but also in seeing projects through from conception to physical reality. There are, however, some disadvantages. Lack of funds or disapproval from government officials can be discouraging. Planners must be able to handle detail as well as have the tenacity to advocate their ideas until problems are solved.

Planners work both indoors and outdoors. They generally work thirty-five to forty hours a week, although those in positions of greater responsibility may work many more hours. Consulting planners set their own hours.

Earnings and Benefits

Salaries vary widely with education, experience, and location. In 2004 the median salary of urban and regional planners was $53,450 per year. Consultants are paid by the hour according to their experience and reputation. Benefits generally include paid holidays and vacations, health insurance, and pension plans. Consultants have to arrange their own benefits.

Where to Go for More Information

American Planning Association
122 S. Michigan Ave., Ste. 1600
Chicago, IL 60603-6107
(312) 431-9100
http://www.planning.org

U.S. Department of Housing and Urban
 Development
451 Seventh St. SW
Washington, DC 20410
(202) 708-1112
http://www.hud.gov

Vocational Counselor

Education and Training	College
Salary	Median—$45,570 per year
Employment Outlook	Very good

Definition and Nature of the Work

Vocational counselors, also called employment counselors, help their clients understand their capabilities and develop career goals. Counselors can then provide the link between people looking for work and employers. To do this, counselors must have an awareness of their clients' potential and also know what skills are in demand in the job market. Unlike agents who work for profit-making employment agencies, vocational counselors work for organizations that provide their services free of charge.

Counselors work in state employment offices, veterans' programs, and private and government-sponsored social service agencies. Those who work with people who have mental or physical disabilities are called rehabilitation counselors. In colleges and universities they may be called college placement counselors.

Counselors first interview their clients to learn about their personalities, education, work experience, skills, and interests. Sometimes they administer achievement, aptitude, and occupational preference tests. In state employment offices and some other agencies, an employment interviewer collects this information for the counselor, who then advises the clients.

Some clients are fully qualified for employment, and counselors simply contact prospective employers. This is often the case in college placement offices. Clients who seek help from social service organizations, on the other hand, usually have had some difficulty in finding or holding jobs. They may have handicaps or addictions; be considered too old to start certain jobs; or lack sufficient training. Some clients may have faced prejudice because of race or gender. Those who have been out of work for a long time may be too discouraged to do well at employment interviews. Counselors may place clients in training programs to develop marketable skills or refer them to other organizations for specific assistance, such as physical rehabilitation. Counselors often coach their clients so they perform well at interviews.

Counselors in junior and senior high schools help students choose careers and get the education and training they need for the jobs they want. They may also help students find part-time or summer jobs or place them in full-time positions after graduation.

Education and Training Requirements

Bachelor's degrees are the minimum requirement for vocational counselors, although many employers require master's degrees in vocational counseling and guidance, social work, sociology, or related fields. Many agencies have at least one staff member with a doctorate in a counseling-related field. A background in interviewing and testing procedures is useful, as is experience in personnel and administrative work.

Getting the Job

Job seekers can apply directly to social service agencies. School placement offices, professional organizations and journals, state employment agencies, newspaper classified ads, and job banks on the Internet are all sources of employment information. Applicants for government jobs must take civil service examinations.

Advancement Possibilities and Employment Outlook

Vocational counselors may take on supervisory or administrative jobs in their agencies or schools. Some become consultants to government and industry, while others teach counseling in colleges and universities. Counselors may need doctorates to teach in colleges or to reach the highest administrative jobs.

The outlook for vocational counselors is very good. Employment is expected to grow faster than the average for all jobs through 2014, largely because of increasing school enrollments and the number of people who must shift careers because of changes in corporate employment. Opportunities may be best in private job-training services; counselors working for the government can be affected by changes in funding.

Working Conditions

Counselors must be able to communicate clearly and listen carefully. They usually work in small offices where they can talk with clients in private. Sometimes they travel to talk with employers or to visit training centers. Because they must be aware of changes in employment practices and training programs, they may spend many hours reading papers and bulletins. Vocational counselors generally work thirty-five to forty hours a week, including evening and weekend work.

Where to Go for More Information

American Counseling Association
5999 Stevenson Ave.
Alexandria, VA 22304-3300
(800) 347-6647
http://www.counseling.org

American Federation of State, County, and
   Municipal Employees
1625 L St. NW
Washington, DC 20036
(202) 429-1000
http://www.afscme.org

Earnings and Benefits

Salaries vary with experience, education, and location. In 2004 the median salary for vocational counselors was $45,570 per year. The top ten percent of counselors earned more than $72,390 per year. Self-employed counselors and counselors working for private firms usually have the highest earnings. Benefits generally include paid holidays and vacations, health insurance, and pension plans.

Books

Exploring the Working World

American Salaries and Wages Survey, 8th ed., Helen S. Fisher. Farmington Hills, MI: Thomson Gale, 2005.

America's Fastest Growing Jobs: Detailed Information on the 140 Fastest Growing Jobs in Our Economy, 8th ed., Michael Farr. Indianapolis, IN: JIST Publishing, 2004.

America's Top 101 Jobs for College Graduates, 6th ed., Michael Farr. Indianapolis, IN: JIST Publishing, 2005.

America's Top 101 Jobs for People without a Four-Year Degree, 7th ed., Michael Farr. Indianapolis, IN: JIST Publishing, 2004.

America's Top 300 Jobs, 9th ed., U.S. Department of Labor. Indianapolis, IN: JIST Publishing, 2004.

Best Career and Education Web Sites: A Quick Guide to Online Job Search, 4th ed., Rachel Singer Gordon and Anne Wolfinger. Indianapolis, IN: JIST Publishing, 2004.

Best Entry-Level Jobs, Ron Lieber and Tom Meltzer. New York: Princeton Review, 2006.

Best Jobs for the 21st Century, 4th ed., Michael Farr and Laurence Shatkin. Indianapolis, IN: JIST Publishing, 2006.

Big Book of Jobs, 2003–2004, U.S. Department of Labor. New York: McGraw-Hill, 2003.

Career Discovery Encyclopedia, 5th ed., 8 vols. Chicago: Ferguson, 2003.

Enhanced Occupational Outlook Handbook, 5th ed., Indianapolis, IN: JIST Publishing, 2005.

Job Hunter's Sourcebook: A Thomson Gale Career Information Guide. Farmington Hills, MI: Thomson Gale, biennial.

Jobs Rated Almanac, 6th ed., Les Krantz. Fort Lee, NJ: Barricade, 2002.

The National JobBank, 2006. Avon, MA: Adams Media, 2006.

Occupational Outlook Handbook series. Washington, DC: United States Government Printing Office, biennial. Briefs, separately published.

Occupational Outlook Quarterly. Washington, DC: United States Government Printing Office. Quarterly publication.

Professional Careers Sourcebook, 7th ed. Farmington Hills, MI: Thomson Gale, 2002.

200 Best Jobs for College Graduates, 3rd ed., Michael Farr and Laurence Shatkin. Indianapolis, IN: JIST Publishing, 2006.

Recommended

Best Jobs for the 21st Century, 4th ed., Michael Farr and Laurence Shatkin. Indianapolis, IN: JIST Publishing, 2006. Lists five hundred jobs and categorizes them into sixty-five "Best Jobs for..." lists. Organizes jobs by category, education required, best growth potential.

Jobs Rated Almanac, 6th ed., Les Krantz. Fort Lee, NJ: Barricade, 2002. Rates 250 jobs and sorts into "best for" and "worst for" rankings. Factors include salary, benefits, and stress level.

300 Best Jobs without a Four-Year Degree, 2nd ed., Michael Farr and Laurence Shatkin. Indianapolis, IN: JIST Publishing, 2006.

VGM's Career Encyclopedia, 5th ed., New York: McGraw-Hill, 2002.

Vocational Careers Sourcebook, 5th ed., Farmington Hills, MI: Thomson Gale, 2002.

Education and Training Opportunities

Acing the College Application: How to Maximize Your Chances for Admission to the College of Your Choice, Michele Hernandez. New York: Ballantine, 2002.

Admission Matters: What Students and Parents Need to Know about Getting Into College, Sally P. Springer and Marion R. Franck. San Francisco: Jossey-Bass, 2005.

Barron's Guide to Graduate Business Schools, Eugene Miller and Neuman F. Pollack. Hauppauge, NY: Barron's Educational Series, revised regularly.

Barron's Guide to Law Schools. Hauppauge, NY: Barron's Educational Series, revised regularly.

Barron's Guide to Medical and Dental Schools, Sol Wischnitzer and Edith Wischnitzer. Hauppauge, NY: Barron's Educational Series, revised regularly.

Barron's Profiles of American Colleges. Hauppauge, NY: Barron's Educational Series, annual.

Bear's Guide to College Degrees by Mail and Internet, 10th ed., John Bear. Berkeley, CA: Ten Speed Press, 2005.

Best 109 Internships, 9th ed., Mark Oldman and Samer Hamadah. New York: Princeton Review, 2003.

The Best 361 Colleges. New York: Princeton Review, annual.

Chronicle Vocational School Manual. Moravia, NY: Chronicle Guidance Publications, annual.

The College Application Essay, Sarah Myers McGinty. New York: The College Board, 2004.

The College Board Book of Majors, 2nd ed. New York: The College Board, 2006.

The College Board Scholarship Handbook. New York: The College Board, annual.

The College Cost and Financial Aid Handbook. New York: The College Board, annual.

College Financial Aid: How to Get Your Fair Share, 6th ed., Peter V. Laurenzo. Albany, NY: Hudson Financial Press, 2002.

The College Handbook. New York: The College Board, annual.

College Majors Handbook with Real Career Paths and Payoffs, 2nd ed., Neeta P. Fogg. Indianapolis, IN: JIST Publishing, 2004.

College Planning for Gifted Students, 3rd ed., Sandra L. Berger. Waco, TX: Prufrock Press, 2006.

College Success Guide: Top 12 Secrets for Student Success, Karine Blackett and Patricia Weiss. Indianapolis, IN: JIST Publishing, 2005.

Complete Book of Colleges. New York: Princeton Review, annual.

Recommended

Acing the College Application: How to Maximize Your Chances for Admission to the College of Your Choice, Michele Hernandez. New York: Ballantine, 2002. Written by former Dartmouth College admissions officer. Frank but reassuring advice on application, essay, and personal interview.

The Insider's Guide to Colleges. New York: St. Martin's Griffin, annual. Surveys students at 320 U.S. and Canadian schools on dorm life, class size, and other campus-related topics.

Vault Guide to Top Internships, Samer Hamadah. New York: Vault, 2005. Provides information on internships offered by 700-plus companies, including Fortune 500 corporations. Nonprofit and government programs also listed.

Fiske Guide to Colleges, Edmund Fiske. Naperville, IL: Sourcebooks, annual.

The Gourman Report: A Rating of Undergraduate Programs in American and International Universities, Jack Gourman. Los Angeles: National Educational Standards, revised regularly.

Guide to College Majors. New York: Princeton Review, 2006.

Guide to the Most Competitive Colleges. Hauppauge, NY: Barron's Educational Series, revised regularly.

How to Choose a College Major, Linda Landis Andrews. New York: McGraw-Hill, 2006.

How to Write Your College Application Essay, Kenneth Nourse. New York: McGraw-Hill, 2001.

The Insider's Guide to Colleges. New York: St. Martin's Griffin, annual.

The Internship Bible, 10th ed. New York: Princeton Review, 2005.

The National Guide to Educational Credit for Training Programs. Washington, DC: American Council on Education, revised regularly.

100 Successful College Application Essays, 2nd ed. New York: New American Library, 2002.

Peterson's Best College Admission Essays, 3rd ed. Princeton, NJ: Thomson Peterson's, 2004.

Peterson's College Money Handbook. Princeton, NJ: Thomson Peterson's, annual.

Peterson's College and University Almanac. Princeton, NJ: Thomson Peterson's, annual.

Peterson's Competitive Colleges. Princeton, NJ: Thomson Peterson's, annual.

Peterson's Financial Aid Answer Book. Princeton, NJ: Thomson Peterson's, annual.

Peterson's Guide to Four-Year Colleges. Princeton, NJ: Thomson Peterson's, annual.

Peterson's Guide to Two-Year Colleges. Princeton, NJ: Thomson Peterson's, annual.

Peterson's Internships. Princeton, NJ: Thomson Peterson's, annual.

Quick Guide to College Majors and Careers, Laurence Shatkin. Indianapolis, IN: JIST Publishing, 2002.

Rugg's Recommendations on the Colleges, Frederick Rugg. Fallbrook, CA: Rugg's Recommendations, annual.

Students' Guide to Colleges: The Definitive Guide to America's Top 100 Schools Written by the Real Experts—the Students Who Attend Them, Jordan Goldman and Colleen Buyers. New York: Penguin, 2005.

The Truth about Getting In: A Top College Advisor Tells You Everything You Need to Know, Katherine Cohen. New York: Hyperion, 2002.

US News Ultimate College Guide. Naperville, IL: Sourcebooks, annual.

Vault Guide to Top Internships, Samer Hamadah. New York, Vault, 2005.

Career Goals

The Career Adventure: Your Guide to Personal Assessment, Career Exploration, and Decision Making, 4th ed., Susan M. Johnston. Upper Saddle, NJ: Prentice-Hall, 2005.

Career Guide to America's Top Industries, 6th ed., U.S. Department of Labor. Indianapolis, IN: JIST Publishing, 2004.

Career Warfare: 10 Rules for Building a Successful Personal Brand and Fighting to Keep It, David F. D'Alessandro and Michele Owens. New York: McGraw-Hill, 2003.

College Majors and Careers: A Resource Guide for Effective Life Planning, 5th ed., Paul Phifer. Chicago: Ferguson, 2003.

Cool Careers for Dummies, Marty Nemko, Paul Edwards, and Sarah Edwards. Foster City, CA: IDG Books, 2001.

Customize Your Career, Roz Usheroff. New York: McGraw-Hill, 2004.

Do What You Are: Discover the Perfect Career for You through the Secrets of Personality Type, 3rd ed., Paul D. Tieger and Barbara Barron-Tieger. New York: Little, Brown, 2001.

50 Best Jobs for Your Personality, Michael Farr and Laurence Shatkin. Indianapolis, IN: JIST Publishing, 2005.

Finding a Career That Works for You: A Step-by-Step Guide to Choosing a Career and Finding a Job, Wilma Fellman. Plantation, FL: Specialty Press, 2000.

Finding Your Perfect Work: The New Career Guide to Making a Living, Creating a Life, 2nd ed., Paul Edwards and Susan Edwards. New York: Penguin, 2003.

The 5 Patterns of Extraordinary Careers: The Guide for Achieving Success and Satisfaction, James M. Citrin and Richard Smith. New York: Crown Business, 2003.

The Global Citizen: A Guide to Creating an International Life and Career, Elizabeth Kruempelmann. Berkeley, CA: Ten Speed Press, 2002.

Guide to Your Career, 5th ed., Alan B. Bernstein. New York: Princeton Review, 2004.

How Hard Are You Knocking? The Job Seeker's Guide to Opening Career Doors, Timothy J. Augustine and Rona Curcio. Winchester, VA: Oakhill Press, 2005.

Job Search and Career Checklists: 101 Proven Time-Saving Checklists to Organize and Plan Your Career Search, Arlene S. Hirsch. Indianapolis, IN: JIST Publishing, 2005.

Recommended

Finding Your Perfect Work: The New Career Guide to Making a Living, Creating a Life, 2nd ed., Paul Edwards and Susan Edwards. New York: Penguin, 2003. Lists types of careers, with emphasis on self-employment opportunities.

What Color Is Your Parachute? A Practical Manual for Job-Hunters and Career-Changers, Richard Nelson Bolles. Berkeley, CA: Ten Speed Press, revised annually. The classic in the genre, and the top-selling career-advice book consistently since the mid-1970s. Updated to reflect twenty-first-century concerns.

Monster Careers: How to Land the Job of Your Life, Jeffrey Taylor and Douglas Hardy. New York: Penguin, 2004.

New Guide for Occupational Exploration: Linking Interests, Learning and Careers, 4th ed., Michael Farr and Laurence Shatkin. Indianapolis, IN: JIST Publishing, 2006.

The Play of Your Life: Your Program for Finding the Career of Your Dreams—And a Step-by-Step Guide to Making It a Reality, Colleen A. Sabatino. New York: Rodale, 2004.

What Color Is Your Parachute? A Practical Manual for Job-Hunters and Career-Changers, Richard Nelson Bolles. Berkeley, CA: Ten Speed Press, revised annually.

What Should I Do with My Life? The True Story of People Who Answered the Ultimate Question, Po Brosnan. New York: Random House, 2002.

Where's My Oasis? The Essential Handbook for Everyone Wanting the Perfect Job, Rowan Manahan. New York: Vermillion, 2004.

Getting the Job and Getting Ahead

Almanac of American Employers, Jack W. Plunkett. Galveston, TX: Plunkett Research Ltd., biennial.

e-Resumes: A Guide to Successful Online Job Hunting, Pat Criscito. Hauppauge, NY: Barron's Educational Series, 2004.

Guide to Internet Job Searching, Margaret Riley Dikel. New York: McGraw-Hill, 2004.

How to Earn What You're Worth: Leveraging Your Goals and Talents to Land Your Dream Job, Sunny Bates. New York: McGraw-Hill, 2004.

How to Get Any Job with Any Major: Career Launch & Re-launch for Everyone Under 30 (or How to Avoid Living in Your Parents' Basement), Donald Asher. Berkeley, CA: Ten Speed Press, 2004.

How to Get Your First Job and Keep It, 2nd ed., Deborah Perlmutter Bloch. New York: McGraw-Hill, 2002.

Insider's Guide to Finding a Job: Expert Advice from America's Top Employers and Recruiters, Wendy S. Enelow and Shelly Goldman. Indianapolis, IN: JIST Publishing, 2004.

International Job Finder: Where the Jobs Are Worldwide, Daniel Lauber and Kraig Rice. River Forest, IL: Planning/Communications, 2002.

International Jobs: Where They Are and How to Get Them, 6th ed., Nina Segal and Eric Kocher. New York: Basic Books, 2003.

Job-Hunting on the Internet, 4th ed., Richard Nelson Bolles and Mark Emery Bolles. Berkeley, CA: Ten Speed Press, 2005.

Job Savvy: How to Be a Success at Work, 3rd ed., LaVerne L. Ludden. Indianapolis, IN: JIST Publishing, 2002.

Job Search Magic: Insider Secrets from America's Career and Life Coach, Susan Britton Whitcomb. Indianapolis, IN: JIST Publishing, 2006.

The Job Search Solution: The Ultimate System for Finding a Great Job Now!, Tony Bashara. New York: AMACOM, 2005.

Job Seeker's Online Goldmine: A Step-by-Step Guidebook to Government and No-Cost Web Tools, Janet E. Wall. Indianapolis, IN: JIST Publishing, 2006.

Knock 'Em Dead 2006: The Ultimate Job Seekers Guide, Martin Yate. Avon, MA: Adams Media, 2006.

National Job Hotline Directory: The Job Finder's Hot List, 3rd ed., Sue Cubbage and Marcia Williams. River Forest, IL: Planning/Communications, 2003.

1000 Best Job Hunting Secrets, Diane Stafford and Moritza Day. Naperville, IL: Sourcebooks, 2004.

Super Job Search: The Complete Manual for Job-Seekers & Career-Changers, 3rd ed., Peter Studner. Los Angeles: Jamenair Ltd., 2003.

10 Insider Secrets to a Winning Job Search: Everything You Need to Get the Job You Want in 24 Hours—Or Less, Todd Bermont. Franklin Lakes, NJ: Career Press, 2004.

Very Quick Job Search: Get a Better Job in Half the Time, 3rd ed., Michael Farr. Indianapolis, IN: JIST Publishing, 2003.

Recommended

How to Get Any Job with Any Major: Career Launch & Re-launch for Everyone Under 30 (or How to Avoid Living in Your Parents' Basement), Donald Asher. Berkeley, CA: Ten Speed Press, 2004. Counsels liberal arts degree-holders on how to package their education and strengths to land a high-paying position.

Knock 'Em Dead 2006: The Ultimate Job Seekers Guide, Martin Yate. Avon, MA: Adams Media, 2006. Offers range of advice for job-hunters at all levels, including resume-building, interview strategies, and salary negotiation tips.

Resumes and Interviews

Adams Job Interview Almanac, 2nd ed., Richard Wallace. Avon, MA: Adams Media Corp., 2005.

Adams Resume Almanac, 2nd ed., Richard Wallace. Avon, MA: Adams Media Corp., 2005.

Amazing Resumes: What Employers Want to See—and How to Say It, Jim Bright and Joanne Earl. Indianapolis, IN: JIST Publishing, 2005.

Competency-Based Resumes: How to Bring Your Resume to the Top of the Pile, Robin Kessler and Linda A. Strasburg. Franklin Lakes, NJ: Career Press, 2004.

Cover Letter Magic, 2nd ed., Wendy S. Enelow and Louise Kursmark. Indianapolis, IN: JIST Publishing, 2004.

Cover Letters That Knock 'Em Dead, 6th ed., Martin Yate. Avon, MA: Adams Media, 2004.

The Elements of Resume Style: Essential Rules and Eye-opening Advice for Writing Resumes and Cover Letters That Work, Scott Bennett. New York: AMACOM, 2005.

Expert Resumes for Career Changers, Wendy S. Enelow and Louise M. Kursmark. Indianapolis, IN: JIST Publishing, 2005.

Fearless Interviewing: How to Win the Job by Communicating with Confidence, Marky Stein. New York: McGraw-Hill, 2002.

Ferguson Guide to Resumes and Job-Hunting Skills, Maurene J. Hinds. Chicago: Ferguson, 2005.

Gallery of Best Resumes: A Collection of Quality Resumes by Professional Resume Writers, 3rd ed., David F. Noble, Ph.D. Indianapolis, IN: JIST Publishing, 2004.

Get the Interview Every Time: Fortune 500 Hiring Professionals' Tips for Writing Winning Resumes and Cover Letters, Brenda Greene. Chicago: Dearborn Trade Publishing, 2004.

How to Interview Like a Top MBA: Job-Winning Strategies from Headhunters, Fortune 100 Recruiters, and Career Counselors, Shel Leanne. New York: McGraw-Hill, 2003.

How to Turn an Interview into a Job, Jeffrey G. Allen. New York: Simon and Schuster, 2004.

McGraw-Hill's Big Red Book of Resumes. New York: McGraw-Hill, 2002.

Monster Careers: Interviewing—Master the Moment That Gets You the Job, Jeffrey Taylor and Doug Hardy. New York: Penguin Books, 2005.

The Resume.com Guide to Writing Unbeatable Resumes, Warren Simons and Rose Curtis. New York: McGraw-Hill, 2004.

The Resume Handbook: How to Write Outstanding Resumes & Cover Letters for Every Situation, 4th ed., Arthur D. Rosenberg and David V. Hizer. Avon, MA: Adams Media, 2003.

Resume Magic: Trade Secrets of a Professional Resume Writer, 2nd ed., Susan Britton Whitcomb. Indianapolis, IN: JIST Publishing, 2003.

Resumes for Dummies, 4th ed., Joyce Lain Kennedy. Indianapolis, IN: Wiley, 2003.

Resumes That Knock 'Em Dead, 6th ed., Martin Yate. Avon, MA: Adams Media, 2004.

301 Smart Answers to Tough Interview Questions, Vicky Oliver. Naperville, IL: Sourcebooks, 2005.

201 Best Questions to Ask on Your Interview, John Kador. New York: McGraw-Hill, 2002.

Winning the Interview Game: Everything You Need to Know to Land the Job, Alan H. Nierenberg. New York: AMACOM, 2005.

Recommended

Resume Magic: Trade Secrets of a Professional Resume Writer, 2nd ed., Susan Britton Whitcomb. Indianapolis, IN: JIST Publishing, 2003. Before and after resume samples provide a how-to on crafting the perfect resume. Includes tips on e-resumes and tricks for scannable-text submissions.

301 Smart Answers to Tough Interview Questions, Vicky Oliver. Naperville, IL: Sourcebooks, 2005. Advice on how to handle the questions designed to unsettle, from explaining gaps in work history to acing arcane trivia volleys.

Mid-Career Options

Change Your Job, Change Your Life: Careering and Re-Careering in the New Boom/Bust Economy, 9th ed., Ron Krannich. Manassas Park, VA: Impact, 2004.

Fearless Career Change, Marky Stein. New York: McGraw-Hill, 2005.

Fire Your Boss, Stephen M. Pollan and Mark Levine. New York: HarperCollins, 2004.

I Don't Know What I Want, But I Know It's Not This: A Step-by-Step Guide to Finding Gratifying Work, Julie Jansen. New York: Penguin Books, 2003.

Over-40 Job Search Guide: 10 Strategies for Making Your Age an Advantage in Your Career, Gail Geary. Indianapolis, IN: JIST Publishing, 2004.

Radical Careering: 100 Truths to Jumpstart Your Job, Your Career, and Your Life, Sally Hogshead. New York: Gotham, 2005.

Second Acts: Creating the Life You Really Want, Building the Career You Truly Desire, Stephen M. Pollan and Mark Levine. New York: HarperCollins, 2003.

Working Identity: Unconventional Strategies for Reinventing Your Career, Hermania Ibarra. Boston: Harvard Business School Press, 2003.

Equality of Opportunity

Dancing on the Glass Ceiling, Nancy Frederick and Candy Deemer. New York: McGraw-Hill, 2004.

Job-Hunting for the So-Called Handicapped or People Who Have Disabilities, 2nd ed., Richard Nelson Bolles and Dale Susan Brown. Berkeley, CA: Ten Speed Press, 2001.

Job Search Handbook for People with Disabilities, 2nd ed., Daniel J. Ryan. Indianapolis, IN: JIST Publishing, 2004.

Lavender Road to Success: The Career Guide for the Gay Community, Kirk Snyder. Berkeley, CA: Ten Speed Press, 2003.

Resources for People with Disabilities, 2nd ed., Shawn Woodyard. Chicago: Ferguson, 2001.

Lists and Indexes of Career and Vocational Information

Encyclopedia of Careers and Vocational Guidance, 13th ed., 5 vols. Chicago: Ferguson, 2006.

O*Net Dictionary of Occupational Titles, 3rd ed. Indianapolis, IN: JIST Publishing, 2004.

Recommended

I Don't Know What I Want, But I Know It's Not This: A Step-by-Step Guide to Finding Gratifying Work, Julie Jansen. New York: Penguin Books, 2003. Experienced career coach identifies the top six reasons people are dissatisfied with their jobs and provides a step-by-step process for finding a career that suits every personality.

Working Identity: Unconventional Strategies for Reinventing Your Career, Hermania Ibarra. Boston: Harvard Business School Press, 2003. Help for those considering a mid-life career change.

Recommended

Dancing on the Glass Ceiling, Nancy Frederick and Candy Deemer. New York: McGraw-Hill, 2004. A former advertising executive teams with a professional executive coach to provide practical as well as inspirational advice for women in the workplace.

Job-Hunting for the So-Called Handicapped or People Who Have Disabilities, 2nd ed., Richard Nelson Bolles and Dale Susan Brown. Berkeley, CA: Ten Speed Press, 2001. From the author of *What Color Is Your Parachute?* Advice for the physically or mentally challenged on finding a career niche.

Internet Sites

Sites with Extensive Links

About.com
http://careerplanning.about.com

Beyond.com
http://www.beyond.com

Jobweb.com
http://www.jobweb.com

JIST Publishing
http://www.jist.com

Job Hunt: Online Job Search Guide and Resource Directory
http://www.job-hunt.org

Vault.com
http://www.vault.com

Vocational Information Center
http://www.khake.com

Career Development Resources

Career Magazine
http://www.careermag.com

Career Resource Homepage
http://www.careerresource.net

Job Hunters Bible
http://www.jobhuntersbible.com

Princeton Review
http://www.princetonreview.com

Quintessential Careers
http://www.quintcareers.com

Online Information and References

AT&T Toll-Free Internet Directory
http://www.tollfree.att.net

The Best Jobs in the USA Today
http://www.bestjobsusa.com

Careers.org
http://www.careers.org

Federal Jobs Digest
http://www.fedworld.gov/jobs/jobsearch.html

Job Finders Online
http://www.planningcommunications.com/jf

Job Safari
http://www.jobsafari.com

Monster Career Center
http://content.monster.com

Occupational Outlook Handbook
http://www.bls.gov/oco

SpherionExchange
http://employee.spherionexchange.com/start.cfm

U.S. Bureau of Labor Statistics Homepage
http://www.bls.gov/home.htm

US News and World Report Career Center
http://www.usnews.com/usnews/biztech/career/career_home.htm

Wall Street Journal Career Journal
http://www.careerjournal.com

Yahoo! Business and Economy
http://dir.yahoo.com/Business_and_Economy

Job Databases and Resume Posting

After College
http://www.aftercollege.com

America's Job Bank
http://www.ajb.org

Career Builder
http://www.careerbuilder.com

Career Mart
http://www.careermart.com

Employment Guide
http://www.employmentguide.com

Yahoo! Hot Jobs
http://hotjobs.yahoo.com

Idealist Nonprofit Career Center
http://www.idealist.org

Job.com
http://www.job.com

JobBank USA
http://www.jobbankusa.com

Job Web
http://www.jobweb.org

Monster Jobs
http://www.monster.com

Monstertrak
http://www.monstertrak.monster.com

NationJob.com
http://www.nationjob.com

Now Hiring
http://www.nowhiring.com

Audiovisual Materials

The following titles include, where possible, the developer's name and location or else the name and location of a distributor. Audiovisual titles may be available through several distributors.

Exploring the Working World

Career Advantage: Strategies for Success series. Video, guide. Princeton, NJ: Films Media Group.

Career Clusters series. Video. Charleston, WV: Cambridge Educational.

Career Exploration series. Video. South Charleston, WV: Meridian Education Corp.

Career Guidance Videos series. Video. South Charleston, WV: Meridian Education Corp.

Career S.E.L.F. Assessment: Finding a Career That Works for You. Video. Charleston, WV: Cambridge Educational.

Careers, Careers, Careers! Video, guide. Princeton, NJ: Films Media Group.

Careers for the 21st Century series. Video, guide. South Charleston, WV: Meridian Education Corp.

Careers without College. Video. Charleston, WV: Cambridge Educational.

The Changing Workplace: Technology and Globalization. Video. Princeton, NJ: Films Media Group.

Choices Today for Career Satisfaction Tomorrow. Video, guide. Charleston, WV: Cambridge Educational.

Complete Job Search System. Video. Charleston, WV: Cambridge Educational.

Connect on the Net: Finding a Job on the Internet. Video. Charleston, WV: Cambridge Educational.

Educational Planning for Your Career. Video. South Charleston, WV: Meridian Education Corp.

The 50 Best Jobs for the 21st Century series. Video. Indianapolis, IN: JIST Publishing.

The JIST Video Guide for Occupational Exploration series. Video. Indianapolis, IN: JIST Publishing.

Internet Careers: College Not Required. Video. Charleston, WV: Cambridge Educational.

Introduction to Career and Educational Exploration. Video. Princeton, NJ: Films Media Group.

JIST TV Series: The Job Search Channel. Video. Indianapolis, IN: JIST Publishing.

Jobs for the 21st Century. Video. Mt. Kisco, NY: Guidance Associates.

Learning for Earning. Video, guide. South Charleston, WV: Meridian Education Corp.

Log On for Success: Using Internet Job Sites. Video, guide. Charleston, WV: Cambridge Educational.

Researching Career Options: New Technologies and Current Techniques. Video. Princeton, NJ: Films Media Group.

School-to-Work Transition. Video. South Charleston, WV: Meridian Education Corp.

Ten Fastest Growing Careers: Jobs for the Future. Video. Mt. Kisco, NY: Guidance Associates.

What Would I Be Good At? Video. Mt. Kisco, NY: Guidance Associates.

What's Out There: How the World of Work is Organized. Video. Princeton, NJ: Films Media Group.

Your Career Search: Taking the First Step. Video. Mt. Kisco, NY: Guidance Associates.

Your Future: Planning Through Career Exploration. Video. South Charleston, WV: Meridian Education Corp.

Getting the Job and Getting Ahead

Career Evaluation. Video. Charleston, WV: Cambridge Educational.

Common Mistakes People Make in Interviews. Video, guide. Charleston, WV: Cambridge Educational.

Exceptional Employee: A Guide to Success on the Job. Video. Charleston, WV: Cambridge Educational.

Exceptional Interviewing Tips: A View from the Inside. Video, workbook. Charleston, WV: Cambridge Educational.

Extraordinary Answers to Common Interview Questions. Video. Charleston, WV: Cambridge Educational.

Finding a Job. Video. Charleston, WV: Cambridge Educational.

First Impressions: Etiquette and Work Habits for New Employees. Video, guide. Charleston, WV: Cambridge Educational.

From Pinkslip to Paycheck: The Road to Reemployment series. Video. Indianapolis, IN: JIST Publishing.

Getting Good Answers to Tough Interview Questions. Video. Indianapolis, IN: JIST Publishing.

Getting the Job You Really Want series. Video, workbook, guide. Indianapolis, IN: JIST Publishing.

How to Find a Job on the Internet. Video. Indianapolis, IN: JIST Publishing.

How to Be a Success at Work series. Video. Indianapolis, IN: JIST Publishing.

The Ideal Resume. Video. Charleston, WV: Cambridge Educational.

If at First: How to Get a Job and Keep It. Video. Mt. Kisco, NY: Guidance Associates.

Interview to Win Your First Job. Video. Indianapolis, IN: JIST Publishing.

Interviewing for a Job. Video. Charleston, WV: Cambridge Educational.

Job Survival Kit. Video. Charleston, WV: Cambridge Educational.

On-the-Job Success series. Video. Indianapolis, IN: JIST Publishing.

Planning Your Career. Video. Charleston, WV: Cambridge Educational.

The Portfolio Resume series. Video. Charleston, WV: Cambridge Educational.

"Quick" Job Search series. Video. Indianapolis, IN: JIST Publishing.

Succeeding on the Job. Video. Charleston, WV: Cambridge Educational.

Success in the Job World series. Video. Indianapolis, IN: JIST Publishing.

Staying on Track in Your Work Search. Video. Princeton, NJ: Films Media Group.

Power Interviewing Skills: Strategies for the Interviewee. Video. Charleston, WV: Cambridge Educational.

Take This Job and Love It: Keys to Surviving Your New Job. Video. Charleston, WV: Cambridge Educational.

Ten Commandments of Resumes. Video. Charleston, WV: Cambridge Educational.

Tough Times Job Strategies. Video, guide. Charleston, WV: Cambridge Educational.

Understanding and Using the O*NET. Video, guide. Charleston, WV: Cambridge Educational.

The Very Quick Job Search Video. Video. Indianapolis, IN: JIST Publishing.

The Video Guide to JIST's Self-Directed Job Search series. Video. Indianapolis, IN: JIST Publishing.

Web Resumes. Video. Charleston, WV: Cambridge Educational.

Computer Software

The following titles include, where possible, the developer's name and location or else the name and location of a distributor. Software titles may be available through several distributors.

Ace the Interview: The Multimedia Job Interview Guide. CD-ROM. Charleston, WV: Cambridge Educational.

Adams Media JobBank FastResume Suite. CD-ROM for Windows. Avon, MA: Adams Media.

Barron's Profiles of American Colleges on CD-ROM. Windows or Macintosh. Hauppauge, NY: Barron's Educational Series.

Cambridge Career Center. CD-ROM. Charleston, WV: Cambridge Educational.

Career Discovery Encyclopedia. CD-ROM. Chicago, IL: Ferguson.

Career Explorer. CD-ROM for Windows. Indianapolis, IN: JIST Publishing.

Career Finder Plus. CD-ROM. Indianapolis, IN: JIST Publishing.

CareerOINKs on the Web. Network. Indianapolis, IN: JIST Publishing.

Careers without College. CD-ROM. Indianapolis, IN: JIST Publishing.

Complete Resume Designer. CD-ROM. Charleston, WV: Cambridge Educational.

Custom Resume Creator. CD-ROM for Windows. Indianapolis, IN: JIST Publishing.

Decisions. CD-ROM. Indianapolis, IN: JIST Publishing.

Electronic Career Planner. CD-ROM for Windows. Indianapolis, IN: JIST Publishing.

Exploring the World of Work. CD-ROM. New York: McGraw-Hill.

JIST Presents Interview Mastery. CD-ROM. Indianapolis, IN: JIST Publishing.

Job Search series. CD-ROM. Indianapolis, IN: JIST Publishing.

Job Survival series. CD-ROM. Indianapolis, IN: JIST Publishing.

The Keys to Interviewing Success: Unlocking Your Professional Future. CD-ROM. Charleston, WV: Cambridge Educational.

Moving on Up: An Interactive Guide to Finding a Great Job. CD-ROM for Windows. Charleston, WV: Cambridge Educational.

Multimedia Career Center. CD-ROM. Charleston, WV: Cambridge Educational.

The Multimedia Career Path. CD-ROM. Charleston, WV: Cambridge Educational.

The Multimedia Guide to Occupational Exploration. CD-ROM. Charleston, WV: Cambridge Educational.

Multimedia Job Search. CD-ROM for Windows. Charleston, WV: Cambridge Educational.

Multimedia Take This Job and Love It. CD-ROM. Charleston, WV: Cambridge Educational.

OOH Career Center. CD-ROM. Charleston, WV: Cambridge Educational.

School-to-Work Career Center. CD-ROM. Charleston, WV: Cambridge Educational.

Success in the World of Work: Succeeding on the Job. CD-ROM. South Charleston, WV: Meridian Education Corp.

Targeting Success. CD-ROM. Indianapolis, IN: JIST Publishing.

General

Books

America's Top Medical, Education, and Human Services Jobs: Detailed Information on Eighty-Eight Major Jobs at All Levels of Education and Training, 5th ed., J. Michael Farr. Indianapolis, IN: JIST Publishing, 2001.

Becoming a Helper, 4th ed., Marianne Schneider Corey and Gerald Corey. Florence, KY: Wadsworth, 2002.

Careers for Caring People and Other Sensitive Types, 2nd ed., Adrian A. Paradis. New York: McGraw-Hill, 2003.

Careers for Good Samaritans and Other Humanitarian Types, 3rd ed., Marjorie Eberts and Margaret Gisler. New York: McGraw-Hill, 2006.

Careers in Nonprofits and Government Agencies, 2006 ed. San Francisco: WetFeet, Inc., 2005.

Great Jobs for Sociology Majors, 2nd ed., Stephen Lambert. New York: McGraw-Hill, 2002.

A Guide to Careers in Community Development, Paul C. Brophy and Alice Shabecoff. Washington, DC: Island Press, 2001.

Vault Guide to the Top Nonprofit and Government Employers, 2006 ed., Laurie Pasiuk. New York: Vault, 2005.

Internet Sites

Community Career Center
http://www.nonprofitjobs.org

Internet Job Source
http://www.statejobs.com

Job Web
http://www.jobweb.com

National Association of Colleges and Employers Jobwire
http://www.naceweb.org/jobwire

The Riley Guide
http://www.rileyguide.com

Audiovisual Materials

Enter Here: Personal, Family and Community Services. Video series. Charleston, WV: Cambridge Educational.

Humanitarian Careers. Video. Indianapolis, IN: JIST Publishing, Inc.

Leading and Influencing Careers. Video series. Indianapolis, IN: JIST Publishing, Inc.

Protective Careers. Video. Indianapolis, IN: JIST Publishing, Inc.

Public and Personal Service. Video. Bloomington, IN: Meridian Educational Corp.

Armed Services

Books

America's Top Military Careers: The Official Guide to Occupations in the Armed Forces, 4th ed., United States Department of Defense. Indianapolis, IN: JIST Publishing, Inc., 2003.

Career Opportunities in the Armed Forces, C.J. Henderson and Jack Dolphin. New York: Facts on File, Inc., 2003.

The Complete Idiot's Guide to Careers in the U.S. Military, Bill Harris. Indianapolis, IN: Alpha Books, 2002.

Military to Federal Career Guide: Ten Steps to Transforming Your Military Experience into a Competitive Federal Resume, Kathryn Troutman. Baltimore: Resume Place, 2005.

Opportunities in Military Careers, rev. ed., Adrian A. Paradis. New York: McGraw-Hill, 2005.

Internet Sites

Air Force
http://www.airforce.com

Army Recruiting
http://www.goarmy.com

Marine Corps Recruiting
http://www.marines.com

Navy Careers
http://www.navy.com

Official Army National Guard Recruitment Site
http://www.1800goguard.com

U.S. Coast Guard
http://www.uscg.mil

Law Enforcement

Books

Career Opportunities in Law Enforcement, Security, and Protective Services, 2nd ed., Susan Echaore-McDavid. New York: Ferguson, 2006.

Careers in Criminal Justice and Related Fields: From Internship to Promotion, 5th ed., J. Scott Harr and Karen M. Hess. Belmont, CA: Thomson, 2005.

Careers in Criminology, Marilyn Morgan. Lincolnwood, IL: Lowell House, 2000.

Criminal Justice: A Brief Introduction, 5th ed., Frank Schmalleger. Upper Saddle River, NJ: Prentice Hall, 2003.

The Field Guide to Law Enforcement, rev. ed., Lloyd L. Weinreb and James D. Whaley. New York: Foundation Press, 2004.

Guide to Careers in Federal Law Enforcement: Profiles of Two Hundred Twenty-five High-Powered Positions and Surefire Tactics for Getting Hired, Thomas H. Ackerman. East Lansing, MI: Hamilton Burrows Press, 2001.

Guide to Law Enforcement Careers, 2nd ed., Donald B. Hutton and Anna Mydlarz. Hauppage, NY: Barron's Educational Series, 2001.

Opportunities in Law Enforcement and Criminal Justice Careers, 2nd ed., James Stinchcomb. New York: McGraw-Hill, 2002.

Seeking Employment in Criminal Justice and Related Fields, 4th ed., J. Scott Harr and Karen M. Hess. New York: Thomson Learning, 2003.

Internet Sites

The Police Officer's Internet Directory
http://www.officer.com

Audiovisual Materials

Becoming a Cop: From Application to the Academy. DVD. Somerset, MA: 911hotjobs.com.

Criminal Justice Careers. Video. Lubbock, TX: CEV Multimedia.

Law Enforcement. Video. New York: Educational Design.

Signal 102: Firefighter I/II Study Helper. CD-ROM. Middlebury, CT: Knightlite Software.

Legal Work

Books

Careers in Law, 3rd ed., Gary Munneke. Chicago: VGM Career Books, 2004.

Careers in Law and Politics, Linda R. Wade. Bear, DE: Mitchell Lane, 2002.

How to Land Your First Paralegal Job: An Insider's Guide to the Fastest-Growing Profession of the New Millennium, 4th ed., Andrea Wagner. Upper Saddle River, NJ: Prentice Hall, 2005.

National Directory of Legal Employers, National Association for Law Placement. New York: Harcourt, 2001.

Paralegal Career Guide, 3rd ed., Chere B. Estrin. Upper Saddle River, NJ: Prentice Hall, 2002.

Should You Really Be a Lawyer?: The Guide to Smart Career Choices before, during, and after Law School, Deborah Schneider and Gary Belasky. Seattle: Decision-Books, 2005.

So You Want to Be a Lawyer: A Practical Guide to Law as a Career, Law School Admission Council. Newtown, PA: Law School Admission Council, 2001.

Vault Guide to Bankruptcy Law Careers, Seth A. Stuhl. New York: Vault, 2003.

Vault Guide to Corporate Law Careers, Zahie El Kouri. New York: Vault, 2003.

Vault Guide to Tax Law Careers, Shannon King Nash. New York: Vault, 2004.

What Can You Do with a Law Degree? A Lawyer's Guide to Career Alternatives Inside, Outside, and Around the Law, 5th ed., Deborah Arron. Seattle: Niche Press, 2003.

Internet Sites

Lawjobs.com
http://www.lawjobs.com

National Federation of Paralegal Associations Online Career Center
http://www.paralegals.org/displaycommon.cfm?an = 20

Public, Civil, and Social Services

Books

The Book of U.S. Government Jobs: Where They Are, What's Available, and How to Get One, 9th ed., Dennis V. Damp. McKees Rock, PA: Bookhaven Press, 2005.

Careers in International Affairs, 7th ed., Maria Pinto Carland and Lisa A. Gihring, eds. Washington, DC: Georgetown University Press, 2003.

Careers in Social Work, 2nd ed., Leon H. Ginsberg. Boston: Allyn & Bacon, 2001.

Federal Personnel Guide: An Annual Publication, Kenneth D. Whitehead, ed. Chevy Chase, MD: Key Communications Group, annual.

Federal Resume Guidebook: Write a Winning Federal Resume to Get in, Get Promoted, and Survive in a Government Job, 3rd ed., Kathryn Kraemer Troutman. Indianapolis: JIST, 2004.

Government Job Finder: Where the Jobs Are in Local, State, and Federal Government, 4th ed., Daniel Lauber and Deborah Verlench. River Forest, IL: Planning/Communications, 2006.

Opportunities in Social Work Careers, Renee Wittenburg. Chicago: VGM, 2003.

The Peace Corps and More: Two Hundred Twenty Ways to Work, Study and Travel at Home and Abroad, Medea Benjamin and Miya Rodolfo-Sioson. San Francisco: Global Exchange, 2003.

Resumes for Social Service Careers, 2nd ed., VGM Career Horizons. Lincolnwood, IL: NTC Publishing Group, 2000.

Social Work Career Development: A Handbook for Job Hunting and Career Planning, 2nd ed., Carol Doelling. Washington, DC: National Association of Social Workers, 2004.

Summary Information on Master of Social Work Programs. Alexandria, VA: Council on Social Work Education, annual.

United States Government Manual, National Archives and Records Administration staff, eds. Baton Rouge, LA: Claitor's Law Books and Publishing Division, annual.

What Social Workers Do, 2nd ed., Margaret Gibelman. Washington, DC: National Association of Social Workers, 2005.

Social Worker, Shirley Brinkerhoff. Broomall, PA: Mason Crest Publishers, 2003.

Washington Information Directory. Washington, DC: Congressional Quarterly, annual.

Internet Sites

Jobs in Government
http://www.jobsingovernment.com

Local Government Institute
http://www.lgi.org

Federal Jobs Digest
http://www.jobsfed.com

FedWorld
http://www.fedworld.gov/jobs/jobsearch.html

U.S. Office of Personnel Management
http://www.opm.gov

Social Work and Social Services Jobs Online
http://gwbweb.wustl.edu/jobs

Audiovisual Materials

Enter Here: Government and Public Administration. Video series. Charleston, WV: Cambridge Educational.

Religious Careers

Books

Opportunities in Religious Service Careers, John O. Nelson. Chicago: VGM, 2004.

Teaching and Library Science

Books

Careers in Education, 4th ed., Roy A. Edelfelt and Alan Reiman. Chicago: VGM, 2004.

Careers in Teaching, J. Barrett Heaton. New York: Rosen, 2005.

Career Opportunities in Library and Information Science, Linda P. Carvell. New York: Ferguson, 2005.

Employment Opportunities in Education: How to Secure Your Career, Jeanne M. Machado. Clifton Park, NY: Thomson Delmar Learning, 2006.

The Information Professional's Guide to Career Development Online, Sarah L. Nesbeitt and Rachel Singer Gordon. Medford, NJ: Information Today, 2002.

Inside Secrets of Finding a Teaching Job: The Most Effective Search Methods for Both New and Experienced Educators, 3rd ed., Jack Warner, Clyde Bryan, and Diane Warner. Indianapolis: JIST, 2006.

Opportunities in Library and Information Science Careers, rev. ed., Blythe Camenson. New York: McGraw-Hill, 2002.

Opportunities in Teaching Careers, rev. ed., Janet Fine. New York: McGraw-Hill, 2005.

Straight from the Stacks: A Firsthand Guide to Careers in Library and Information Science, Laura Townsend Kane. Chicago: American Library Association, 2003.

Internet Sites

American Library Association
http://www.ala.org/education

Council for Advancement and Support of Education Career Center
http://www.case.org/jobs

The information in this directory was generated from the IPEDS (Integrated Postsecondary Education Data System) database of the U.S. Department of Education. It includes only regionally or nationally accredited institutions offering postsecondary occupational training in public and community services. Because college catalogs and directories of colleges and universities are readily available elsewhere, this directory does not include institutions that offer only bachelor's and advanced degrees.

Armed Services

ALABAMA

John C Calhoun State Community
 College
Hwy. 31 N
Decatur 35602

TEXAS

Wayland Baptist University
1900 West Seventh
Plainview 79072

WEST VIRGINIA

The University of Charleston
2300 MacCorkle Ave. SE
Charleston 25304

Custodial Services

CALIFORNIA

Center for Employment Training,
 Gilroy
7800 Arroyo Circle
Gilroy 95020

Center for Employment Training,
 Salinas
421 Monterey St.
Salinas 93901

Center for Employment Training, Santa
 Ana
120 West Fifth St.
Santa Ana 92701

Center for Employment Training,
 Spring St.
426 Spring St.
Los Angeles 90013

ILLINOIS

Illinois Valley Community College
815 North Orlando Smith Ave.
Oglesby 61348-9692

MINNESOTA

Century Community and Technical
 College
3300 Century Ave. N
White Bear Lake 55110

South Central Technical College,
 Faribault
1225 Southwest Third St.
Faribault 55021

PENNSYLVANIA

Philadelphia Elwyn Institute
4040 Market St.
Philadelphia 19104-3003

Fire Control Technology

ALABAMA

Chattahoochee Valley Community
 College
2602 College Dr.
Phenix City 36869

Community College of the Air Force
130 West Maxwell Blvd.
Montgomery 36112-6613

Jefferson State Community College
2601 Carson Rd.
Birmingham 35215-3098

ALASKA

University of Alaska, Anchorage
3211 Providence Dr.
Anchorage 99508

University of Alaska, Fairbanks
Signers Hall
Fairbanks 99775

ARIZONA

Glendale Community College
6000 West Olive Ave.
Glendale 85302

Mesa Community College
1833 West Southern Ave.
Mesa 85202

Phoenix College
1202 West Thomas Rd.
Phoenix 85013

Pima Community College
2202 West Anklam Rd.
Tucson 85709-0001

Yavapai College
1100 East Sheldon St.
Prescott 86301

ARKANSAS

Black River Technical College
Hwy. 304
P.O. Box 468
Pocahontas 72455

CALIFORNIA

Allan Hancock College
800 South College Dr.
Santa Maria 93454

American River College
4700 College Oak Dr.
Sacramento 95841

Bakersfield College
1801 Panorama Dr.
Bakersfield 93305-1299

Butte College
3536 Butte Campus Dr.
Oroville 95965

Cabrillo College
6500 Soquel Dr.
Aptos 95003

Chabot College
25555 Hesperian Blvd.
Hayward 94545

College of San Mateo
1700 West Hillsdale Blvd.
San Mateo 94402

Crafton Hills College
11711 Sand Canyon Rd.
Yucaipa 92399-1799

El Camino College
16007 Crenshaw Blvd.
Torrance 90506

Fresno City College
1101 East University Ave.
Fresno 93741

Long Beach City College
4901 East Carson St.
Long Beach 90808

Merced College
3600 M St.
Merced 95348-2898

Mission College
3000 Mission College Blvd.
Santa Clara 95054-1897

Monterey Peninsula College
980 Fremont St.
Monterey 93940-4799

Mount San Antonio College
1100 North Grand
Walnut 91789

Oxnard College
4000 South Rose Ave.
Oxnard 93033

Rancho Santiago Community College
 District
17th at Bristol
Santa Ana 92706

Rio Hondo College
3600 Workman Mill Rd.
Whittier 90601-1699

San Diego Miramar College
10440 Black Mountain Rd.
San Diego 92126-2999

Santa Rosa Junior College
1501 Mendocino Ave.
Santa Rosa 95401-4395

Shasta College
P.O. Box 496006
Redding 96049

Sierra College
5000 Rocklin Rd.
Rocklin 95677

COLORADO

Aims Community College
Box 69
Greeley 80632

Arapahoe Community College
2500 West College Dr.
Littleton 80160-9002

Red Rocks Community College
13300 West Sixth Ave.
Lakewood 80228

FLORIDA

Broward Community College
225 East Las Olas Blvd.
Fort Lauderdale 33301

Daytona Beach Community College
1200 Volusia Ave.
Daytona Beach 32114

Edison Community College
8099 College Pkwy. SW
Fort Myers 33906-6210

Florida Community College at
 Jacksonville
501 West State St.
Jacksonville 32202

Indian River Community College
3209 Virginia Ave.
Fort Pierce 34981

Lake County Area Vocational Technical
 Center
2001 Kurt St.
Eustis 32726

Lively Technical Center
500 North Appleyard Dr.
Tallahassee 32304

Miami-Dade Community College
300 Northeast Second Ave.
Miami 33132

Palm Beach Community College
4200 Congress Ave.
Lake Worth 33461

Pasco-Hernando Community College
36727 Blanton Rd.
Dade City 33523-7599

Sarasota County Technical Institute
4748 Beneva Rd.
Sarasota 34233-1798

Seminole Community College
100 Weldon Blvd.
Sanford 32773-6199

South Technical Education Center
1300 Southwest 30th Ave.
Boynton Beach 33426-9099

William T McFatter Vocational
 Technical Center
6500 Nova Dr.
Davie 33317

GEORGIA

Dekalb College
3251 Panthersville Rd.
Decatur 30034

HAWAII

Honolulu Community College
874 Dillingham Blvd.
Honolulu 96817

ILLINOIS

City Colleges of Chicago, Central Office
226 West Jackson
Chicago 60606

College of Du Page
425 22nd St.
Glen Ellyn 60137-6599

Illinois Central College
One College Dr.
East Peoria 61635-0001

Investigations Institute
2155 Stonington Ave.
Ste. 118
Hoffman Estates 60195-2057

Joliet Junior College
1215 Houbolt Rd.
Joliet 60431

Lincoln Land Community College
Shepherd Rd.
Springfield 62194-9256

Moraine Valley Community College
10900 South 88th Ave.
Palos Hills 60465-0937

Prairie State College
202 Halsted St.
Chicago Heights 60411

Southeastern Illinois College
3575 College Rd.
Harrisburg 62946

INDIANA

Ivy Tech State College, Central Indiana
One West 26th St.
Indianapolis 46206-1763

IOWA

Des Moines Community College
2006 Ankeny Blvd.
Ankeny 50021

Kirkwood Community College
P.O. Box 2068
Cedar Rapids 52406

KANSAS

Johnson County Community College
12345 College Blvd.
Overland Park 66210-1299

LOUISIANA

Delgado Community College
501 City Pk Ave.
New Orleans 70119

Louisiana State University, Eunice
P.O. Box 1129
Eunice 70535

MAINE

Southern Maine Technical College
Fort Rd.
South Portland 04106

MASSACHUSETTS

Bristol Community College
777 Elsbree St.
Fall River 02720

Middlesex Community College
Springs Rd.
Bedford 01730

North Shore Community College
One Ferncroft Rd.
Danvers 01923

Tad Technical Institute
45 Spruce St.
Chelsea 02150

MICHIGAN

Delta College
University Center 48710

Henry Ford Community College
5101 Evergreen Rd.
Dearborn 48128

Lansing Community College
419 North Capitol Ave.
Lansing 48901-7210

Macomb Community College
14500 Twelve Mile Rd.
Warren 48093-3896

MINNESOTA

Lake Superior College
2101 Trinity Rd.
Duluth 55811

MISSOURI

Saint Louis Community College, Forest Park
5600 Oakland Ave.
Saint Louis 63110

NEBRASKA

Southeast Community College Area
1111 O St.
Ste. 111
Lincoln 68520

NEVADA

Community College of Southern Nevada
3200 East Cheyenne Ave.
Las Vegas 89030

Truckee Meadows Community College
7000 Dandini Blvd.
Reno 89512

NEW JERSEY

Mercer County Community College
1200 Old Trenton Rd.
Trenton 08690

NEW YORK

Corning Community College
Spencer Hill
Corning 14830

Monroe Community College
1000 East Henrietta Rd.
Rochester 14623

Onondaga Community College
4941 Onondaga Rd.
Syracuse 13215

Suffolk County Community College, Ammerman Campus
533 College Rd.
Selden 11784

NORTH CAROLINA

Central Piedmont Community College
P.O. Box 35009
Charlotte 28235-5009

Guilford Technical Community College
Box 309
Jamestown 27282

OHIO

Columbus State Community College
550 East Spring St.
Columbus 43216

Lakeland Community College
7700 Clocktower Dr.
Kirtland 44094-5198

University of Akron, Main Campus
302 Buchtel Common
Akron 44325-4702

OKLAHOMA

Oklahoma State University, Oklahoma City
900 North Portland
Oklahoma City 73107

OREGON

Chemeketa Community College
4000 Lancaster Dr. NE
Salem 97305

Portland Community College
P.O. Box 19000
Portland 97280-0990

RHODE ISLAND

Community College of Rhode Island
400 East Ave.
Warwick 02886-1807

Providence College
River Ave. and Eaton St.
Providence 02918

TEXAS

Austin Community College
5930 Middle Fiskville Rd.
Austin 78752

Collin County Community College
2200 West University Dr.
McKinney 75070

Houston Community College System
22 Waugh Dr.
Houston 77270-7849

San Antonio College
1300 San Pedro Ave.
San Antonio 78284

Tarrant County Junior College
1500 Houston St.
Fort Worth 76102

WASHINGTON

Bates Technical College
1101 South Yakima Ave.
Tacoma 98405

Spokane Community College
North 1810 Greene Ave.
Spokane 99207

WISCONSIN

Blackhawk Technical College
P.O. Box 5009
Janesville 53547

Fox Valley Technical College
1825 North Bluemound Dr.
Appleton 54913-2277

Madison Area Technical College
3550 Anderson St.
Madison 53704

Milwaukee Area Technical College
700 West State St.
Milwaukee 53233-1443

Northeast Wisconsin Technical College
2740 West Mason St.
P.O. Box 19042
Green Bay 54307-9042

Legal Services Technology

ALABAMA

Gadsden State Community College
1001 George Wallace Dr.
Gadsden 35902-0227

George C Wallace State Community College, Hanceville
801 Main St. NW
Hanceville 35077-2000

Huntsville Business Institute, School of Court Reporting
4900 Corporate Dr.
Ste. G1
Huntsville 35805

James H. Faulkner State Community College
1900 U.S. Hwy. 31 S
Bay Minette 36507

John C Calhoun State Community College
Hwy. 31 N
Decatur 35602

Samford University
800 Lakeshore Dr.
Ste. 2240
Birmingham 35229-2240

ALASKA

Charter College
2221 East Northern Lights Blvd.
Ste. 120
Anchorage 99508

University of Alaska, Anchorage
3211 Providence Dr.
Anchorage 99508

ARIZONA

Academy of Business College
2525 West Beryl Ave.
Phoenix 85021

Apollo College, Westside
2701 West Bethany Home Rd.
Phoenix 85017

Interstate Career College
6367 East Tanque Verde Rd.
Ste. 100
Tucson 85715

Lamson Junior College
1126 North Scottsdale Rd.
Ste. 17
Tempe 85281-1700

Paralegal Institute
2933 West Indian School Rd.
Phoenix 85061-1408

Phoenix College
1202 West Thomas Rd.
Phoenix 85013

Pima Community College
2202 West Anklam Rd.
Tucson 85709-0001

ARKANSAS

Westark College
P.O. Box 3649
Fort Smith 72913

CALIFORNIA

American River College
4700 College Oak Dr.
Sacramento 95841

Cerritos College
11110 Alondra Blvd.
Norwalk 90650

City College of San Francisco
50 Phelan Ave.
San Francisco 94112

Coastline Community College
11460 Warner Ave.
Fountain Valley 92708

College of the Redwoods
7351 Tompkins Hill Rd.
Eureka 95501-9302

College of the Sequoias
915 South Mooney Blvd.
Visalia 93277

De Anza College
21250 Stevens Creek Blvd.
Cupertino 95014

El Camino College
16007 Crenshaw Blvd.
Torrance 90506

Fresno City College
1101 East University Ave.
Fresno 93741

Fullerton College
321 East Chapman Ave.
Fullerton 92832-2095

Humphreys College
3600 Sisk Rd.
Ste. 3A
Modesto 95356

Kensington College
2428 North Grand Ave.
Ste. D
Santa Ana 92705-8708

Napa Valley College
2277 Napa Vallejo Hwy.
Napa 94558

Newbridge College
1840 East 17th St.
Ste. 140
Santa Ana 92705

Pasadena City College
1570 East Colorado Blvd.
Pasadena 91106

Platt College Los Angeles, Inc.
2920 Inland Empire Blvd.
Ontario 91764

Rancho Santiago Community College
District
17th at Bristol
Santa Ana 92706

Rio Hondo College
3600 Workman Mill Rd.
Whittier 90601-1699

Saint Mary's College of California
P.O. Box 3554
Moraga 94575

San Joaquin College of Law
901 Fifth St.
Clovis 93612

Skyline College
3300 College Dr.
San Bruno 94066

Southern California College of Business
and Law
595 West Lambert Rd.
Brea 92821

Southwestern College
900 Otay Lakes Rd.
Chula Vista 91910

University of Northern California,
Lorenzo Patino School Law
1012 J St.
Sacramento 95814-2501

University of San Francisco
2130 Fulton St.
San Francisco 94117-1080

University of West Los Angeles
1155 West Arbor Vitae St.
Inglewood 90301-2902

Watterson College
150 South Los Robles Blvd.
Ste. 100
Pasadena 91101

West Los Angeles College
4800 Freshman Dr.
Culver City 90230

West Valley College
14000 Fruitvale Ave.
Saratoga 95070

COLORADO

Arapahoe Community College
2500 West College Dr.
Littleton 80160-9002

Blair College
828 Wooten Rd.
Colorado Springs 80915

College of the Canons
Forge Rd. Industrial Park
Canon City 81212

Community College of Aurora
16000 East Centre Tech Pkwy.
Aurora 80011-9036

Community College of Denver
P.O. Box 173363
Denver 80217

Denver Paralegal Institute
1401 19th St.
Denver 80202-1213

Denver Paralegal Institute, Colorado
Springs
105 East Vermijo Ave.
Ste. 415
Colorado Springs 80903-2012

Pikes Peak Community College
5675 South Academy Blvd.
Colorado Springs 80906-5498

CONNECTICUT

Branford Hall Career Institute
One Summit Pl.
Branford 06405

Briarwood College
2279 Mount Vernon Rd.
Southington 06489

Connecticut Institute for Paralegal
Studies
26 Sixth St.
Stamford 06905

Huntington Institute, Inc.
193 Broadway
Norwich 06360

Manchester Community Technical
College
60 Bidwell St.
Manchester 06040-1046

Morse School of Business
275 Asylum St.
Hartford 06103

Naugatuck Valley Community-
Technical College
750 Chase Pkwy.
Waterbury 06708

Norwalk Community-Technical College
188 Richards Ave.
Norwalk 06854

Sacred Heart University
5151 Park Ave.
Fairfield 06432-1023

Teikyo Post University
800 Country Club Rd.
P.O. Box 2540
Waterbury 06723-2540

University of Bridgeport
380 University Ave.
Bridgeport 06601

University of Hartford
200 Bloomfield Ave.
West Hartford 06117

DELAWARE

Delaware Technical and Community
College, Owens
Box 610
Georgetown 19947

FLORIDA

Atlantic Coast Institute
5225 West Broward Blvd.
Fort Lauderdale 33317

Broward Community College
225 East Las Olas Blvd.
Fort Lauderdale 33301

Daytona Beach Community College
1200 Volusia Ave.
Daytona Beach 32114

Florida Community College at
Jacksonville
501 West State St.
Jacksonville 32202

Florida Metropolitan University, Tampa
College
3319 West Hillsborough Ave.
Tampa 33614

Florida Metropolitan University, Tampa
College, Lakeland
1200 U.S. Hwy. 98 S
Ste. 45
Lakeland 33801

Florida Metropolitan University, Tampa
College, Pinellas
2471 McMullen Booth Rd.
Clearwater 33759

Gulf Coast Community College
5230 West Hwy. 98
Panama City 32401

Hillsborough Community College
P.O. Box 31127
Tampa 33631-3127

Indian River Community College
3209 Virginia Ave.
Fort Pierce 34981

International College
2654 Tamiami Trail E
Naples 34112

Jones College, Jacksonville
5353 Arlington Expwy.
Jacksonville 32211

Keiser College
1500 Northwest 49th St.
Ste. 114
Fort Lauderdale 33309

Manatee Community College
5840 26th St. W
Bradenton 34207

Miami-Dade Community College
300 Northeast Second Ave.
Miami 33132

Okaloosa-Walton Community College
100 College Blvd.
Niceville 32578

Orlando College
5421 Diplomat Cir.
Orlando 32810

Palm Beach Community College
4200 Congress Ave.
Lake Worth 33461

Pensacola Junior College
1000 College Blvd.
Pensacola 32504

Saint Petersburg Junior College
8580 66 St. N
Pinellas Park 34665

Santa Fe Community College
3000 Northwest 83rd St.
Gainesville 32606

Seminole Community College
100 Weldon Blvd.
Sanford 32773-6199

South College
1760 North Congress Ave.
West Palm Beach 33409

Southern College
5600 Lake Underhill Rd.
Orlando 32807

Tallahassee Community College
444 Appleyard Dr.
Tallahassee 32304-2895

Valencia Community College
P.O. Box 3028
Orlando 32802

Webster College, Inc.
2127 Grand Blvd.
Holiday 34691

GEORGIA

Athens Area Technical Institute
U.S. Hwy. 29 N
Athens 30610-0399

HAWAII

Kapiolani Community College
4303 Diamond Head Rd.
Honolulu 96816

IDAHO

Lewis-Clark State College
500 Eighth Ave.
Lewiston 83501

ILLINOIS

Elgin Community College
1700 Spartan Dr.
Elgin 60123

Illinois Central College
One College Dr.
East Peoria 61635-0001

MacCormac College
506 South Wabash
Chicago 60605

Midstate College
244 Southwest Jefferson
Peoria 61602

Robert Morris College
180 North Lasalle St.
Chicago 60601

Sanford-Brown College
3237 West Chain of Rocks Rd.
Granite 62040

South Suburban College
15800 South State St.
South Holland 60473

William Rainey Harper College
1200 West Algonquin Rd.
Palatine 60067-7398

INDIANA

Ball State University
2000 University Ave.
Muncie 47306

Ivy Tech State College, Central Indiana
One West 26th St.
Indianapolis 46206-1763

Professional Careers Institute
2611 Waterfront Pkwy. & East Dr.
Indianapolis 46214-2028

Sawyer College, Hammond
6040 Hohman Ave.
Hammond 46320

Sawyer College, Merrillville
3803 East Lincoln Hwy.
Merrillville 46410

University of Indianapolis
1400 East Hanna Ave.
Indianapolis 46227

Vincennes University
1002 North First St.
Vincennes 47591

IOWA

American Institute of Commerce
2302 West First St.
Cedar Falls 50613

Des Moines Community College
2006 Ankeny Blvd.
Ankeny 50021

Kirkwood Community College
P.O. Box 2068
Cedar Rapids 52406

KANSAS

The Brown Mackie College
100 East Santa Fe
Ste. 300
Olathe 66061

The Brown Mackie College
126 South Santa Fe St.
Salina 67402-1787

Johnson County Community College
12345 College Blvd.
Overland Park 66210-1299

Kansas City Kansas Community College
7250 State Ave.
Kansas City 66112

Washburn University of Topeka
1700 College Ave.
Topeka 66621

Wichita State University
1845 Fairmount
Wichita 67260

KENTUCKY

Eastern Kentucky University
Lancaster Ave.
Richmond 40475

Kentucky Career Institute
8095 Connector Dr.
Florence 41022-0143

Midway College
512 Stephens St.
Midway 40347-1120

Sullivan College
3101 Bardstown Rd.
Louisville 40205

University of Louisville
2301 South Third St.
Louisville 40292-0001

LOUISIANA

Baton Rouge College
2834 South Sherwood Forest
Ste. B12
Baton Rouge 70816

McNeese State University
4100 Ryan St.
Lake Charles 70609

Nicholls State University
University Station
La Hwy. 1
Thibodaux 70310

Remington College
303 Rue Louis XIV
Lafayette 70508

Tulane University of Louisiana
6823 Saint Charles Ave.
New Orleans 70118

MAINE

Beal College
629 Main St.
Bangor 04401

Casco Bay College
477 Congress St.
Portland 04101

MARYLAND

Abbie Business Institute
5310 Spectrum Dr.
Frederick 21703

Anne Arundel Community College
101 College Pkwy.
Arnold 21012

Baltimore City Community College
2901 Liberty Heights Ave.
Baltimore 21215

Dundalk Community College
7200 Sollers Point Rd.
Dundalk 21222

Frederick Community College
7932 Opossumtown Pike
Frederick 21702

Hagerstown Business College
18618 Crestwood Dr.
Hagerstown 21742

Montgomery College of Takoma Park
Takoma Ave. and Fenton St.
Takoma Park 20912

Prince Georges Community College
301 Largo Rd.
Largo 20774-2199

Villa Julie College
Green Spring Valley Rd.
Stevenson 21153

MASSACHUSETTS

Aquinas College at Milton
303 Adams St.
Milton 02186

Bay Path College
588 Longmeadow St.
Longmeadow 01106

Becker College, Worcester
61 Sever St.
Worcester 01615-0071

Fisher College
118 Beacon St.
Boston 02116

Kinyon-Campbell Business School
1041 Pearl St.
Brockton 02401

Kinyon-Campbell Business School
59 Linden St.
New Bedford 02740

Massachusetts Bay Community College
50 Oakland St.
Wellesley Hills 02181

Middlesex Community College
Springs Rd.
Bedford 01730

Mount Ida College
777 Dedham St.
Newton Centre 02159

North Shore Community College
One Ferncroft Rd.
Danvers 01923

Northern Essex Community College
Elliott Way
Haverhill 01830-2399

Quincy College
34 Coddington St.
Quincy 02169

Stonehill College
Washington St.
North Easton 02357

MICHIGAN

Academy of Court Reporting
26111 Evergreen Rd.
Southfield 48076-4481

American Institute for Paralegal
Studies, Inc.
17515 West Nine Mile Rd.
Ste. 775
Southfield 48075

Delta College
University Center 48710

Ferris State University
901 South State St.
Big Rapids 49307

Gogebic Community College
East 4946 Jackson Rd.
Ironwood 49938

Great Lakes Junior College of Business
310 South Washington Ave.
Saginaw 48607

Henry Ford Community College
5101 Evergreen Rd.
Dearborn 48128

Jackson Community College
2111 Emmons Rd.
Jackson 49201-8399

Kellogg Community College
450 North Ave.
Battle Creek 49017

Lansing Community College
419 North Capitol Ave.
Lansing 48901-7210

Macomb Community College
14500 Twelve Mile Rd.
Warren 48093-3896

Montcalm Community College
2800 College Dr.
Sidney 48885

Mott Community College
1401 East Court St.
Flint 48503

Northwestern Michigan College
1701 East Front St.
Traverse City 49686

Oakland Community College
2480 Opdyke Rd.
Bloomfield Hills 48304-2266

Oakland University
Rochester Hills 48309-4401

Southwestern Michigan College
58900 Cherry Grove Rd.
Dowagiac 49047-9793

University of Detroit, Mercy
P.O. Box 19900
Detroit 48219-0900

MINNESOTA

Inver Hills Community College
2500 80th St. E
Inver Grove Heights 55076

North Hennepin Community College
7411 85th Ave. N
Brooklyn Park 55445

Northland Community and Technical
College
Hwy. 1 E
Thief River Falls 56701

MISSISSIPPI

Mississippi Gulf Coast Community
College
Central Office
P.O. Box 67
Perkinston 39573

MISSOURI

Drury College
900 North Benton Ave.
Springfield 65802

Missouri Western State College
4525 Downs Dr.
Saint Joseph 64507

Penn Valley Community College
3201 Southwest Trafficway
Kansas City 64111

Rockhurst College
1100 Rockhurst Rd.
Kansas City 64110-2561

Vatterott College
3925 Industrial Dr.
Saint Ann 63074

Webster University
470 East Lockwood
Saint Louis 63119-3194

William Jewell College
500 College Hill
Liberty 64068

MONTANA

May Technical College
1306 Central Ave.
Billings 59103

May Technical College, Great Falls
1807 Third St. NW
Great Falls 59404

University of Great Falls
1301 Twentieth St. S
Great Falls 59405-4996

NEBRASKA

College of Saint Mary
1901 South 72nd St.
Omaha 68124

Metropolitan Community College Area
5300 North 30th St.
Omaha 68111

Nebraska College of Business
3350 North 90th
Omaha 68134

NEVADA

Community College of Southern
Nevada
3200 East Cheyenne Ave.
Las Vegas 89030

Morrison College
140 Washington St.
Reno 89503

NEW HAMPSHIRE

Hesser College
Three Sundial Ave.
Manchester 03103

McIntosh College
23 Cataract Ave.
Dover 03820

New Hampshire Community Technical
College, Nashua
505 Amherst St.
Nashua 03061-2052

New Hampshire Technical Institute
11 Institute Dr.
Concord 03301

NEW JERSEY

Bergen Community College
400 Paramus Rd.
Paramus 07652

Brookdale Community College
765 Newman Springs Rd.
Lincroft 07738-1599

Burlington County College
Rte. 530
Pemberton 08068

Cittone Institute
100 Canal Pointe Blvd.
Princeton 08540

Cumberland County College
College Dr.
P.O. Box 517
Vineland 08360

Horizon Institute of Paralegal Studies
453 North Wood Ave.
Linden 07036

Katharine Gibbs School
80 Kingsbridge Rd.
Piscataway 08854

Mercer County Community College
1200 Old Trenton Rd.
Trenton 08690

Middlesex County College
155 Mill Rd.
Edison 08818-3050

Omega Institute
7050 Rte. 38 E
Pennsauken 08109

Sussex County Community College
College Hill
Newton 07860

NEW MEXICO

Albuquerque Career Institute
11300 Lomas Blvd. NE
Albuquerque 87112

Albuquerque Technical Vocational
Institute
525 Buena Vista SE
Albuquerque 87106

San Juan College
4601 College Blvd.
Farmington 87402

Santa Fe Community College
South Richards Ave.
Santa Fe 87502

NEW YORK

Broome Community College
P.O. Box 1017
Binghamton 13902

Corning Community College
Spencer Hill
Corning 14830

Erie Community College, City Campus
121 Ellicott St.
Buffalo 14203

Herkimer County Community College
Reservoir Rd.
Herkimer 13350-1598

Nassau Community College
One Education Dr.
Garden City 11530

Rennert Bilingual
216 East 45th St.
17 Fl.
New York 10017

Schenectady County Community
College
Washington Ave.
Schenectady 12305

The Sobelsohn School
370 Seventh Ave.
New York 10001

Suffolk County Community College,
Ammerman Campus
533 College Rd.
Selden 11784

Suffolk County Community College,
Western Campus
Crooked Hill Rd.
Brentwood 11717

Tompkins-Cortland Community
College
170 North St.
Dryden 13053

NORTH CAROLINA

Cape Fear Community College
411 North Front St.
Wilmington 28401

Carteret Community College
3505 Arendell St.
Morehead City 28557

Central Carolina Community College
1105 Kelly Dr.
Sanford 27330

Central Piedmont Community College
P.O. Box 35009
Charlotte 28235-5009

Coastal Carolina Community College
444 Western Blvd.
Jacksonville 28546-6877

Davidson County Community College
297 Davidson Community College Rd.
Lexington 27292

Durham Technical Community College
1637 Lawson St.
Durham 27703

Fayetteville Technical Community
College
2201 Hull Rd.
Fayetteville 28303-0236

Forsyth Technical Community College
2100 Silas Creek Pkwy.
Winston Salem 27103

Guilford Technical Community College
Box 309
Jamestown 27282

Johnston Community College
P.O. Box 2350
Smithfield 27577-2350

Kings College
322 Lamar Ave.
Charlotte 28204

Pitt Community College
Hwy. 11 S
P.O. Drawer 7007
Greenville 27835-7007

Rockingham Community College
P.O. Box 38
Hwy. 65W County Home Rd.
Wentworth 27375-0038

Southwestern Community College
447 College Dr.
Sylva 28779

Western Piedmont Community College
1001 Burkemont Ave.
Morganton 28655-9978

NORTH DAKOTA

Interstate Business College
520 East Main Ave.
Bismarck 58501

OHIO

Academy of Court Reporting
614 Superior Ave. NW
Cleveland 44113

Academy of Court Reporting, Akron
2930 West Market St.
Akron 44333

Academy of Court Reporting, Columbus
630 East Broad St.
Columbus 43215

American School of Technology
2100 Morse Rd.
Bldg. 4599
Columbus 43229

Columbus Paraprofessional Institute
1900 East Grandville Rd.
Bldg. A
Ste. 210
Columbus 43229

Columbus State Community College
550 East Spring St.
Columbus 43216

Dyke College
112 Prospect Ave.
Cleveland 44115

Lakeland Community College
7700 Clocktower Dr.
Kirtland 44094-5198

Lima Technical College
4240 Campus Dr.
Lima 45804

Muskingum Area Technical College
1555 Newark Rd.
Zanesville 43701

Raedel College and Industrial Welding
School
14 Lincoln Way W
Massilon 44647

Sawyer College of Business, West
13027 Lorain Ave.
Cleveland 44111

Sawyer College of Business
3150 Mayfield Rd.
Cleveland Heights 44118

Sinclair Community College
444 West Third St.
Dayton 45402

Technology Education College
288 South Hamilton Rd.
Columbus 43213

Tri-County Vocational School
15675 St. Rte. 691
Nelsonville 45764

University of Akron, Main Campus
302 Buchtel Common
Akron 44325-4702

University of Cincinnati, Main Campus
P.O. Box 210127
Cincinnati 45221-0127

University of Toledo
2801 West Bancroft
Toledo 43606

OKLAHOMA

City College, Inc.
1370 North Interstate Dr.
Norman 73072

Rogers University, Claremore
1701 West Will Rogers Blvd.
Claremore 74017

Rose State College
6420 Southeast 15th
Midwest City 73110

OREGON

College of Legal Arts
527 Southwest Hall
Ste. 308
Portland 97201

Pioneer Pacific College
25195 Southwest Parkway Ave.
Wilsonville 97070

Portland Community College
P.O. Box 19000
Portland 97280-0990

Western Business College
425 Southwest Washington
Portland 97204

PENNSYLVANIA

Academy of Medical Arts and Business
2301 Academy Dr.
Harrisburg 17112

American Center for Technical Arts
1930 Chestnut St.
Philadelphia 19103

American Center for Technical Arts and
Sciences
100 East Lancaster Ave.
Wayne 19087

Central Pennsylvania Business School
College Hill Rd.
Summerdale 17093-0309

Community College of Allegheny
County
800 Allegheny Ave.
Pittsburgh 15233-1895

Duffs Business Institute
110 Ninth St.
Pittsburgh 15222

Gannon University
109 West Sixth St.
Erie 16541

Harrisburg Area Community College,
Harrisburg
One Hacc Dr.
Harrisburg 17110

Luzerne County Community College
1333 South Prospect St.
Nanticoke 18634

Manor Junior College
700 Fox Chase Rd.
Jenkintown 19046

Mount Aloysius College
7373 Admiral Peary Hwy.
Cresson 16630-1999

Peirce College
1420 Pine St.
Philadelphia 19102

Pennsylvania College of Technology
One College Ave.
Williamsport 17701

Pennsylvania State University, Main
Campus
201 Old Main
University Park 16802

Robert Morris College
Narrows Run Rd.
Coraopolis 15108-1189

Star Technical Institute, Kingston
212 Wyoming Ave.
Kingston 18704

Western School of Health & Business
Careers
One Monroeville Center
Ste. 250
Monroeville 15146

Western School of Health & Business
Careers
421 Seventh Ave.
Pittsburgh 15219

Westmoreland County Community
College
Youngwood 15697-1895

RHODE ISLAND

Johnson and Wales University
8 Abbott Park Place
Providence 02903-3376

Katharine Gibbs School
178 Butler Ave.
Providence 02906

SOUTH CAROLINA

Florence Darlington Technical College
P.O. Box 100548
Florence 29501-0548

Greenville Technical College
Station B
P.O. Box 5616
Greenville 29606-5616

Midlands Technical College
P.O. Box 2408
Columbia 29202

Trident Technical College
P.O. Box 118067
Charleston 29423-8067

SOUTH DAKOTA

Kilian Community College
224 North Phillips Ave.
Sioux Falls 57104-6014

National American University
321 Kansas City St.
Rapid City 57701

Nettleton Career College
100 South Spring Ave.
Sioux Falls 57104

TENNESSEE

Chattanooga State Technical
   Community College
4501 Amnicola Hwy.
Chattanooga 37406

Cleveland State Community College
P.O. Box 3570
Cleveland 37320-3570

Pellissippi State Technical Community
   College
P.O. Box 22990
Knoxville 37933-0990

State Technical Institute at Memphis
5983 Macon Cove
Memphis 38134

TEXAS

Austin Community College
5930 Middle Fiskville Rd.
Austin 78752

Center for Advanced Legal Studies
3910 Kirby
Ste. 200
Houston 77098

Collin County Community College
2200 West University Dr.
McKinney 75070

Del Mar College
101 Baldwin
Corpus Christi 78404-3897

El Centro College
Main and Lamar
Dallas 75202

El Paso Community College
P.O. Box 20500
El Paso 79998

Grayson County College
6101 Grayson Dr.
Denison 75020

Houston Community College System
22 Waugh Dr.
Houston 77270-7849

Midland College
3600 North Garfield
Midland 79705

North Harris Montgomery Community
   College District
250 North Sam Houston Pkwy. E
Ste. 300
Houston 77060

San Antonio College
1300 San Pedro Ave.
San Antonio 78284

Southern Careers Institute, Inc.
2301 South Congress
Ste. 27
Austin 78704

Southern Methodist University
6425 Boaz St.
Dallas 75275-0221

Southwestern Paralegal Institutes
4888 Loop Central Dr.
Ste. 800
Houston 77081

Tarrant County Junior College
1500 Houston St.
Fort Worth 76102

Texas School of Business, Inc.
711 Airtex Dr.
Houston 77073

Texas School of Business, Southwest,
   Inc.
10250 Bissonnet
Houston 77036

Tyler Junior College
1327 South Baxter Ave.
Tyler 75711

UTAH

Mountain West College, Salt Lake City
3098 Highland Dr.
Salt Lake City 84106

Utah Valley State College
800 West, 1200 South
Orem 84058

Westminster College of Salt Lake City
1840 South, 1300 East
Salt Lake City 84105

VERMONT

Champlain College
163 South Willard St.
Burlington 05401

VIRGINIA

Commonwealth College
301 Centre Pointe Dr.
Virginia Beach 23462

Para-Legal Institute
9402a Lee Hwy.
Fairfax 22031

University of Richmond
28 Westhampton Way
Richmond 23173

WASHINGTON

Clark College
1800 East McLoughlin Blvd.
Vancouver 98663-3598

Edmonds Community College
20000 68th Ave. W
Lynnwood 98036

Highline Community College
P.O. Box 98000
Des Moines 98198-9800

Pierce College
9401 Farwest Dr. SW
Lakewood 98498

Spokane Community College
North 1810 Greene Ave.
Spokane 99207

WEST VIRGINIA

The College of West Virginia
500 South Kanawha St.
Beckley 25801

Marshall University
400 Hal Greer Blvd.
Huntington 25755

University of Charleston
2300 MacCorkle Ave. SE
Charleston 25304

West Virginia Business College
116 Pennsylvania Ave.
Nutterfort 26301

West Virginia Business College
1052 Main St.
Wheeling 26003

West Virginia Career College
148 Willey St.
Morgantown 26505

WISCONSIN

Chippewa Valley Technical College
620 West Clairemont Ave.
Eau Claire 54701

Lakeshore Technical College
1290 North Ave.
Cleveland 53015

MBTI Business Training Institute
606 West Wisconsin Ave.
Milwaukee 53203

Milwaukee Area Technical College
700 West State St.
Milwaukee 53233-1443

Northeast Wisconsin Technical College
2740 West Mason St.
P.O. Box 19042
Green Bay 54307-9042

WYOMING

Casper College
125 College Dr.
Casper 82601

Laramie County Community College
1400 East College Dr.
Cheyenne 82007

Library Assistant Technology

CALIFORNIA

Foothill College
12345 El Monte Rd.
Los Altos Hills 94022

Fresno City College
1101 East University Ave.
Fresno 93741

Palomar College
1140 West Mission
San Marcos 92069-1487

Sacramento City College
3835 Freeport Blvd.
Sacramento 95822

ILLINOIS

City Colleges of Chicago, Wilbur Wright
   College
4300 North Narragansett
Chicago 60634

College of Du Page
425 22nd St.
Glen Ellyn 60137-6599

Police Science and Law Enforcement Technology

ALABAMA

Community College of the Air Force
130 West Maxwell Blvd.
Montgomery 36112-6613

Gadsden State Community College
1001 George Wallace Dr.
Gadsden 35902-0227

George C Wallace State Community
   College, Hanceville
801 Main St. NW
Hanceville 35077-2000

John C Calhoun State Community
   College
Hwy. 31 N
Decatur 35602

ALASKA

University of Alaska, Southeast
11120 Glacier Hwy.
Juneau 99801

ARIZONA

Arizona Institute of Business and
   Technology
925 South Gilbert Rd.
Ste. 210
Mesa 85204

Arizona Western College
P.O. Box 929
Yuma 85366

Central Arizona College
8470 North Overfield Rd.
Coolidge 85228-9778

Glendale Community College
6000 West Olive Ave.
Glendale 85302

Mesa Community College
1833 West Southern Ave.
Mesa 85202

Phoenix College
1202 West Thomas Rd.
Phoenix 85013

Pima Community College
2202 West Anklam Rd.
Tucson 85709-0001

ARKANSAS

East Arkansas Community College
1700 Newcastle Rd.
Forrest City 72335

Garland County Community College
101 College Dr.
Hot Springs 71913

CALIFORNIA

California Career School
1100 Technology Circle
Anaheim 92805

Chaffey Community College
5885 Haven Ave.
Rancho Cucamonga 91737-3002

City College of San Francisco
50 Phelan Ave.
San Francisco 94112

Contra Costa College
2600 Mission Bell Dr.
San Pablo 94806

De Anza College
21250 Stevens Creek Blvd.
Cupertino 95014

Fresno City College
1101 East University Ave.
Fresno 93741

Fullerton College
321 East Chapman Ave.
Fullerton 92832-2095

Imperial Valley College
P.O. Box 158
Imperial 92251-0158

Lassen Community College
Hwy. 139
P.O. Box 3000
Susanville 96130

Mount San Antonio College
1100 North Grand
Walnut 91789

Napa Valley College
2277 Napa Vallejo Hwy.
Napa 94558

Palomar College
1140 West Mission
San Marcos 92069-1487

Rancho Santiago Community College
   District
1530 West 17th St.
Santa Ana 92706

Rio Hondo College
3600 Workman Mill Rd.
Whittier 90601-1699

Royal Security Training Academy
1510 Balsam Dr.
Pomona 91766

Sacramento City College
3835 Freeport Blvd.
Sacramento 95822

Safety First Security Training Academy
1649 Van Ness Ave.
Ste. 102
Fresno 93721

San Diego Miramar College
10440 Black Mountain Rd.
San Diego 92126-2999

San Joaquin Valley College
201 New Stine Rd.
Bakersfield 93309

San Joaquin Valley College
295 East Sierra Ave.
Fresno 93710-3616

San Joaquin Valley College
8400 West Mineral King Ave.
Visalia 93291

Santa Rosa Junior College
1501 Mendocino Ave.
Santa Rosa 95401-4395

Shasta College
P.O. Box 496006
Redding 96049

Sierra College
5000 Rocklin Rd.
Rocklin 95677

Solano County Community College
District
4000 Suisun Valley Rd.
Suisun 94585-3197

Southwestern College
900 Otay Lakes Rd.
Chula Vista 91910

Victor Valley College
18422 Bear Valley Rd.
Victorville 92392-9699

COLORADO

Aims Community College
Box 69
Greeley 80632

Colorado Mountain College
P.O. Box 10001
Glenwood Springs 81602

Delta-Montrose Area Vocational
Technical Center
1765 U.S. Hwy. 50
Delta 81416

Denver Institute of Technology
7350 North Broadway
Denver 80221

Morgan Community College
17800 County Rd. 20
Fort Morgan 80701

Nakazono Security Training
1780 South Bellaire St.
Denver 80222

Trinidad State Junior College
600 Prospect St.
Trinidad 81082

CONNECTICUT

Housatonic Community-Technical
College
510 Barnum Ave.
Bridgeport 06608

Manchester Community-Technical
College
60 Bidwell St.
P.O. Box 1045
Manchester 06040-1046

Northwestern Connecticut Community-
Technical College
Park Place E
Winsted 06098

Norwalk Community-Technical College
188 Richards Ave.
Norwalk 06854

Tunxis Community-Technical College
Rtes. 6 and 177
Farmington 06032

DELAWARE

Delaware Technical and Community
College, Owens
Box 610
Georgetown 19947

Delaware Technical and Community
College, Stanton-Wilmington
400 Stanton-Christiana Rd.
Newark 19702

FLORIDA

Brevard Community College
1519 Clearlake Rd.
Cocoa 32922

Central Florida Community College
3001 Southwest College Rd.
Ocala 34474

Chipola Junior College
3094 Indian Circle
Marianna 32446

Daytona Beach Community College
1200 Volusia Ave.
Daytona Beach 32114

Florida Community College at
Jacksonville
501 West State St.
Jacksonville 32202

Indian River Community College
3209 Virginia Ave.
Fort Pierce 34981

Lake City Community College
Rte. 19
Box 1030
Lake City 32025

Lake County Area Vocational Technical
Center
2001 Kurt St.
Eustis 32726

Lively Technical Center
500 North Appleyard Dr.
Tallahassee 32304

Manatee Vocational Technical Center
5603 34th St. W
Bradenton 34210

Miami-Dade Community College
300 Northeast Second Ave.
Miami 33132

North Florida Community College
Turner Davis Dr.
Madison 32340

Palm Beach Community College
4200 Congress Ave.
Lake Worth 33461

Pasco-Hernando Community College
36727 Blanton Rd.
Dade City 33523-7599

Santa Fe Community College
3000 Northwest 83rd St.
Gainesville 32606

Sarasota County Technical Institute
4748 Beneva Rd.
Sarasota 34233-1798

Seminole Community College
100 Weldon Blvd.
Sanford 32773-6199

South Florida Community College
600 West College Dr.
Avon Park 33825

William T McFatter Vocational
Technical Center
6500 Nova Dr.
Davie 33317

Withlacoochee Technical Institute
1201 West Main St.
Inverness 32650

GEORGIA

Columbus State University
4225 University Ave.
Columbus 31907-5645

Floyd College
P.O. Box 1864
Rome 30162-1864

Georgia Military College, Fort Gordon
Center
P.O. Box 7258
Fort Gordon 30905

Georgia Military College, Main Campus
201 East Greene St.
Milledgeville 31061-3398

Interactive Learning Systems
4814 Old National Hwy.
College Park 30337

Interactive Learning Systems
200 Cleveland Rd.
Ste. 5 and 6
Bogart 30622

Interactive Learning Systems
4814 Old National Hwy.
College Park 30337

HAWAII

Hawaii Community College
200 West Kawili St.
Hilo 96720-4091

Honolulu Community College
874 Dillingham Blvd.
Honolulu 96817

IDAHO

College of Southern Idaho
P.O. Box 1238
Twin Falls 83301

Eastern Idaho Technical College
1600 South, 2500 East
Idaho Falls 83404

Idaho State University
741 South Seventh Ave.
Pocatello 83209

North Idaho College
1000 West Garden Ave.
Coeur D'Alene 83814

Ricks College
Rexburg 83460-4107

ILLINOIS

Belleville Area College
2500 Carlyle Rd.
Belleville 62221

Black Hawk College
6600 34th Ave.
Moline 61265

City Colleges of Chicago, Harold
Washington College
30 East Lake St.
Chicago 60601

City Colleges of Chicago, Richard J
Daley College
7500 South Pulaski Rd.
Chicago 60652

City Colleges of Chicago, Wilbur Wright
College
4300 North Narragansett
Chicago 60634

College of Du Page
425 22nd St.
Glen Ellyn 60137-6599

College of Lake County
19351 West Washington St.
Grayslake 60030-1198

Danville Area Community College
2000 East Main St.
Danville 61832

Illinois Central College
One College Dr.
East Peoria 61635-0001

Illinois Valley Community College
815 North Orlando Smith Ave.
Oglesby 61348-9692

John A Logan College
700 Logan College Rd.
Carterville 62918

Joliet Junior College
1215 Houbolt Rd.
Joliet 60431

Kankakee Community College
P.O. Box 888
Kankakee 60901

Kaskaskia College
27210 College Rd.
Centralia 62801

Lake Land College
5001 Lake Land Blvd.
Mattoon 61938

Lewis and Clark Community College
5800 Godfrey Rd.
Godfrey 62035

Lincoln Land Community College
Shepherd Rd.
Springfield 62194-9256

Moraine Valley Community College
10900 South 88th Ave.
Palos Hills 60465-0937

Morton College
3801 South Central Ave.
Cicero 60804

Northwestern University
633 Clark St.
Evanston 60208

Oakton Community College
1600 East Golf Rd.
Des Plaines 60016

Parkland College
2400 West Bradley Ave.
Champaign 61821

Rend Lake College
468 North Ken Graz Pkwy.
Ina 62846

Richland Community College
One College Park
Decatur 62521

Rock Valley College
3301 North Mulford Rd.
Rockford 61114

Sauk Valley Community College
173 Illinois Rte. 2
Dixon 6102i

Shawnee Community College
8364 Shawnee College Rd.
Ullin 62992

South Suburban College
15800 South State St.
South Holland 60473

Southeastern Illinois College
3575 College Rd.
Harrisburg 62946

Southern Illinois University,
Carbondale
Faner Hall 2179
Carbondale 62901-4512

Triton College
2000 Fifth Ave.
River Grove 60171

Waubonsee Community College
Rte. 47 at Harter Rd.
Sugar Grove 60554-0901

William Rainey Harper College
1200 West Algonquin Rd.
Palatine 60067-7398

INDIANA

Indiana State University
210 North Seventh St.
Terre Haute 47809

Indiana University, Kokomo
2300 South Washington
Kokomo 46902

Indiana University, Purdue University,
Fort Wayne
2101 Coliseum Blvd. E
Fort Wayne 46805

Indiana University, South Bend
1700 Mishawaka Ave.
South Bend 46615

Sawyer College, Merrillville
3803 East Lincoln Hwy.
Merrillville 46410

Vincennes University
1002 North First St.
Vincennes 47591

IOWA

Des Moines Community College
2006 Ankeny Blvd.
Ankeny 50021

Hawkeye Community College
1501 East Orange Rd.
Waterloo 50704

Indian Hills Community College
525 Grandview
Ottumwa 52501

Iowa Lakes Community College
19 South Seventh St.
Estherville 51334

Iowa Valley Community College
Box 536
Marshalltown 50158

Iowa Western Community College
2700 College Rd.
Box 4C
Council Bluffs 51502

Kirkwood Community College
P.O. Box 2068
Cedar Rapids 52406

North Iowa Area Community College
500 College Dr.
Mason City 50401

Western Iowa Tech Community College
4647 Stone Ave.
P.O. Box 5199
Sioux City 51102-5199

KANSAS

Barton County Community College
245 Northeast 30th Rd.
Great Bend 67530

Butler County Community College
901 South Haverhill Rd.
El Dorado 67042

Cowley County Community College
125 South Second St.
Arkansas City 67005

Garden City Community College
801 Campus Dr.
Garden City 67846

Hutchinson Community College
1300 North Plum St.
Hutchinson 67501

Johnson County Community College
12345 College Blvd.
Overland Park 66210-1299

Seward County Community College
Box 1137
Liberal 67905-1137

KENTUCKY

Eastern Kentucky University
Lancaster Ave.
Richmond 40475

Hopkinsville Community College
North Dr.
Hopkinsville 42240

Northern Kentucky University
University Dr.
Highland Heights 41099

University of Louisville
2301 South Third St.
Louisville 40292-0001

LOUISIANA

Bossier Parish Community College
2719 Airline Dr. N
Bossier City 71111

Delgado Community College
501 City Park Ave.
New Orleans 70119

Grambling State University
100 Main St.
Grambling 71245

Louisiana State University, Eunice
P.O. Box 1129
Eunice 70535

Nicholls State University
University Station
La Hwy. 1
Thibodaux 70310

Southern University and A & M College
Baton Rouge 70813

MAINE

Southern Maine Technical College
Fort Rd.
South Portland 04106

University of Maine
Office of Institutional Studies
Orono 04469

University of Maine at Augusta
46 University Dr.
Augusta 04330-9410

MARYLAND

Allegany College of Maryland
12401 Willowbrook Rd. SE
Cumberland 21502

Anne Arundel Community College
101 College Pkwy.
Arnold 21012

Catonsville Community College
800 South Rolling Rd.
Catonsville 21228

Chesapeake College
P.O. Box 8
Wye Mills 21679-0008

Essex Community College
7201 Rossville Blvd.
Baltimore 21237

Hagerstown Junior College
11400 Robinwood Dr.
Hagerstown 21742-6590

Harford Community College
401 Thomas Run Rd.
Bel Air 21015

Montgomery College of Rockville
51 Mannakee St.
Rockville 20850

Prince Georges Community College
301 Largo Rd.
Largo 20774-2199

Wor-Wic Community College
32000 Campus Dr.
Salisbury 21801-7131

MASSACHUSETTS

Becker College, Worcester
61 Sever St.
Worcester 01615-0071

Berkshire Community College
1350 West St.
Pittsfield 01201-5786

Bunker Hill Community College
250 New Rutherford Ave.
Boston 02129

Cape Cod Community College
2240 Iyanough Rd.
West Barnstable 02668-1599

Dean College
99 Main St.
Franklin 02038

Greenfield Community College
One College Dr.
Greenfield 01301-9739

Holyoke Community College
303 Homestead Ave.
Holyoke 01040

Massachusetts Bay Community College
50 Oakland St.
Wellesley Hills 02181

Massasoit Community College
One Massasoit Blvd.
Brockton 02402

Middlesex Community College
Springs Rd.
Bedford 01730

Mount Wachusett Community College
444 Green St.
Gardner 01440

North Shore Community College
One Ferncroft Rd.
Danvers 01923

Northeastern University
360 Huntington Ave.
Boston 02115

Northern Essex Community College
Elliott Way
Haverhill 01830-2399

Quincy College
34 Coddington St.
Quincy 02169

Quinsigamond Community College
670 West Boylston St.
Worcester 01606

Springfield Technical Community
College
One Armory Square
Springfield 01105

MICHIGAN

Alpena Community College
666 Johnson St.
Alpena 49707

Delta College
University Center 48710

Grand Rapids Community College
143 Bostwick Ave. NE
Grand Rapids 49503-3295

Jackson Community College
2111 Emmons Rd.
Jackson 49201-8399

Kalamazoo Valley Community College
6767 West O Ave.
Kalamazoo 49009

Kellogg Community College
450 North Ave.
Battle Creek 49017

Kirtland Community College
10775 North Saint Helen Rd.
Roscommon 48653

Lake Michigan College
2755 East Napier Ave.
Benton Harbor 49022-8099

Lake Superior State University
650 West Easterday Ave.
Sault Sainte Marie 49783

Lansing Community College
419 North Capitol Ave.
Lansing 48901-7210

Macomb Community College
14500 Twelve Mile Rd.
Warren 48093-3896

Madonna University
36600 Schoolcraft Rd.
Livonia 48150

Montcalm Community College
2800 College Dr.
Sidney 48885

Mott Community College
1401 East Court St.
Flint 48503

Muskegon Community College
221 South Quarterline Rd.
Muskegon 49442

Northern Michigan University
1401 Presque Isle
Marquette 49855

Northwestern Michigan College
1701 East Front St.
Traverse City 49686

Oakland Community College
2480 Opdyke Rd.
Bloomfield Hills 48304-2266

Schoolcraft College
18600 Haggerty Rd.
Livonia 48152

Suomi College
601 Quincy St.
Hancock 49930

Washtenaw Community College
P.O. D1
Ann Arbor 48106-1610

West Shore Community College
3000 North Stiles Rd.
Scottville 49454

MINNESOTA

Alexandria Technical College
1601 Jefferson St.
Alexandria 56308

Fond Du Lac Tribal and Community
College
2101 14th St.
Cloquet 55720

Hibbing Community College
1515 East 25th St.
Hibbing 55746

Inver Hills Community College
2500 80th St. E
Inver Grove Heights 55076

Mankato State University
South Rd. and Ellis Ave.
Mankato 56002-8400

Normandale Community College
9700 France Ave. S
Bloomington 55431

North Hennepin Community College
7411 85th Ave. N
Brooklyn Park 55445

Northland Community and Technical
College
Hwy. 1 E
Thief River Falls 56701

Rochester Community and Technical
College
851 30th Ave. SE
Rochester 55904-4999

MISSISSIPPI

Mississippi Gulf Coast Community
College
Central Office
P.O. Box 67
Perkinston 39573

MISSOURI

Jefferson College
1000 Viking Dr.
Hillsboro 63050

Missouri Southern State College
3950 East Newman Rd.
Joplin 64801-1595

Missouri Western State College
4525 Downs Dr.
Saint Joseph 64507

Penn Valley Community College
3201 Southwest Trafficway
Kansas City 64111

Three Rivers Community College
Three Rivers Blvd.
Poplar Bluff 63901

MONTANA

Dawson Community College
300 College Dr.
Glendive 59330

NEBRASKA

Metropolitan Community College Area
5300 North 30th St.
Omaha 68111

Northeast Community College
801 East Benjamin
P.O. Box 469
Norfolk 68702-0469

NEVADA

Community College of Southern
   Nevada
3200 East Cheyenne Ave.
Las Vegas 89030

Truckee Meadows Community College
7000 Dandini Blvd.
Reno 89512

Western Nevada Community College
2201 West College Pkwy.
Carson City 89703

NEW HAMPSHIRE

Hesser College
Three Sundial Ave.
Manchester 03103

NEW JERSEY

Atlantic Community College
5100 Black Horse Pike
Mays Landing 08330-2699

Bergen Community College
400 Paramus Rd.
Paramus 07652

Brookdale Community College
765 Newman Springs Rd.
Lincroft 07738-1599

Burlington County College
Rte. 530
Pemberton 08068

Camden County College
P.O. Box 200
Blackwood 08012

County College of Morris
214 Center Grove Rd.
Randolph 07869

Essex County College
303 University Ave.
Newark 07102

Gloucester County College
1400 Tanyard Rd.
Sewell 08080

Mercer County Community College
1200 Old Trenton Rd.
Trenton 08690

Middlesex County College
155 Mill Rd.
Edison 08818-3050

Ocean County College
College Dr.
Toms River 08753

Passaic County Community College
One College Blvd.
Paterson 07505-1179

Raritan Valley Community College
P.O. Box 3300 Lamington Rd.
Somerville 08876

Union County College
1033 Springfield Ave.
Cranford 07016

NEW MEXICO

Albuquerque Technical Vocational
   Institute
525 Buena Vista SE
Albuquerque 87106

New Mexico State University, Main
   Campus
P.O. Box 30001
Dept. 3Z
Weddell Dr.
Las Cruces 88003

Santa Fe Community College
6401 Richards Ave.
Santa Fe 87505

University of New Mexico, Gallup
   Branch
200 College Rd.
Gallup 87301

NEW YORK

Adirondack Community College
Bay Rd.
Queensbury 12804

Broome Community College
P.O. Box 1017
Binghamton 13902

Canisius College
2001 Main St.
Buffalo 14208

Cayuga County Community College
Franklin St.
Auburn 13021

Clinton Community College
136 Clinton Point Dr.
Plattsburgh 12901

Columbia-Greene Community College
4400 Rte. 23
Hudson 12534

CUNY John Jay College Criminal
   Justice
899 Tenth Ave.
New York 10019

Dutchess Community College
53 Pendell Rd.
Poughkeepsie 12601

Erie Community College, North
   Campus
Main St. and Youngs Rd.
Williamsville 14221

Hilbert College
5200 South Park Ave.
Hamburg 14075-1597

Jamestown Community College
525 Falconer St.
Jamestown 14701

Marist College
290 North Rd.
Poughkeepsie 12601

Monroe Community College
1000 East Henrietta Rd.
Rochester 14623

Orange County Community College
115 South St.
Middletown 10940

Rockland Community College
145 College Rd.
Suffern 10901

Suffolk County Community College,
   Ammerman Campus
533 College Rd.
Selden 11784

Suffolk County Community College,
   Eastern Campus
Speonk Riverhead Rd.
Riverhead 11901

Suffolk County Community College,
   Western Campus
Crooked Hill Rd.
Brentwood 11717

Sullivan County Community College
Le Roy Rd.
P.O. Box 4002
Loch Sheldrake 12759-4002

SUNY College of Technology at Canton
Cornell Drive
Canton 13617

SUNY College of Technology at
   Farmingdale
Melville Rd.
Farmingdale 11735-1021

SUNY Westchester Commmunity
   College
75 Grasslands Rd.
Valhalla 10595

Superior Career Institute, Inc.
254 West 29th St.
3rd Fl.
New York 10011

Tompkins-Cortland Community
   College
170 North St.
Dryden 13053

NORTH CAROLINA

Alamance Community College
P.O. Box 8000
Graham 27253

American Institute of Applied Science
P.O. Box 639
Youngsville 27596

Asheville Buncombe Technical
   Community College
340 Victoria Rd.
Asheville 28801

Beaufort County Community College
Box 1069
Washington 27889

Brunswick Community College
P.O. Box 30
Supply 28462

Cape Fear Community College
411 North Front St.
Wilmington 28401

Carteret Community College
3505 Arendell St.
Morehead City 28557

Catawba Valley Community College
2550 Hwy. 70 SE
Hickory 28602-0699

Central Carolina Community College
1105 Kelly Dr.
Sanford 27330

Central Piedmont Community College
P.O. Box 35009
Charlotte 28235-5009

Cleveland Community College
137 South Post Rd.
Shelby 28152

Coastal Carolina Community College
444 Western Blvd.
Jacksonville 28546-6877

College of the Albemarle
1208 North Road St.
Elizabeth City 27906-2327

Craven Community College
800 College Ct.
New Bern 28562

Davidson County Community College
297 Davidson Community College Rd.
Lexington 27292

Durham Technical Community College
1637 Lawson St.
Durham 27703

Fayetteville Technical Community
   College
2201 Hull Rd.
Fayetteville 28303-0236

Forsyth Technical Community College
2100 Silas Creek Pkwy.
Winston Salem 27103

Gaston College
201 Hwy. 321 S
Dallas 28034

Guilford Technical Community College
Box 309
Jamestown 27282

Halifax Community College
P.O. Drawer 809
Weldon 27890

Haywood Community College
Freedlander Dr.
Clyde 28721

James Sprunt Community College
P.O. Box 398
Kenansville 28349

Johnston Community College
P.O. Box 2350
Smithfield 27577-2350

Mayland Community College
P.O. Box 547
Spruce Pine 28777

Mitchell Community College
500 West Broad
Statesville 28677

Montgomery Community College
P.O. Box 787
Troy 27371

Pitt Community College
Hwy. 11 S
P.O. Drawer 7007
Greenville 27835-7007

Randolph Community College
629 Industrial Park Ave.
Asheboro 27204

Richmond Community College
P.O. Box 1189
Hamlet 28345

Robeson Community College
P.O. Box 1420
Lumberton 28359

Rowan-Cabarrus Community College
Box 1595
Salisbury 28145-1595

Southeastern Community College
4564 Chadburn Hwy.
Whiteville 28472

Stanly Community College
141 College Dr.
Albemarle 28001

Vance-Granville Community College
State Rd. 1126
P.O. Box 917
Henderson 27536

Wake Technical Community College
9101 Fayetteville Rd.
Raleigh 27603-5696

Wayne Community College
3000 Wayne Memorial Dr.
Goldsboro 27533-8002

Western Piedmont Community College
1001 Burkemont Ave.
Morganton 28655-9978

Wilson Technical Community College
902 Herring Ave.
Wilson 27893

NORTH DAKOTA

Minot State University
500 University Ave. W
Minot 58707

United Tribes Technical College
3315 University Dr.
Bismarck 58501

University of North Dakota, Lake
  Region
1801 North College Dr.
Devils Lake 58301

OHIO

Brentley Institute, Inc.
P.O. Box 20724
Cleveland 44120

Butler County JVS District, D Russel
  Lee Career Center
3603 Hamilton Middletown Rd.
Hamilton 45011

Central Ohio Technical College
1179 University Dr.
Newark 43055-1767

Columbus State Community College
550 East Spring St.
Columbus 43216

Cuyahoga Community College District
700 Carnegie Ave.
Cleveland 44115-2878

Delaware Joint Vocational School
  District
4565 Columbus Pke.
Delaware 43015

Eastland Career Center
4465 South Hamilton Rd.
Groveport 43125

Edison State Community College
1973 Edison Dr.
Piqua 45356

Gallia Jackson Vinton JVSD
Box 157
Rio Grande 45674

Hocking Technical College
3301 Hocking Pkwy.
Nelsonville 45764

Jefferson Community College
4000 Sunset Blvd.
Steubenville 43952-3598

Lakeland Community College
7700 Clocktower Dr.
Kirtland 44094-5198

Lima Technical College
4240 Campus Dr.
Lima 45804

Lorain County Community College
1005 Abbe Rd. N
Elyria 44035

Midwest Technical Schools, Inc.
7009 Taylorsville Rd.
Ste. B
Huber Heights 45424

Muskingum Area Technical College
1555 Newark Rd.
Zanesville 43701

North Central Technical College
2441 Kenwood Circle
P.O. Box 698
Mansfield 44901

Ohio University, Chillicothe Branch
571 West Fifth St.
Chillicothe 45601

Owens Community College, Findlay
  Campus
300 Davis St.
Findlay 45840

Owens Technical College
39335 Oregon Rd.
Toledo 43699-1947

Sinclair Community College
444 West Third St.
Dayton 45402

Southern Hills Joint Vocational School
  District
9193 Hamer Rd.
Georgetown 45121

Terra State Community College
2830 Napoleon Rd.
Fremont 43420

University of Akron, Main Campus
302 Buchtel Common
Akron 44325-4702

University of Cincinnati, Main Campus
P.O. Box 210127
Cincinnati 45221-0127

University of Toledo
2801 West Bancroft
Toledo 43606

Youngstown State University
One University Plz.
Youngstown 44555

OKLAHOMA

Cameron University
2800 Gore Blvd.
Lawton 73505

Central Oklahoma Area Vocational
  Technical School
Three Court Circle
Drumright 74030

Central Oklahoma Area Vocational
  Technical School
1720 South Main
Sapulpa 74030

Connors State College
Rte. 1
Box 1000
Warner 74469

Northeastern Oklahoma Agricultural
  and Mechanical College
200 I St. NE
Miami 74354

Northern Oklahoma College
Box 310 Tonkawa
Tonkawa 74653

Oklahoma State University, Oklahoma
  City
900 North Portland
Oklahoma City 73107

Platt College
309 South Ann Arbor
Oklahoma City 73128

Platt College
3801 South Sheridan
Tulsa 74145

Redlands Community College
1300 South Country Club Rd.
El Reno 73036-5304

Rogers University, Claremore
1701 West Will Rogers Blvd.
Claremore 74017

Rose State College
6420 Southeast 15th
Midwest City 73110

Tulsa Community College
6111 East Skelly Dr.
Tulsa 74135

OREGON

Blue Mountain Community College
P.O. Box 100
Pendleton 97801

Clackamas Community College
19600 Molalla Ave.
Oregon City 97045

Lane Community College
4000 East 30th Ave.
Eugene 97405

Linn-Benton Community College
6500 Southwest Pacific Blvd.
Albany 97321

Pioneer Pacific College
25195 Southwest Parkway Ave.
Wilsonville 97070

Rogue Community College
3345 Redwood Hwy.
Grants Pass 97527

Southwestern Oregon Community
  College
1988 Newmark Ave.
Coos Bay 97420

Treasure Valley Community College
650 College Blvd.
Ontario 97914

PENNSYLVANIA

Advanced Career Training
McClatchy Bldg.
2nd Fl.
Southwest Corner 69th
Upper Darby 19082

American Center Technical Arts
1930 Chestnut St.
Philadelphia 19103

Bucks County Community College
Swamp Rd.
Newtown 18940

Community College of Allegheny
  County
800 Allegheny Ave.
Pittsburgh 15233-1895

Community College of Beaver County
One Campus Dr.
Monaca 15061

Community College of Philadelphia
1700 Spring Garden St.
Philadelphia 19130

Delaware County Community College
901 South Media Line Rd.
Media 19063-1094

Harrisburg Area Community College,
  Harrisburg
One Hacc Dr.
Harrisburg 17110

Lackawanna Junior College
501 Vine St.
Scranton 18509

Lehigh Carbon Community College
4525 Education Park Dr.
Schnecksville 18078-2598

Lion Investigation Academy
434 Clearfield St.
Freemansburg 18017

Luzerne County Community College
1333 South Prospect St.
Nanticoke 18634

Mercyhurst College
501 East 38th St.
Erie 16546

Montgomery County Community
  College
340 Dekalb Pike
Blue Bell 19422

Suburban Academy of Law
  Enforcement
3550 William Penn Hwy.
Pittsburgh 15235

Westmoreland County Community
  College
Youngwood 15697-1895

York College Pennsylvania
Country Club Rd.
York 17405-7199

RHODE ISLAND

Community College of Rhode Island
400 East Ave.
Warwick 02886-1807

SOUTH CAROLINA

Central Carolina Technical College
506 North Guignard Dr.
Sumter 29150

Florence Darlington Technical College
P.O. Box 100548
Florence 29501-0548

Horry-Georgetown Technical College
P.O. Box 1966
Conway 29526

Midlands Technical College
P.O. Box 2408
Columbia 29202

Orangeburg Calhoun Technical College
3250 Saint Matthews Rd.
Orangeburg 29118

Piedmont Technical College
P.O. Drawer 1467
Greenwood 29648

Tri-County Technical College
P.O. Box 587
Pendleton 29670

Trident Technical College
P.O. Box 118067
Charleston 29423-8067

SOUTH DAKOTA

Western Dakota Technical Institute
800 Mickelson Dr.
Rapid City 57701

TENNESSEE

East Tennessee State University
P.O. Box 70734
Johnson City 37614-0734

Roane State Community College
276 Patton Ln.
Harriman 37748

Shelby State Community College
P.O. Box 40568
Memphis 38174-0568

Tennessee Technological University
900 North Dixie Ave.
Cookeville 38505

Walters State Community College
500 South Davy Crockett Pkwy.
Morristown 37813-6899

TEXAS

Alvin Community College
3110 Mustang Rd.
Alvin 77511

Austin Community College
5930 Middle Fiskville Rd.
Austin 78752

Bee County College
3800 Charco Rd.
Beeville 78102

Central Texas College
P.O. Box 1800
Killeen 76540-1800

Del Mar College
101 Baldwin
Corpus Christi 78404-3897

El Centro College
Main and Lamar
Dallas 75202

El Paso Community College
P.O. Box 20500
El Paso 79998

Grayson County College
6101 Grayson Dr.
Denison 75020

Kilgore College
1100 Broadway
Kilgore 75662-3299

Lamar University, Beaumont
4400 Mlk.
P.O. Box 10001
Beaumont 77710

Laredo Community College
West End Washington St.
Laredo 78040

McLennan Community College
1400 College Dr.
Waco 76708

Navarro College
3200 West Seventh
Corsicana 75110

Northeast Texas Community College
Fm 1735
Mount Pleasant 75456

Odessa College
201 West University
Odessa 79764

San Antonio College
1300 San Pedro Ave.
San Antonio 78284

San Jacinto College, Central Campus
8060 Spencer Hwy.
Pasadena 77505

San Jacinto College, North Campus
5800 Uvalde
Houston 77049

South Plains College
1401 College Ave.
Levelland 79336

Southwest Texas Junior College
2401 Garner Field Rd.
Uvalde 78801

Tarrant County Junior College
1500 Houston St.
Fort Worth 76102

Texas Security Officers Institute
6906 Atwell
Ste. 209
Houston 77081

Texas Southmost College
80 Fort Brown
Brownsville 78520

Trinity Valley Community College
500 South Prairieville
Athens 75751

Tyler Junior College
1327 South Baxter Ave.
Tyler 75711

Wayland Baptist University
1900 West Seventh
Plainview 79072

Weatherford College
308 East Park Ave.
Weatherford 76086

UTAH

Bridgerland Applied Technology Center
1301 North, 600 West
Logan 84321

Salt Lake Community College
P.O. Box 30808
Salt Lake City 84130

Southern Utah University
351 West Center
Cedar City 84720

Weber State University
3750 Harrison Blvd.
Ogden 84408

VERMONT

Champlain College
163 South Willard St.
Burlington 05401

VIRGINIA

Central Virginia Community College
3506 Wards Rd.
Lynchburg 24502

Danville Community College
1008 South Main St.
Danville 24541

Germanna Community College
2130 Germanna Hwy.
Locust Grove 22508

J Sargeant Reynolds Community
College
P.O. Box 85622
Richmond 23285-5622

John Tyler Community College
13101 Jefferson Davis Hwy.
Chester 23831-5399

Mountain Empire Community College
Drawer 700
Big Stone Gap 24219

New River Community College
Drawer 1127
Dublin 24084-1127

Northern Virginia Community College
4001 Wakefield Chapel Rd.
Annandale 22003

Paul D Camp Community College
100 North College Dr.
P.O. Box 737
Franklin 23851

Southside Virginia Community College
109 Campus Dr.
Alberta 23821

Southwest Virginia Community College
Box South V C C
Richlands 24641

Thomas Nelson Community College
P.O. Box 9407
Hampton 23670

Tidewater Community College
121 College Pl.
Norfolk 23510

Virginia Highlands Community College
P.O. Box 828
Abingdon 24212-0828

Virginia School of Polygraph
7909 Brookfield Rd.
Norfolk 23518

Virginia Western Community College
3095 Colonial Ave.
Roanoke 24015

Wytheville Community College
1000 East Main St.
Wytheville 24382

WASHINGTON

Bellevue Community College
3000 Landerholm Circle SE
Bellevue 98007-6484

Columbia Basin College
2600 North 20th Ave.
Pasco 99301

Everett Community College
801 Wetmore Ave.
Everett 98201

Green River Community College
12401 Southeast 320th St.
Auburn 98092

Olympic College
1600 Chester Ave.
Bremerton 98337-1699

Shoreline Community College
16101 Greenwood Ave. N
Seattle 98133

Spokane Community College
North 1810 Greene Ave.
Spokane 99207

WEST VIRGINIA

Bluefield State College
219 Rock St.
Bluefield 24701

Fairmont State College
1201 Locust Ave.
Fairmont 26554

Southern West Virginia Community
and Technical College
Box 2900
Mt. Gay 25637

West Virginia State College
Rte. 25
Institute 25112

WISCONSIN

Blackhawk Technical College
P.O. Box 5009
Janesville 53547

Chippewa Valley Technical College
620 West Clairemont Ave.
Eau Claire 54701

Fox Valley Technical College
1825 North Bluemound Dr.
Appleton 54913-2277

Gateway Technical College
3520 30th Ave.
Kenosha 53144-1690

Good, Armstrong, and Associates, Ltd.
2142 South 55th St.
Milwaukee 53219

Lakeshore Technical College
1290 North Ave.
Cleveland 53015

Madison Area Technical College
3550 Anderson St.
Madison 53704

Mid-State Technical College
500 32nd St. N
Wisconsin Rapids 54494

Milwaukee Area Technical College
700 West State St.
Milwaukee 53233-1443

Moraine Park Technical College
235 North National Ave.
Fond Du Lac 54936-1940

Nicolet Area Technical College
Hwy. G S
Rhinelander 54501

Northcentral Technical College
1000 Campus Dr.
Wausau 54401-1899

Northeast Wisconsin Technical College
2740 West Mason St.
P.O. Box 19042
Green Bay 54307-9042

Waukesha County Technical College
800 Main St.
Pewaukee 53072

Western Wisconsin Technical College
304 North Sixth St.
P.O. Box 908
La Crosse 54602-0908

WYOMING

Casper College
125 College Dr.
Casper 82601

Sheridan College
3059 Coffeen Ave.
Sheridan 82801

ARIZONA

Phoenix College
1202 West Thomas Rd.
Phoenix 85013

CALIFORNIA

Allan Hancock College
800 South College Dr.
Santa Maria 93454

Antelope Valley College
3041 West Ave. K
Lancaster 93536

Butte College
3536 Butte Campus Dr.
Oroville 95965

Cabrillo College
6500 Soquel Dr.
Aptos 95003

Cerritos College
11110 Alondra Blvd.
Norwalk 90650

Chabot College
25555 Hesperian Blvd.
Hayward 94545

Citrus College
1000 West Foothill Blvd.
Glendora 91741-1899

College of Marin
835 College Ave.
Kentfield 94904

College of San Mateo
1700 West Hillsdale Blvd.
San Mateo 94402

College of the Canyons
26455 Rockwell Canyon Rd.
Santa Clarita 91355

College of the Desert
43-500 Monterey St.
Palm Desert 92260

College of the Redwoods
7351 Tompkins Hill Rd.
Eureka 95501-9302

College of the Sequoias
915 South Mooney Blvd.
Visalia 93277

Cosumnes River College
8401 Center Pkwy.
Sacramento 95823-5799

Cuesta College
P.O. Box 8106
San Luis Obispo 93403-8106

Diablo Valley College
321 Golf Club Rd.
Pleasant Hill 94523

El Camino College
16007 Crenshaw Blvd.
Torrance 90506

Fresno City College
1101 East University Ave.
Fresno 93741

Fullerton College
321 East Chapman Ave.
Fullerton 92832-2095

Golden West College
15744 Golden W
Huntington Beach 92647

Grossmont College
8800 Grossmont College Dr.
El Cajon 92020

Hartnell College
156 Homestead Ave.
Salinas 93901

Long Beach City College
4901 East Carson St.
Long Beach 90808

Los Angeles Southwest College
1600 West Imperial Hwy.
Los Angeles 90047

Los Angeles Valley College
5800 Fulton Ave.
Van Nuys 91401

Mendocino College
P.O. Box 3000
Ukiah 95482

Merced College
3600 M St.
Merced 95348-2898

Merritt College
12500 Campus Dr.
Oakland 94619

Modesto Junior College
435 College Ave.
Modesto 95350-5800

Monterey Peninsula College
980 Fremont St.
Monterey 93940-4799

Moorpark College
7075 Campus Rd.
Moorpark 93021

Mount San Jacinto College
1499 North State St.
San Jacinto 92583

Pasadena City College
1570 East Colorado Blvd.
Pasadena 91106

Porterville College
100 East College Ave.
Porterville 93257

Rancho Santiago Community College
District
1530 West 17th St.
Santa Ana 92706

Riverside Community College
4800 Magnolia Ave.
Riverside 92506-1299

San Joaquin Delta College
5151 Pacific Ave.
Stockton 95207

Santa Monica College
1900 Pico Blvd.
Santa Monica 90405-1628

Southwestern College
900 Otay Lakes Rd.
Chula Vista 91910

Ventura College
4667 Telegraph Rd.
Ventura 93003

West Los Angeles College
4800 Freshman Dr.
Culver City 90230

West Valley College
14000 Fruitvale Ave.
Saratoga 95070

Yuba College
2088 North Beale Rd.
Marysville 95901

COLORADO

Aims Community College
Box 69
Greeley 80632

Arapahoe Community College
2500 West College Dr.
Littleton 80160-9002

Colorado Northwestern Community
College
500 Kennedy Dr.
Rangely 81648-3598

Pikes Peak Community College
5675 South Academy Blvd.
Colorado Springs 80906-5498

Pueblo Community College
900 West Orman Ave.
Pueblo 81004

Red Rocks Community College
13300 West Sixth Ave.
Lakewood 80228

Trinidad State Junior College
600 Prospect St.
Trinidad 81082

CONNECTICUT

Connecticut Institute of Technology
Two Elizabeth St.
West Haven 06516

DELAWARE

Delaware Technical and Community
College, Stanton-Wilmington
400 Stanton-Christiana Rd.
Newark 19702

FLORIDA

Edison Community College
8099 College Pkwy. SW
Fort Myers 33906-6210

Florida Community College at
Jacksonville
501 West State St.
Jacksonville 32202

Indian River Community College
3209 Virginia Ave.
Fort Pierce 34981

Miami-Dade Community College
300 Northeast Second Ave.
Miami 33132

Pensacola Junior College
1000 College Blvd.
Pensacola 32504

Polk Community College
999 Ave. H NE
Winter Haven 33881

Seminole Community College
100 Weldon Blvd.
Sanford 32773-6199

HAWAII

Honolulu Community College
874 Dillingham Blvd.
Honolulu 96817

Maui Community College
310 Kaahumanu Ave.
Kahului 96732

IDAHO

Idaho State University
741 South Seventh Ave.
Pocatello 83209

ILLINOIS

Lake Land College
5001 Lake Land Blvd.
Mattoon 61938

INDIANA

Indiana University, Purdue University,
Fort Wayne
2101 Coliseum Blvd. E
Fort Wayne 46805

Indiana University, Purdue University,
Indianapolis
355 North Lansing
Indianapolis 46202

IOWA

Iowa Western Community College
2700 College Rd.
Box 4C
Council Bluffs 51502

LOUISIANA

Delgado Community College
501 City Park Ave.
New Orleans 70119

Louisiana Technical College, T H Harris
Campus
337 East South St.
Opelousas 70570

MAINE

University of Maine
Office of Institutional Studies
Orono 04469

MASSACHUSETTS

Hebrew College
43 Hawes St.
Brookline 02146

Lincoln Institute of Land Policy
113 Brattle St.
Cambridge 02138-3400

Massasoit Community College
One Massasoit Blvd.
Brockton 02402

Quinsigamond Community College
670 West Boylston St.
Worcester 01606

Springfield Technical Community
College
One Armory Square
Springfield 01105

University of Massachusetts, Lowell
One University Ave.
Lowell 01854

Wentworth Institute of Technology
550 Huntington Ave.
Boston 02115

MICHIGAN

Alpena Community College
666 Johnson St.
Alpena 49707

Ferris State University
901 South State St.
Big Rapids 49307

Grand Rapids Community College
143 Bostwick Ave. NE
Grand Rapids 49503-3295

Henry Ford Community College
5101 Evergreen Rd.
Dearborn 48128

Lansing Community College
419 North Capitol Ave.
Lansing 48901-7210

Michigan Technological University
1400 Townsend Dr.
Houghton 49931-1295

MINNESOTA

Lake Superior College
2101 Trinity Rd.
Duluth 55811

Saint Paul Technical College
235 Marshall Ave.
Saint Paul 55102

MISSISSIPPI

Northeast Mississippi Community
College
Cunningham Blvd.
Booneville 38829

MISSOURI

Mineral Area College
P.O. Box 1000
Park Hills 63601-1000

Park College
8700 River Park Dr.
Parkville 64152-3795

MONTANA

University of Great Falls
1301 Twentieth St. S
Great Falls 59405-4996

NEW HAMPSHIRE

New Hampshire Technical Institute
11 Institute Dr.
Concord 03301

University of New Hampshire, Main
Campus
Thompson Hall
Durham 03824

NEW JERSEY

Mercer County Community College
1200 Old Trenton Rd.
Trenton 08690

Middlesex County College
155 Mill Rd.
Edison 08818-3050

Ocean County College
College Dr.
Toms River 08753

Thomas A Edison State College
101 West State St.
Trenton 08608-1176

NEW MEXICO

Albuquerque Technical Vocational
Institute
525 Buena Vista SE
Albuquerque 87106

NEW YORK

Broome Community College
P.O. Box 1017
Binghamton 13902

Columbia-Greene Community College
4400 Rte. 23
Hudson 12534

Corning Community College
Spencer Hill
Corning 14830

CUNY Bronx Community College
West 181 St. & University Ave.
Bronx 10453

CUNY College of Staten Island
2800 Victory Blvd.
Staten Island 10314

CUNY Hostos Community College
500 Grand Concourse
Bronx 10451

CUNY New York City Technical College
300 Jay St.
Brooklyn 11201

Erie Community College, City Campus
121 Ellicott St.
Buffalo 14203

Erie Community College, North
Campus
Main St. and Youngs Rd.
Williamsville 14221

Finger Lakes Community College
4355 Lake Shore Dr.
Canandaigua 14424

Fulton-Montgomery Community
College
2805 State Hwy. 67
Johnstown 12095

Genesee Community College
One College Rd.
Batavia 14020

Herkimer County Community College
Reservoir Rd.
Herkimer 13350-1598

Hudson Valley Community College
80 Vandenburgh Ave.
Troy 12180

Jefferson Community College
Outer Coffeen St.
Watertown 13601

Mater Dei College
5428 St. Hwy. 37
Ogdensburg 13669

Mohawk Valley Community College
1101 Sherman Dr.
Utica 13501

Monroe Community College
1000 East Henrietta Rd.
Rochester 14623

Nassau Community College
One Education Dr.
Garden City 11530

Niagara County Community College
3111 Saunders Settlement Rd.
Sanborn 14132

North Country Community College
20 Winona Ave.
P.O. Box 89
Saranac Lake 12983

Onondaga Community College
4941 Onondaga Rd.
Syracuse 13215

Paul Smith's College of Arts and Science
New York 12970

Rochester Institute of Technology
One Lomb Memorial Dr.
Rochester 14623-5603

Saint John's University, New York
8000 Utopia Pkwy.
Jamaica 11439

Schenectady County Community
College
Washington Ave.
Schenectady 12305

SUNY College of Technology at
Farmingdale
Melville Rd.
Farmingdale 11735-1021

SUNY College of Technology at Canton
Cornell Drive
Canton 13617

SUNY Ulster County Community
College
Cottekill Rd.
Stone Ridge 12484

SUNY Westchester Commmunity
College
75 Grasslands Rd.
Valhalla 10595

NORTH CAROLINA

Central Piedmont Community College
P.O. Box 35009
Charlotte 28235-5009

Gaston College
201 Hwy. 321 S
Dallas 28034

Guilford Technical Community College
Box 309
Jamestown 27282

Wake Technical Community College
9101 Fayetteville Rd.
Raleigh 27603-5696

NORTH DAKOTA

North Dakota State College of Science
800 North Sixth St.
Wahpeton 58076

OHIO

Cincinnati State Technical and
Community College
3520 Central Pkwy.
Cincinnati 45223

Clark State Community College
570 East Leffel Ln.
Springfield 45505

Columbus State Community College
550 East Spring St.
Columbus 43216

Ohio University, Eastern Campus
National Rd. W
Saint Clairsville 43950

Ohio University, Main Campus
Athens 45701

Ohio University, Southern Campus
1804 Liberty Ave.
Ironton 45638

Sinclair Community College
444 West Third St.
Dayton 45402

Stark State College of Technology
6200 Frank Ave. NW
Canton 44720

University of Akron, Main Campus
302 Buchtel Common
Akron 44325-4702

University of Akron, Wayne College
1901 Smucker Rd.
Orrville 44667

University of Cincinnati, Main Campus
P.O. Box 210127
Cincinnati 45221-0127

University of Toledo
2801 West Bancroft
Toledo 43606

Urbana University
College Way
Urbana 43078

OKLAHOMA

Platt College
3801 South Sheridan
Tulsa 74145

OREGON

Blue Mountain Community College
P.O. Box 100
Pendleton 97801

Clackamas Community College
19600 Molalla Ave.
Oregon City 97045

Oregon Institute of Technology
3201 Campus Dr.
Klamath Falls 97601-8801

PENNSYLVANIA

Bucks County Community College
Swamp Rd.
Newtown 18940

Harrisburg Area Community College,
Harrisburg
One Hacc Dr.
Harrisburg 17110

Lehigh Carbon Community College
4525 Education Park Dr.
Schnecksville 18078-2598

Pennsylvania College of Technology
One College Ave.
Williamsport 17701

Pennsylvania Institute of Technology
800 Manchester Ave.
Media 19063

Westmoreland County Community
College
Youngwood 15697-1895

RHODE ISLAND

Roger Williams University
One Old Ferry Rd.
Bristol 02809-2923

SOUTH CAROLINA

Florence Darlington Technical College
P.O. Box 100548
Florence 29501-0548

Horry-Georgetown Technical College
P.O. Box 1966
Conway 29526

Spartanburg Methodist College
1200 Textile Dr.
Spartanburg 29301-0009

Spartanburg Technical College
P.O. Box 4386
Spartanburg 29305

Trident Technical College
P.O. Box 118067
Charleston 29423-8067

University of South Carolina at Aiken
171 University Pkwy.
Aiken 29801

University of South Carolina at
Lancaster
P.O. Box 889
Lancaster 29720

TENNESSEE

Pellissippi State Technical Community
College
P.O. Box 22990
Knoxville 37933-0990

TEXAS

San Antonio College
1300 San Pedro Ave.
San Antonio 78284

Tarrant County Junior College
1500 Houston St.
Fort Worth 76102

Texarkana College
2500 North Robison Rd.
Texarkana 75599

VERMONT

Southern Vermont College
Monument Rd.
Bennington 05201

Vermont Technical College
P.O. Box 500
Randolph Center 05061

VIRGINIA

J Sargeant Reynolds Community
College
P.O. Box 85622
Richmond 23285-5622

New River Community College
Drawer 1127
Dublin 24084-1127

Thomas Nelson Community College
P.O. Box 9407
Hampton 23670

Tidewater Community College
121 College Pl.
Norfolk 23510

WASHINGTON

Bates Technical College
1101 South Yakima Ave.
Tacoma 98405

Centralia College
600 West Locust St.
Centralia 98531

Spokane Community College
North 1810 Greene Ave.
Spokane 99207

Spokane Falls Community College
West 3410 Fort George Wright Dr.
Spokane 99224

Walla Walla Community College
500 Tausick Way
Walla Walla 99362

Yakima Valley Community College
P.O. Box 1647
Yakima 98907

WEST VIRGINIA

Bluefield State College
219 Rock St.
Bluefield 24701

WISCONSIN

Madison Area Technical College
3550 Anderson St.
Madison 53704

Mid-State Technical College
500 32nd St. N
Wisconsin Rapids 54494

Moraine Park Technical College
235 North National Ave.
Fond Du Lac 54936-1940

Northeast Wisconsin Technical College
2740 West Mason St.
P.O. Box 19042
Green Bay 54307-9042

WYOMING

Laramie County Community College
1400 East College Dr.
Cheyenne 82007

Public Service Technology

ALABAMA

Samford University
800 Lakeshore Dr.
Ste. 2240
Birmingham 35229-2240

COLORADO

Parks College
9065 Grant St.
Denver 80229

CONNECTICUT

Manchester Community Technical
College
60 Bidwell St.
Manchester 06040-1046

FLORIDA

Daytona Beach Community College
1200 Volusia Ave.
Daytona Beach 32114

Valencia Community College
P.O. Box 3028
Orlando 32802

HAWAII

Denver Business College
419 South St.
Ste. 174
Honolulu 96813

INDIANA

Indiana University, Purdue University,
Indianapolis
355 North Lansing
Indianapolis 46202

IOWA

Des Moines Community College
2006 Ankeny Blvd.
Ankeny 50021

Iowa Valley Community College
Box 536
Marshalltown 50158

Kirkwood Community College
P.O. Box 2068
Cedar Rapids 52406

MAINE

University of Maine
Office of Institutional Studies
Orono 04469

MASSACHUSETTS

Berkshire Community College
1350 West St.
Pittsfield 01201-5786

Holyoke Community College
303 Homestead Ave.
Holyoke 01040

Lincoln Institute of Land Policy
113 Brattle St.
Cambridge 02138-3400

Quinsigamond Community College
670 West Boylston St.
Worcester 01606

MICHIGAN

Delta College
University Center 48710

MINNESOTA

Minneapolis Community and Technical
College
1501 Hennepin Ave.
Minneapolis 55403-1779

North Hennepin Community College
7411 85th Ave. N
Brooklyn Park 55445

NEW MEXICO

University of New Mexico, Gallup
Campus
200 College Rd.
Gallup 87301

NEW YORK

Cazenovia College
Cazenovia 13035

Corning Community College
Spencer Hill
Corning 14830

Fulton-Montgomery Community
College
2805 St. Hwy. 67
Johnstown 12095

Genesee Community College
One College Rd.
Batavia 14020

Herkimer County Community College
Reservoir Rd.
Herkimer 13350-1598

Hilbert College
5200 South Park Ave.
Hamburg 14075-1597

Hudson Valley Community College
80 Vandenburgh Ave.
Troy 12180

Jamestown Community College
525 Falconer St.
Jamestown 14701

Jefferson Community College
Outer Coffeen St.
Watertown 13601

Mater Dei College
5428 St. Hwy. 37
Ogdensburg 13669

Medaille College
18 Agassiz Circle
Buffalo 14214

Mohawk Valley Community College
1101 Sherman Dr.
Utica 13501

Monroe Community College
1000 East Henrietta Rd.
Rochester 14623

Niagara County Community College
3111 Saunders Settlement Rd.
Sanborn 14132

Onondaga Community College
4941 Onondaga Rd.
Syracuse 13215

Rochester Institute of Technology
One Lomb Memorial Dr.
Rochester 14623-5603

Schenectady County Community
College
Washington Ave.
Schenectady 12305

Suffolk County Community College,
Ammerman Campus
533 College Rd.
Selden 11784

SUNY College of Technology at Alfred
Alfred 14802

SUNY Empire State College
Two Union Ave.
Saratoga Springs 12866

SUNY Ulster County Community
College
Cottekill Rd.
Stone Ridge 12484

SUNY Westchester Commmunity
College
75 Grasslands Rd.
Valhalla 10595

Tompkins-Cortland Community
College
170 North St.
Dryden 13053

Touro College
27-33 West 23rd St.
New York 10010

OHIO

Vocational Guidance Services
2239 East 55th St.
Cleveland 44103

OKLAHOMA

Kiamichi AVTS SD #7, Hugo
107 South 15th
Box 699
Hugo 74743

Metro Area Vocational Technical
Center, School District 22
1900 Springlake Dr.
Oklahoma City 73111

PENNSYLVANIA

Community College of Philadelphia
1700 Spring Garden St.
Philadelphia 19130

Sawyer School
717 Liberty Ave.
Pittsburgh 15222

TENNESSEE

Shelby State Community College
P.O. Box 40568
Memphis 38174-0568

Tennessee Technology Center at
Morristown
821 West Louise Ave.
Morristown 37813

TEXAS

Houston Community College System
22 Waugh Dr.
Houston 77270-7849

WISCONSIN

Milwaukee Area Technical College
700 West State St.
Milwaukee 53233-1443

Religious Occupations

CALIFORNIA

Booker T Crenshaw Christian College &
School Ministry, Inc.
3134 Franklin Ave.
San Diego 92113

Golden Gate Baptist Seminary
201 Seminary Dr.
Mill Valley 94941-3197

International School of Theology
24600 Arrowhead Springs Rd.
San Bernardino 92414

The Master's College
21726 Placerita Cyn Rd.
Santa Clarita 91321-1200

Pacific Coast Baptist Bible College
1100 South Valley Center
San Dimas 91773

The Salvation Army College for
Officers' Training
30840 Hawthorne Blvd.
Rancho Palos Verdes 90274

San Jose Christian College
790 South 12th St.
P.O. Box 1090
San Jose 95108

Trinity Life Bible College
5225 Hillsdale at Madison
Sacramento 95842

COLORADO

Nazarene Bible College
1111 Academy Park Loop
Colorado Springs 80910-3717

FLORIDA

Florida Baptist Theological College
5400 College Dr.
Graceville 32440

Florida Christian College, Inc.
1011 Bill Beck Blvd.
Kissimmee 34744

Gospel Crusade Institute of Ministry
1200 Glory Way Blvd.
Rte. 2
P.O. Box 279
Bradenton 34202

United Bible College & Seminary
P.O. Box 585284
Orlando 32858

Zoe College, Inc.
6501 Arlington Expy.
Bldg. A
Ste. 120
Jacksonville 32211

GEORGIA

Beulah Heights Bible College
892-906 Berne St. SE
Atlanta 30316

IDAHO

Boise Bible College
8695 Marigold St.
Boise 83714

Northwest Nazarene College
623 Holly St.
Nampa 83686-5897

ILLINOIS

Lincoln Christian College and
Seminary
100 Campus View Dr.
Lincoln 62656-2111

Moody Bible Institute
820 North Lasalle Blvd.
Chicago 60610

INDIANA

Indiana Wesleyan University
4201 South Washington St.
Marion 46953

IOWA

Emmaus Bible College
2570 Asbury Rd.
Dubuque 52001

KANSAS

Hesston College
Box 3000
Hesston 67062

Manhattan Christian College
1415 Anderson Ave.
Manhattan 66502

KENTUCKY

Clear Creek Baptist Bible College
300 Clear Creek Rd.
Pineville 40977-9752

Kentucky Mountain Bible College
Box 10
Vancleve 41385

Southern Baptist Theological Seminary
2825 Lexington Rd.
Louisville 40280

LOUISIANA

New Orleans Baptist Theological
Seminary
3939 Gentilly Blvd.
New Orleans 70126

World Evangelism Bible College and
Seminary
8919 World Ministry Ave.
Baton Rouge 70810

MARYLAND

Ner Israel Rabbinical College
400 Mount Wilson Ln.
Baltimore 21208

Washington Bible College
6511 Princess Garden Pkwy.
Lanham 20706-3599

MASSACHUSETTS

Baptist Bible College East
950 Metropolitan Ave.
Hyde Park 02136

Gordon-Conwell Theological Seminary
130 Essex St.
South Hamilton 01982

MICHIGAN

Reformed Bible College
3333 East Beltline NE
Grand Rapids 49525

Sacred Heart Major Seminary
2701 Chicago Blvd.
Detroit 48206

MINNESOTA

Association Free Lutheran Bible School
3110 East Medicine Lake Blvd.
Plymouth 55441-3099

North Central Bible College
910 Elliot Ave. S
Minneapolis 55404

Oak Hills Bible College
1600 Oak Hills Rd. SW
Bemidji 56601

MISSISSIPPI

Southeastern Baptist College
4229 Hwy. 15 N
Laurel 39440

MISSOURI

Baptist Bible College
628 East Kearney
Springfield 65803

Berean University
1445 Boonville Ave.
Springfield 65802

Central Bible College
3000 North Grant
Springfield 65803-1096

Midwestern Baptist Theological
  Seminary
5001 North Oak Trafficway
Kansas City 64118

Ozark Christian College
1111 North Main St.
Joplin 64801

NEBRASKA

Grace University
1311 South Ninth St.
Omaha 68108-3629

Platte Valley Bible College
305 East 16th St.
Scotts Bluff 69363

NEW JERSEY

College of Saint Elizabeth
Two Convent Rd.
Morristown 07960-6989

NEW MEXICO

Nazarene Indian Bible College
2315 Markham Rd. SW
P.O. Box 12295
Albuquerque 87195

NEW YORK

Elim Bible Institute
7245 College St.
Lima 14485

Practical Bible College
400 Riverside Dr.
Bible School Park 13737-0601

Word of Life Bible Institute
Rte. 9
Pottersville 12860

NORTH CAROLINA

East Coast Bible College
6900 Wilkinson Blvd.
Charlotte 28214

Roanoke Bible College
714 First St.
Elizabeth City 27909-3926

Southeastern Baptist Theological
  Seminary
Box 1889
Wake Forest 27588-1889

OHIO

Cincinnati Bible College & Seminary
2700 Glenway Ave.
Cincinnati 45204-3200

Circleville Bible College
1476 Lancaster Pike
Circleville 43113

OKLAHOMA

Hillsdale Free Will Baptist College
3701 South I-35
Moore 73160

Oklahoma Baptist University
500 West University
Shawnee 74801

Southwestern College of Christian
  Ministries
P.O. Box 340
Bethany 73008

OREGON

Eugene Bible College
2155 Bailey Hill Rd.
Eugene 97405

Multnomah College and Bilblical
  Seminary
8435 Northeast Glisan St.
Portland 97220

Portland Bible College
9201 Northeast Fremont
Portland 97220

Western Baptist College
5000 Deer Park Dr. SE
Salem 97301

PENNSYLVANIA

Baptist Bible College and Seminary
538 Venard Rd.
Clarks Summit 18411

Lancaster Bible College
901 Eden Rd.
Lancaster 17601

Saint Charles Borromeo Seminary
100 East Wynnewood Rd.
Wynnewood 19096

Valley Forge Christian College
1401 Charlestown Rd.
Phoenixville 19460

RHODE ISLAND

Zion Bible Institute
27 Middle Hwy.
Barrington 02806

SOUTH CAROLINA

Bob Jones University
Greenville 29614

Columbia International University
7435 Monticello Rd.
Columbia 29230

TENNESSEE

Emmanuel Bible College
610 Boscobel St.
Nashville 37206

Memphis School of Preaching
3950 Forest Hill Irene Rd.
Memphis 38125-2560

Mid America Baptist Seminary
2216 Germantown Rd. S
Germantown 38138

Tennessee Temple University
1815 Union Ave.
Chattanooga 37404

United Theological Seminary, Scarritt-
  Bennett Center
19th Ave. S
Nashville 37203

TEXAS

International Christian Institute &
  Graduate School
P.O. Box 720405
Houston 71727

Texas Bible College
816 Evergreen
Houston 77023

VIRGINIA

The Catholic Distance University
120 East Colonial Hwy.
Hamilton 20158-9012

Eastern Mennonite University
1200 Park Rd.
Harrisonburg 22801-2462

WASHINGTON

Lutheran Bible Institute of Seattle
4221 228th SE
Issaquah 98029

Puget Sound Christian College
410 Fourth Ave. N
Edmonds 98020-3171

WEST VIRGINIA

Appalachian Bible College
Box ABC
Bradley 25818-1353

Social Work and Recreation Technology

ALABAMA

Community College of the Air Force
130 West Maxwell Blvd.
Montgomery 36112-6613

Lawson State Community College
3060 Wilson Rd. SW
Birmingham 35221

ARIZONA

Pima Community College
2202 West Anklam Rd.
Tucson 85709-0001

CALIFORNIA

Alexander Training Institute of San
  Francisco
30 Grant Ave.
San Francisco 94108

Allan Hancock College
800 South College Dr.
Santa Maria 93454

Diablo Valley College
321 Golf Club Rd.
Pleasant Hill 94523

Fresno City College
1101 East University Ave.
Fresno 93741

Imperial Valley College
P.O. Box 158
Imperial 92251-0158

COLORADO

Aims Community College
Box 69
Greeley 80632

FLORIDA

Charlotte Vocational Technical Center
18300 Toledo Blade Blvd.
Port Charlotte 33948-3399

IDAHO

Ricks College
Rexburg 83460-4107

ILLINOIS

City Colleges of Chicago, Kennedy-King
6800 South Wentworth Ave.
Chicago 60621

College of Du Page
425 22nd St.
Glen Ellyn 60137-6599

Elgin Community College
1700 Spartan Dr.
Elgin 60123

Rock Valley College
3301 North Mulford Rd.
Rockford 61114

South Suburban College
15800 South State St.
South Holland 60473

INDIANA

Indiana University East
2325 Chester Blvd.
Richmond 47374

KANSAS

Allen County Community College
1801 North Cottonwood
Iola 66749

Cloud County Community College
2221 Campus Dr.
Box 1002
Concordia 66901-1002

Colby Community College
1255 South Range
Colby 67701

Kansas City Area Vocational Technical
  School
2220 North 59th St.
Kansas City 66104

Kaw Area Technical School
5724 Huntoon
Topeka 66604

Neosho County Community College
800 West 14th St.
Chanute 66720

North Central Kansas Technical College
Hwy. 24
P.O. Box 507
Beloit 67420

Salina Area Vocational Technical
  School
2562 Scanlan Ave.
Salina 67401

Wichita Area Technical College
201 North Water
Wichita 67202-1292

KENTUCKY

Hopkinsville Community College
North Dr.
Hopkinsville 42240

Jefferson Community College
109 East Broadway
Louisville 40202

Owensboro Community College
4800 New Hartford Rd.
Owensboro 42303

MASSACHUSETTS

Dean College
99 Main St.
Franklin 02038

Massasoit Community College
One Massasoit Blvd.
Brockton 02402

Mount Ida College
777 Dedham St.
Newton Centre 02159

MICHIGAN

Delta College
University Center 48710

Grand Rapids Community College
143 Bostwick Ave. NE
Grand Rapids 49503-3295

Macomb Community College
14500 Twelve Mile Rd.
Warren 48093-3896

Mott Community College
1401 East Court St.
Flint 48503

MINNESOTA

Inver Hills Community College
2500 80th St. E
Inver Grove Heights 55076

MISSISSIPPI

Mississippi Gulf Coast Community
College
Central Office
P.O. Box 67
Perkinston 39573

MISSOURI

Jefferson College
1000 Viking Dr.
Hillsboro 63050

Saint Louis Community College, Forest
Park
5600 Oakland Ave.
Saint Louis 63110

MONTANA

Blackfeet Community College
Hwy. 2 And 89
Browning 59417-0819

NEBRASKA

Metropolitan Community College Area
5300 North 30th St.
Omaha 68111

NEW JERSEY

Brookdale Community College
765 Newman Springs Rd.
Lincroft 07738-1599

Camden County College
P.O. Box 200
Blackwood 08012

Essex County College
303 University Ave.
Newark 07102

Hudson County Community College
25 Journal Sq.
Jersey City 07306

Ocean County College
College Dr.
Toms River 08753

NEW MEXICO

Northern New Mexico Community
College
1002 North Onate St.
Espanola 87532

NORTH CAROLINA

Central Piedmont Community College
P.O. Box 35009
Charlotte 28235-5009

Halifax Community College
P.O. Drawer 809
Weldon 27890

Wayne Community College
3000 Wayne Memorial Dr.
Goldsboro 27533-8002

OHIO

Clark State Community College
570 East Leffel Ln.
Springfield 45505

Columbus State Community College
550 East Spring St.
Columbus 43216

Edison State Community College
1973 Edison Dr.
Piqua 45356

Washington State Community College
710 Colegate Dr.
Marietta 45750

OKLAHOMA

Caddo-Kiowa Area Vocational Technical
School
P.O. Box 190
Fort Cobb 73038

Connors State College
Rte. 1
Box 1000
Warner 74469

Francis Tuttle Area Vocational
Technical Center
12777 North Rockwell Ave.
Oklahoma City 73142-2789

Metro Area Vocational Technical School
District 22
1900 Springlake Dr.
Oklahoma City 73111

OREGON

Chemeketa Community College
4000 Lancaster Dr. NE
Salem 97305

Lane Community College
4000 East 30th Ave.
Eugene 97405

Portland Community College
P.O. Box 19000
Portland 97280-0990

Rogue Community College
3345 Redwood Hwy.
Grants Pass 97527

PENNSYLVANIA

Community College of Allegheny
County
800 Allegheny Ave.
Pittsburgh 15233-1895

Harrisburg Area Community College,
Harrisburg
One Hacc Dr.
Harrisburg 17110

Keystone College
P.O. Box 50
La Plume 18440-0200

Pennsylvania State University, Main
Campus
201 Old Main
University Park 16802

RHODE ISLAND

Community College of Rhode Island
400 East Ave.
Warwick 02886-1807

SOUTH CAROLINA

Denmark Technical College
P.O. Box 327
Solomon Blatt Blvd.
Denmark 29042

Florence Darlington Technical College
P.O. Box 100548
Florence 29501-0548

Midlands Technical College
P.O. Box 2408
Columbia 29202

Piedmont Technical College
P.O. Drawer 1467
Greenwood 29648

Trident Technical College
P.O. Box 118067
Charleston 29423-8067

TEXAS

Austin Community College
5930 Middle Fiskville Rd.
Austin 78752

VERMONT

Champlain College
163 South Willard St.
Burlington 05401

WASHINGTON

Spokane Falls Community College
West 3410 Fort George Wright Dr.
Spokane 99224

WEST VIRGINIA

The College of West Virginia
500 South Kanawha St.
Beckley 25801

Teacher and Teacher's Aide Training

ALABAMA

Bishop State Community College
351 North Broad St.
Mobile 36608

Community College of the Air Force
130 West Maxwell Blvd.
Montgomery 36112-6613

Gadsden State Community College
1001 George Wallace Dr.
Gadsden 35902-0227

John C Calhoun State Community
College
Hwy. 31 N
Decatur 35602

Shoals Community College
800 George Wallace Blvd.
Muscle Shoals 35662

ARIZONA

Berlitz Language Centers
3333 East Camelback Rd.
Ste. 160
Phoenix 85018

Eastern Arizona College
Church St.
Thatcher 85552-0769

Mesa Community College
1833 West Southern Ave.
Mesa 85202

Opportunities Industrialization Center,
Phoenix
39 East Jackson St.
Phoenix 85004

Pima Community College
2202 West Anklam Rd.
Tucson 85709-0001

ARKANSAS

Black River Technical College
Hwy. 304
Box 468
Pocahontas 72455

Quapaw Technical Institute
200 Mid America Blvd.
Hot Springs 71913

CALIFORNIA

Allan Hancock College
800 South College Dr.
Santa Maria 93454

Antelope Valley College
3041 West Ave. K
Lancaster 93536

Berlitz Language Centers
323 North Beverly Dr.
Beverly Hills 90210

Berlitz Language Centers
1475 South Bascom Ave.
Campbell 95008

Berlitz Language Centers
800 Wilshire Blvd.
Los Angeles 90017

Berlitz Language Centers
430 Cambridge Ave.
Palo Alto 94306

Berlitz Language Centers
600 South Lake Ave.
Pasadena 91106

Berlitz Language Centers
7801 Mission Center Ct.
San Diego 92108

Berlitz Language Centers
180 Montgomery
San Francisco 94104

Berlitz Language Centers
616 Santa Monica Blvd.
Santa Monica 90401

Berlitz Language Centers
2355 Crenshaw Blvd.
Park Del Amo Bldg.
Torrance 90501

Berlitz Language Centers
1646 North California Blvd.
Ste. P112
Walnut Creek 94596

Berlitz Language Centers
6415 Independence Ave.
Woodland Hills 91367

Cerritos College
11110 Alondra Blvd.
Norwalk 90650

Chaffey Community College
5885 Haven Ave.
Rancho Cucamonga 91737-3002

City College of San Francisco
50 Phelan Ave.
San Francisco 94112

College of Alameda
555 Atlantic Ave.
Alameda 94501

College of the Canyons
26455 Rockwell Canyon Rd.
Santa Clarita 91355

Compton Community College
1111 East Artesia Blvd.
Compton 90221

D-Q University
Rd. 31
P.O. Box 409
Davis 95617-0409

El Camino College
16007 Crenshaw Blvd.
Torrance 90506

Golden West College
15744 Golden West
Huntington Beach 92647

Hartnell College
156 Homestead Ave.
Salinas 93901

Imperial Valley College
P.O. Box 158
Imperial 92251-0158

Long Beach City College
4901 East Carson St.
Long Beach 90808

Mira Costa College
One Barnard Dr.
Oceanside 92056-3899

Modesto Junior College
435 College Ave.
Modesto 95350-5800

Monterey Institute of International
Studies
425 Van Buren
Monterey 93940

Montessori Training Center of San
Diego
4544 Pocahontas Ave.
San Diego 92117

Montessori Western Teacher Training
Program
6202 Cerulean St.
Garden Grove 92645

Mount Saint Mary's College
12001 Chalon Rd.
Los Angeles 90049

Napa Valley College
2277 Napa Vallejo Hwy.
Napa 94558

Pasadena City College
1570 East Colorado Blvd.
Pasadena 91106

Rudolf Steiner College
9200 Fair Oaks Blvd.
Fair Oaks 95628

Saint Giles Language Teaching Center
One Hallidie Plaza
Ste. 350
San Francisco 94102

San Diego City College
1313 12th Ave.
San Diego 92101

Santa Monica College
1900 Pico Blvd.
Santa Monica 90405-1628

Santa Monica Montessori Institute
1909 Colorado Ave.
Santa Monica 90404

Santa Rosa Junior College
1501 Mendocino Ave.
Santa Rosa 95401-4395

Shasta College
P.O. Box 496006
Redding 96049

Sierra College
5000 Rocklin Rd.
Rocklin 95677

Southwestern College
900 Otay Lakes Rd.
Chula Vista 91910

Ventura College
4667 Telegraph Rd.
Ventura 93003

Vista College
2020 Milvia St.
Berkeley 94704-1183

Yuba College
2088 North Beale Rd.
Marysville 95901

COLORADO

Berlitz Language Centers
55 Madison St.
Ste. 175
Denver 80206

College of the Canons
Forge Rd. Industrial Pk.
Canon City 81212

CONNECTICUT

Berlitz Language Centers
350 Bedford St.
Stamford 06901

Berlitz Language Centers
61 South Main St.
West Hartford 06107

Berlitz Language Centers
125 Main St.
Ste. 370
Westport 06880

Manchester Community Technical
College
60 Bidwell St.
P.O. Box 1045
Manchester 06040-1046

DISTRICT OF COLUMBIA

Berlitz Language Centers
1050 Connecticut Ave. NW
Washington 20036

The Washington Montessori Institute
2119 South St. NW
Washington 20008

FLORIDA

Berlitz Language Centers
396 Alhambra Circle
Coral Gables 33134

Berlitz Language Centers
2400 East Commercial Blvd.
Ste 100
Fort Lauderdale 33308-4022

Berlitz Language Centers
777 Brickell Ave.
Ste. 970
Miami 33131-2807

Berlitz Language Centers
100 West Kennedy Blvd.
Tampa 33602

GEORGIA

Andrew College
413 College St.
Cuthbert 31740-1395

Berlitz Language Centers
3400 Peachtree Rd. NE
Atlanta 30326

Dekalb Technical Institute
495 North Indian Creek Dr.
Clarkston 30021

National Center for Montessori
Education, Atlanta
2175 Norcross Tucker Rd.
Norcross 30071

Reinhardt College
7300 Reinhardt College Pkwy.
Waleska 30183

South College
709 Mall Blvd.
Savannah 31406

HAWAII

Brigham Young University, Hawaii
Campus
55-220 Kulanui St.
Laie 96762

Hawaii Community College
200 West Kawili St.
Hilo 96720-4091

IDAHO

College of Southern Idaho
P.O. Box 1238
Twin Falls 83301

North Idaho College
1000 West Garden Ave.
Coeur D'Alene 83814

Ricks College
Rexburg 83460-4107

ILLINOIS

Berlitz Language Centers
Two North Lasalle
Ste. 1810
Chicago 60602

Berlitz Language Centers, Water Tower
Place
845 North Michigan Ave.
Ste. 1345
Chicago 60611

Berlitz Language Centers
1821 Walden Office Square
Ste. 230
Schaumburg 60173

Berlitz Language Centers
950 Green Bay Rd.
Winnetka 60093

Montessori Education Center
Associated
302 South Grant
Hinsdale 60521

Spanish Coalition for Jobs, Inc.
2011 West Pershing Rd.
Chicago 60609

INDIANA

Ancilla College
P.O. Box 1
Donaldson 46513

Anderson University
1100 East Fifth St.
Anderson 46012-3462

Berlitz Language Centers
8888 Keystone Crossing
Ste. 848
Indianapolis 46240

Indiana University, Purdue University,
Fort Wayne
2101 Coliseum Blvd. E
Fort Wayne 46805

Vincennes University
1002 North First St.
Vincennes 47591

IOWA

Kirkwood Community College
P.O. Box 2068
Cedar Rapids 52406

KANSAS

Allen County Community College
1801 North Cottonwood
Iola 66749

Barton County Community College
245 Northeast 30th Rd.
Great Bend 67530

Butler County Community College
901 South Haverhill Rd.
El Dorado 67042

Cloud County Community College
2221 Campus Dr.
Box 1002
Concordia 66901-1002

Coffeyville Community College
400 West 11th St.
Coffeyville 67337

Colby Community College
1255 South Range
Colby 67701

Cowley County Community College
125 South Second St.
Arkansas City 67005

Dodge City Community College
2501 North 14th Ave.
Dodge City 67801

Fort Scott Community College
2108 South Horton
Fort Scott 66701

Garden City Community College
801 Campus Dr.
Garden City 67846

Highland Community College
P.O. Box 68
Highland 66035-0068

Hutchinson Community College
1300 North Plum St.
Hutchinson 67501

Independence Community College
Brookside Dr. and College Ave.
Independence 67301

Kansas City Kansas Community College
7250 State Ave.
Kansas City 66112

Pratt Community College
348 Northeast St. Rte. 61
Pratt 67124

Seward County Community College
Box 1137
Liberal 67905-1137

KENTUCKY

Midway College
512 Stephens St.
Midway 40347-1120

LOUISIANA

Delgado Community College
501 City Park Ave.
New Orleans 70119

Southern University, Shreveport-Bossier
City Campus
3050 Martin L King Dr.
Shreveport 71107

MAINE

University of Maine at Farmington
86 Main St.
Farmington 04938

MARYLAND

Allegany Community College of
Maryland
12401 Willowbrook Rd. SE
Cumberland 21502

Anne Arundel Community College
101 College Pkwy.
Arnold 21012

Berlitz Language Centers
Two North Charles St.
Ste. 760
Baltimore 21201

Berlitz Language Centers
11300 Rockville Pike
Ste. 911
Rockville 20852

Catonsville Community College
800 South Rolling Rd.
Catonsville 21228

Chesapeake College
P.O. Box 8
Wye Mills 21679-0008

Dundalk Community College
7200 Sollers Point Rd.
Dundalk 21222

Essex Community College
7201 Rossville Blvd.
Baltimore 21237

Frederick Community College
7932 Opossumtown Pike
Frederick 21702

Hagerstown Junior College
11400 Robinwood Dr.
Hagerstown 21742-6590

Harford Community College
401 Thomas Run Rd.
Bel Air 21015

Howard Community College
10901 Little Patuxent Pkwy.
Columbia 21044

Montgomery College of Rockville
51 Mannakee St.
Rockville 20850

Prince Georges Community College
301 Largo Rd.
Largo 20774-2199

MASSACHUSETTS

Aquinas College at Newton
15 Walnut Park
Newton 02158

Bay Path College
588 Longmeadow St.
Longmeadow 01106

Becker College, Worcester
61 Sever St.
Worcester 01615-0071

Berlitz Language Centers
437 Boylston St.
Boston 02116

Berlitz Language Centers
40 Washington St.
Wellesley Hills 02181

Bristol Community College
777 Elsbree St.
Fall River 02720

Cape Cod Community College
2240 Iyanough Rd.
West Barnstable 02668-1599

Dean College
99 Main St.
Franklin 02038

Endicott College
376 Hale St.
Beverly 01915

Fisher College
118 Beacon St.
Boston 02116

Greenfield Community College
One College Dr.
Greenfield 01301-9739

Hebrew College
43 Hawes St.
Brookline 02146

Lasell College
1844 Commonwealth Ave.
Newton 02166

Middlesex Community College
Springs Rd.
Bedford 01730

Mount Wachusett Community College
444 Green St.
Gardner 01440

North Shore Community College
One Ferncroft Rd.
Danvers 01923

Quinsigamond Community College
670 West Boylston St.
Worcester 01606

Springfield Technical Community
College
One Armory Square
Springfield 01105

Wheelock College
200 the Riverway
Boston 02215

MICHIGAN

Alpena Community College
666 Johnson St.
Alpena 49707

Berlitz Language Centers
30700 Telegraph Rd.
Bingham Farms 48025

Delta College
University Center 48710

Ferris State University
901 South State St.
Big Rapids 49307

Gogebic Community College
East 4946 Jackson Rd.
Ironwood 49938

Grand Rapids Community College
143 Bostwick Ave. NE
Grand Rapids 49503-3295

Kalamazoo Valley Community College
6767 West O Ave.
Kalamazoo 49009

Monroe County Community College
1555 South Raisinville Rd.
Monroe 48161

Muskegon Community College
221 South Quarterline Rd.
Muskegon 49442

Schoolcraft College
18600 Haggerty Rd.
Livonia 48152

Southwestern Michigan College
58900 Cherry Grove Rd.
Dowagiac 49047-9793

MINNESOTA

Berlitz Language Centers
6600 France Ave. S
Ste. 190
Minneapolis 55435

College of Saint Catherine, Minneapolis
601 25th Ave. S
Minneapolis 55454

Rochester Community and Technical
College
851 30th Ave. SE
Rochester 55904-4999

MISSISSIPPI

Coahoma Community College
3240 Friars Point Rd.
Clarksdale 38614

Mary Holmes College
Hwy. 50 W
West Point 39773

Mississippi Gulf Coast Community
College
Central Office
P.O. Box 67
Perkinston 39573

Northeast Mississippi Community
College
Cunningham Blvd.
Booneville 38829

Northwest Mississippi Community
College
510 North Panola Hwy. 51 N
Senatobia 38668

MISSOURI

Berlitz Language Centers
200 South Hanley Rd.
Saint Louis 63105

Crowder College
601 Laclede
Neosho 64850

Saint Charles County Community
College
4601 Mid Rivers Mall Dr.
Saint Peter's 63376

NEBRASKA

Central Community College Area
P.O. Box 4903
Grand Island 68802

Northeast Community College
801 East Benjamin
P.O. Box 469
Norfolk 68702-0469

NEW HAMPSHIRE

Hesser College
Three Sundial Ave.
Manchester 03103

NEW JERSEY

Bergen Community College
400 Paramus Rd.
Paramus 07652

Berlitz Language Centers
400 Alexander Pk.
Princeton 08540

Berlitz Language Centers
40 West Ridgewood Ave.
Ridgewood 07450

Berlitz Language Centers
47 Maple St.
Summit 07901

Brookdale Community College
765 Newman Springs Rd.
Lincroft 07738-1599

Cumberland County College
College Dr.
P.O. Box 517
Vineland 08360

Essex County College
303 University Ave.
Newark 07102

Gloucester County College
1400 Tanyard Rd.
Sewell 08080

NEW MEXICO

New Mexico Junior College
5317 Lovington Hwy.
Hobbs 88240

University of New Mexico, Gallup
Campus
200 College Rd.
Gallup 87301

NEW YORK

Berlitz Language Centers
41 Mineola Blvd.
Mineola 11501

Berlitz Language Centers
61 Broadway
Ste. 1630
New York 10006

Berlitz Language Centers
40 West 51st St.
New York 10020

Berlitz Language Centers
36 Main St. W
Rochester 14614

Berlitz Language Centers
One North Broadway
White Plains 10601

Cazenovia College
Cazenovia 13035

CUNY Borough of Manhattan
Community College
199 Chambers St.
New York 10007

CUNY Bronx Community College
West 181st St. & University Ave.
Bronx 10453

CUNY Hostos Community College
500 Grand Concourse
Bronx 10451

CUNY Kingsborough Community
College
2001 Oriental Blvd.
Brooklyn 11235

Iona College
715 North Ave.
New Rochelle 10801

Maria College of Albany
700 New Scotland Ave.
Albany 12208

Mater Dei College
5428 St. Hwy. 37
Ogdensburg 13669

Siena College
515 Loudon Rd.
Loudonville 12211

Trocaire College
360 Choate Ave.
Buffalo 14220

Villa Maria College, Buffalo
240 Pine Ridge Rd.
Buffalo 14225-3999

NORTH CAROLINA

Berlitz Language Centers
5821 Fairview Rd.
Ste. 105
Charlotte 28209

Berlitz Language Centers
5974A Six Forks Rd.
Raleigh 27609

Campbell University, Inc.
P.O. Box 97
Buies Creek 27506

Chowan College
Murfreesboro 27855

Isothermal Community College
P.O. Box 804
Spindale 28160

Vance-Granville Community College
State Rd. 1126
P.O. Box 917
Henderson 27536

OHIO

Berlitz Language Centers
156 South Main St.
Akron 44308

Berlitz Language Centers
503 Race St. Skywalk
Cincinnati 45202

Berlitz Language Centers
815 Superior
Ste. 100
Cleveland 44115

Bowling Green State University,
Firelands
901 Rye Beach Rd.
Huron 44839

Cuyahoga Community College District
700 Carnegie Ave.
Cleveland 44115-2878

Lorain County Community College
1005 Abbe Rd. N
Elyria 44035

Montessori Teacher Education
Collaborative
11424 Bellflower Rd. NE
Cleveland 44106

Sinclair Community College
444 West Third St.
Dayton 45402

University of Akron, Main Campus
302 Buchtel Common
Akron 44325-4702

University of Rio Grande
North College St.
Rio Grande 45674

OKLAHOMA

Bacone College
2299 Old Bacome Rd.
Muskogee 74403-1597

Carl Albert State College
1507 South McKenna
Poteau 74953-5208

Connors State College
Rte. 1
P.O. Box 1000
Warner 74469

Eastern Oklahoma State College
1301 West Main St.
Wilburton 74578

Northeastern Oklahoma Agricultural
and Mechanical College
200 I St. NE
Miami 74354

Northern Oklahoma College
Box 310 Tonkawa
Tonkawa 74653

Pontotoc Area Vocational Technical
School
601 West 33rd
Ada 74820

Redlands Community College
1300 South Country Club Rd.
El Reno 73036-5304

Rogers University, Claremore
1701 West Will Rogers Blvd.
Claremore 74017

Rose State College
6420 Southeast 15th
Midwest City 73110

Seminole State College
2701 Boren Blvd.
Seminole 74868

Tulsa Community College
6111 East Skelly Dr.
Tulsa 74135

Western Oklahoma State College
2801 North Main St.
Altus 73521-1397

OREGON

Montessori Institute Northwest
1404 Seventh St.
Ste. 13
Oregon City 97045

Portland Community College
P.O. Box 19000
Portland 97280-0990

PENNSYLVANIA

Berlitz Language Centers
1608 Walnut St.
Philadelphia 19103

Berlitz Language Centers
355 Fifth Ave.
Ste. 1511
Pittsburgh 15222

Berlitz Language Centers
230 Sugartown Rd.
Ste. 103
Wayne 19087

Bucks County Community College
Swamp Rd.
Newtown 18940

Butler County Community College
College Dr. Oak Hills
Butler 16003-1203

Community College of Allegheny
County
800 Allegheny Ave.
Pittsburgh 15233-1895

Community College of Philadelphia
1700 Spring Garden St.
Philadelphia 19130

Delaware County Community College
901 South Media Line Rd.
Media 19063-1094

Harrisburg Area Community College,
Harrisburg
One Hacc Dr.
Harrisburg 17110

Keystone College
P.O. Box 50
La Plume 18440-0200

Lehigh Carbon Community College
4525 Education Park Dr.
Schnecksville 18078-2598

Luzerne County Community College
1333 South Prospect St.
Nanticoke 18634

Manor Junior College
700 Fox Chase Rd.
Jenkintown 19046

Montgomery County Community
College
340 Dekalb Pike
Blue Bell 19422

Northampton County Area Community
College
3835 Green Pond Rd.
Bethlehem 18020-7599

Reading Area Community College
P.O. Box 1706
Reading 19603-1706

RHODE ISLAND

Community College of Rhode Island
400 East Ave.
Warwick 02886-1807

TENNESSEE

Hiwassee College
225 Hiwassee College Dr.
Madisonville 37354

Jackson State Community College
2046 North Pkwy.
Jackson 38301

TEXAS

Amarillo College
P.O. Box 447
Amarillo 79178

Angelina College
P.O. Box 1768
Lufkin 75902-1768

Berlitz Language Centers
8400 North Mopac
Austin 78759

Berlitz Language Centers
17194 Preston Rd.
Ste. 207
Dallas 75248

Berlitz Language Centers
3100 Richmond Ave.
Ste. 101
Houston 77098

Berlitz Language Centers
5815 Callaghan Rd.
San Antonio 78228

Cisco Junior College
Rte. 3
Box 3
Cisco 76437

College of the Mainland
1200 Amburn Rd.
Texas City 77591

Del Mar College
101 Baldwin
Corpus Christi 78404-3897

El Paso Community College
P.O. Box 20500
El Paso 79998

Frank Phillips College
P.O. Box 5118
Borger 79008-5118

Galveston College
4015 Ave. Q
Galveston 77550

Grayson County College
6101 Grayson Dr.
Denison 75020

Hill College
P.O. Box 619
Hillsboro 76645

Houston Montessori Center
9601 Katy Fwy.
Ste. 350
Houston 77024-1330

Howard County Junior College District
1001 Birdwell Ln.
Big Spring 79720

Kilgore College
1100 Broadway
Kilgore 75662-3299

King's Way Missionary Institute
401 South Kings Hwy.
McAllen 78501

McLennan Community College
1400 College Dr.
Waco 76708

Navarro College
3200 West Seventh
Corsicana 75110

North Harris Montgomery Community
College District
250 North Sam Houston Pkwy. E
Ste. 300
Houston 77060

Panola College
1109 West Panola St.
Carthage 75633

Richland College
12800 Abrams Rd.
Dallas 75243-2199

San Jacinto College, Central Campus
8060 Spencer Hwy.
Pasadena 77505

San Jacinto College, North Campus
5800 Uvalde
Houston 77049

Southwest Texas Junior College
2401 Garner Field Rd.
Uvalde 78801

Temple College
2600 South First St.
Temple 76504-7435

Texas Southmost College
80 Fort Brown
Brownsville 78520

Trinity Valley Community College
500 South Prairieville
Athens 75751

Tyler Junior College
1327 South Baxter Ave.
Tyler 75711

Weatherford College
308 East Park Ave.
Weatherford 76086

Wharton County Junior College
911 Boling Hwy.
Wharton 77488

UTAH

Dixie College
225 South, 700 East
Saint George 84770

VERMONT

Champlain College
163 South Willard St.
Burlington 05401

Community College of Vermont
Box 120
Waterbury 05676

VIRGINIA

Berlitz Language Centers
2070 Chain Bridge Rd.
Ste. 140
Vienna 22182

J Sargeant Reynolds Community
College
P.O. Box 85622
Richmond 23285-5622

Northern Virginia Community College
4001 Wakefield Chapel Rd.
Annandale 22003

Saint Paul's College
115 College Dr.
Lawrenceville 23868

Southern Virginia College
One College Hill Dr.
Buena Vista 24416

Tidewater Community College
121 College Pl.
Norfolk 23510

Virginia Western Community College
3095 Colonial Ave.
Roanoke 24015

WASHINGTON

Berlitz Language Centers
400 112th Ave. NE
Ste. 285
Bellevue 98009

WEST VIRGINIA

Opportunities Industrialization Center,
North Central West Virginia
120 Jackson St.
Fairmont 26554

WISCONSIN

Berlitz Language Centers
111 East Wisconsin Ave.
Ste. 740
Milwaukee 53202

Milwaukee Area Technical College
700 West State St.
Milwaukee 53233-1443

Northcentral Technical College
1000 Campus Dr.
Wausau 54401-1899

Opportunities Industrialization Center
2835 North 32nd St.
Milwaukee 53210

Waukesha County Technical College
800 Main St.
Pewaukee 53072

WYOMING

Casper College
125 College Dr.
Casper 82601

Central Wyoming College
2660 Peck Ave.
Riverton 82501

Eastern Wyoming College
3200 West C St.
Torrington 82240

Laramie County Community College
1400 East College Dr.
Cheyenne 82007

Northwest Community College
231 West Sixth St.
Powell 82435

Sheridan College
3059 Coffeen Ave.
Sheridan 82801

Western Wyoming Community College
2500 College Dr.
Rock Springs 82902

Index

All jobs mentioned in this volume are listed and cross-referenced in the index. Entries that appear in all capital letters have occupational profiles. For example, ADULT EDUCATION WORKER, BUILDING CUSTODIAN, CRIMINOLOGIST and so on are profiles in this volume. Entries that are not capitalized refer to jobs that do not have a separate profile but for which information is given.

Under some capitalized entries there is a section titled "Profile includes." This lists jobs that are mentioned in the profile. For example, in the case of CUSTOMS WORKER, jobs that are described in the profile are Customs agent, Import specialist, and Inspector.

Some entries are followed by a job title in parentheses after the page number on which it can be found. This job title is the occupational profile in which the entry is discussed. For instance, the Consular officer entry is followed by the profile title (Foreign service worker).